TODAY'S MYTHS AND TOMORROW'S REALITIES

Richard M. Millard

TODAY'S MYTHS AND TOMORROW'S REALITIES

Overcoming Obstacles to Academic Leadership in the 21st Century

 Jossey-Bass Publishers

San Francisco • Oxford • 1991

TODAY'S MYTHS AND TOMORROW'S REALITIES
Overcoming Obstacles to Academic Leadership in the 21st Century
by Richard M. Millard

Copyright © 1991 by: Jossey-Bass Inc., Publishers
350 Sansome Street
San Francisco, California 94104
&
Jossey-Bass Limited
Headington Hill Hall
Oxford OX3 0BW

Library of Congress Cataloging-in-Publication Data

Millard, Richard M.
 Today's myths and tomorrow's realities : overcoming obstacles to
academic leadership in the 21st century / Richard M. Millard.
  p.   cm. — (The Jossey-Bass higher and adult education series)
 Includes bibliographical references and index.
 ISBN 1-55542-361-2
 1. Education, Higher—United States—Aims and objectives.
 2. Education, Higher—United States—History—20th century.
 3. Educational planning—United States.   4. Educational change—
United States.   I. Title.   II. Series.
 LA227.4.M55   1991
 378.73—dc20   91-11251
                                                                CIP

Manufactured in the United States of America

The paper in this book meets the guidelines for
permanence and durability of the Committee on
Production Guidelines for Book Longevity of
the Council on Library Resources.

JACKET DESIGN BY WILLI BAUM

FIRST EDITION

Code 9164

THE JOSSEY-BASS

HIGHER AND ADULT EDUCATION SERIES

Consulting Editor
Adult and Continuing Education

Alan B. Knox
University of Wisconsin, Madison

Contents

Contents

Preface

IN THE LAST HALF OF THE TWENTIETH CENTURY, HIGHER EDUCATION in the United States has undergone an amazing transformation from what was prior to World War II a relatively small, essentially elitist, largely private post–high school enterprise serving primarily eighteen- to twenty-four-year-old full-time resident students to an expanded system with more than twelve and a half million students that comes close to providing what Ernest Boyer (1987) has described as the "first system of universal access to higher education" (p. 27). Through research and broader and better education of the work force, it has contributed immeasurably to the economic health and welfare of the nation and the world.

In spite of such achievement, however, higher education has for the past few years been subject to extensive criticism and doubts about its continuing ability to effectively meet the changing and developing needs of the nation. These criticisms have come not solely or even primarily from the academic community but also from state and federal agencies, special commissions, the U.S. Congress, state legislators, and governors. While the current round of criticisms was first leveled at elementary and secondary education in the early 1980s, it quickly spread to higher education. Somewhat ironically, a number of reports and published criticisms, rather than focusing on the need for change to address changing conditions, have tended to call for a return to an earlier, simpler conception of higher education and its functions and have thus become part of the problem rather than its solution.

The thesis of *Today's Myths and Tomorrow's Realities* is that the evolution of higher education should be accelerated to meet the conditions of a changed and changing world, not retarded or reversed. The book rejects the view that higher education has failed, has fallen from a previous state of grace, or has declined or even that it has become unresponsive to changing conditions. It calls for recognition that there are problems and challenges that higher education must face if it is to continue to have a major impact on social, economic, and political development in the twenty-first century and that unless it meets these challenges, not only higher education but the nation is in serious trouble.

Some of these challenges result from the history and success of higher education itself over recent decades — its rapid enrollment expansion, its move to a much broader sense of egalitarian service to society, its contribution to economic development through research and human resource development, and its greatly increased prominence as a focus of public and political concern. At this point, however, most of the challenges come from changing societal and economic conditions — the shift from an industrial to an information and service society with increased demand for a more literate and better-educated work force, demographic changes in age distribution of the population and the size of minority and immigrant groups, and increasing international economic competitiveness, among other factors.

If the challenges are to be met and higher education is to enhance its leadership role in the twenty-first century, certain assumptions with varying degrees of prevalence in the academic community need to be challenged. These assumptions are usually rooted in tradition and, on the positive side, frequently involve elements of insight and important cautions. However, taken at face value or as absolutes, they might better be called myths that inhibit administrators and faculty from realistically dealing with changing conditions, reinforce the status quo, and/or reinforce an elitist conception of the function of higher education in society.

The primary purpose of this book is to identify and critique a number of the more prevalent of these myths and to suggest, without abandoning the elements of insight and cautions they may reflect, a framework for transcending them through modification, correction, or in some cases replacement in the light of the relevance of higher education to the current and developing climate in which it exists. The list of myths to be considered is meant to be not exhaustive but rather illustrative. Out of the identification and review of these myths are developed some guidelines for transcending them and general perspectives regarding the possible role of higher education in dealing with the realities of the twenty-first century.

The idea for and essential structure of this book grew out of a series of conversations that involved Thurman White, then executive director of the Oklahoma Network for Continuing Higher Education and one of the deans of the continuing higher education movement in America, Lynn Luckow, then editor for Adult and Continuing Education and now president and chief executive officer of Jossey-Bass, and myself. We were soon joined by Arlon Elser of the W. K. Kellogg Foundation. We first considered the possibility of a book on the foundation-funded project the Oklahoma Network for Continuing Higher Education and its implications for postsecondary education nationally. However, we agreed that it might be far more useful to look at some of the myths, assumptions, or barriers that impede or hinder higher or postsecondary educational institutions from effectively shifting gears to meet some of the changed and changing conditions of an information and learning society, of a world in which life-span learning has in fact become the mainstream and in which the ivory tower has become an anachronism. Aspects not only of the Oklahoma project but of other current or recent foundation-funded projects would be used to illustrate means of overcoming some of the barriers. In addition, examples would be drawn from the author's life-long involvement in higher and postsecondary educational concerns.

Overview of the Contents

The book deals with seven families of myths, each of which involves a broad area of postsecondary educational concerns.

The introductory chapter, Chapter One, sets the stage by reviewing some of the changing conditions and criticisms that are part of the higher education environment as we approach the end of the century. It specifies that by *myths* we mean beliefs, attitudes, or assumptions indigenous to the higher education community that, while they may have grown out of experience and may contain some valid insights, taken at face value may distort the facts in such a way as to inhibit effective action in meeting current and emerging higher education needs. The discussion then focuses on the relevance to academic and social responsibility of dealing effectively with the myths at both institutional and state levels. The areas of nontraditional and continuing education, the chapter suggests, provide some of the more enlightened approaches to dealing with many of the myths. Finally, some of the W. K. Kellogg Foundation–sponsored projects and the Oklahoma Network for Continuing Higher Education project in particular are cited as examples of important attempts to overcome some of the hurdles set by the myths.

Chapter Two presents a discussion of the first family of myths, those designated as "academic sacred cows." These are the myths most clearly rooted in tradition and in many ways serve as the foundation for a number of the myths that follow. The first and perhaps most basic myth is the Golden Era Myth, which involves veneration of the past and its use as normative for the present. It is the myth that tends to permeate a number of recent reports. Aside from the difficulty in finding a golden era, holders of the myth tend to overlook the fact that even if you find it, in the words of Thomas Wolfe, you can't go home again. This in no way, however, undermines the importance of the past for understanding the present. The second, related myth is that the only legitimate reform of higher education comes from within the academy—the Reform from Within Myth. This myth tends to be historically inaccurate and to underestimate the role of interaction between higher education and its environment. The third is the Traditional College Student Myth—the assumption that the "real" college students on whom we should concentrate are the eighteen- to twenty-four-year-old resident students. This myth disregards current student demography, yet continued allegiance to it tends to shape the structure and central focus of many institutions. The fourth, the Centrality of the University Myth, involves the assumption that the "university," particularly the research university, is the paradigm for all postsecondary education. This is a Procrustean view that overlooks the legitimate diversity of institutions and the fact that they need to be considered in the light of their missions as these in turn are related to diverse educational needs. The fifth, the Transfer of Credit Myth, would restrict the transfer of academic credit to "comparable" institutions and programs. Such a view confuses substantive knowledge and attained competence with formal institutional course equivalence. The sixth and seventh myths, the Older Student Myth — that older students dilute program quality — and the Continuing Education Myth — that adult and continuing education programs are primarily either auxiliary money-making enterprises or "public services" — confuse ability with age, overlook the demography of current students, and mix short-range convenience with long-term advantage.

Chapter Three focuses on the second family of myths, those that involve matters of turf and institutional ethnocentrism, the last stronghold of rugged institutionalism. The first of these, the Autonomy Myth, is the academic equivalent of "What is good for General Motors is good for the country." It tends to confuse reasonable institutional autonomy to carry out institutional missions with freedom from accountability and responsibility to both the academic and wider communities, including the political community. According to the Competition Myth, a laissez-faire approach toward students, faculty, and funding is central to institutional achievement. However, such a position neglects the cooperative base and public responsibility of the academic enterprise. The third myth in this family, the State Board Myth, is the view that statewide higher education boards are inherently repressive and intrusive and should be opposed whenever possible. Such a view overlooks not only the reasons for establishing such boards but the legitimate overriding interest of the states in ensuring that the diversity of postsecondary educational needs are being addressed.

The third family of myths, discussed in Chapter Four, relates to the curriculum and involves issues at the center of much of the current controversy. These include the Liberal Arts Contamination Myth—that the liberal arts and general education are being contaminated by vocationalism, professionalism, and career interests; the Professional Education Exclusion Myth—that professional programs overload students with technical courses, thus slighting or eliminating liberal education; the Curricular Absolutes Myth—that there are curricular absolutes that characterize all "real" undergraduate higher education; and the Feet of the Master Myth—that truly effective education can take place only on campus in the classes of the master professor or his or her designee. These assumptions tend to overlook a number of factors: first, that liberal education can no longer be defined in terms of a specific set of courses but involves development of skills, attitudes, knowledge achievements, experiences, and competencies related to career in the broad sense, which includes life work, life plan, and life-style; second, that professional education itself may have liberal outcomes, and some arts and science education may be highly restrictive; third, that the paradigm for integrating liberal and professional education and thus the aim of education in the broad sense may well be relevance to full career development; and, fourth, that as desirable as residency may be for some students, the critical question is not the when or even the how of instruction but whether the student has attained the appropriate skills, experiences, attitudes, and competencies and is committed to their further development.

Chapter Five is concerned with the fourth family of myths, those related to what is meant by quality, the range of its applicability, and its measurement. The first of these myths is the Reputational Input Myth—the view that quality is defined or determined by reputation, selectivity, and resources. Such a view clearly confuses achievement of educational objectives with factors that may have little to do with such achievement and rules out the recognition that one can equally demand and expect quality in various types of institutions, programs, and even courses, including remedial courses. The Research-Publication Myth defines faculty quality in terms of research and publication, which may indeed be relevant in whole or in part for some institutions but overlooks the fact that faculty quality is function-specific and for any institution involves relevance or appropriateness to institutional and program objectives. The Undergraduate Focus Myth is evidenced in some of the more recent reports even from the political community that assume that the quality issue is primarily a matter of undergraduate curriculum and degrees. To focus primarily or solely on undergraduate curriculum is to forget that quality issues apply to institutions as a whole and their various activities, not to undergraduate education alone. Both the Nontraditional Education Myth and the Noncredit Course Myth, while involving somewhat different clientele and educational objectives, rest on the assumption that anything different from traditional classes for credit on campus is per se qualitatively inferior. Such views overlook not only some thirty years of development of nontraditional programs but the nature of the current student body, the role of educational technologies, and the growing importance of continuing professional education. Finally, the Assessment Myth has two sides. It takes the form of assuming that, on the one hand, effective assessment of student learning is a panacea that will solve all current quality problems or, on the other hand, that it is a fad that will go away with shifts in academic and political interest. Assessment has always been essential both to recognition of quality and to providing information relevant to its improvement. It is neither a panacea nor a fad but a means of determining whether educational objectives have been achieved.

Chapter Six discusses the fifth family of myths, those that have to do with conceptions of equity. The first of the equity myths is that equity and quality are antithetical concepts — the Equity Versus Quality Myth. This view tends to identify equity as access. While access is essential to equity, equity involves considerably more than access alone. Access to poor or second-rate programs only perpetuates inequality. Equity requires quality. The second myth — the Higher Admissions Standards Myth — assumes that high admissions standards ensure both quality and equity by providing student comparability in ability to benefit. This easily becomes an exclusionist or elitist concept of equity. Far more important for equity than admission standards are completion or exit requirements. Closely related to the admissions standards myth is the view that remedial work is not a college's business — the Remedial Work Myth. Such a position would educationally disenfranchise those in the population who most need additional education. Remedial education is a necessity if the educational and human resource needs of the country are to be met now and in the next century. Further, to ensure equity, the quality of remedial education should be equal or superior to that of other types of programs. Finally, the Value-Added Myth involves the assumption that what is important is the progress that students make beyond their point of entry rather than the achievement of particular educational objectives. Value added is a necessary but not a sufficient condition of educational equity and quality. However, taken by itself, value added perpetuates inequality by confusing progress toward objectives with their achievement.

The sixth family of myths, discussed in Chapter Seven, embodies concerns about what are sometimes conceived to be the negative impacts of the rapid development of educational technologies. The first of these — the Sanctity of the Classroom Myth — is that the new technologies somehow change, undermine, or destroy the uniqueness of the classroom and the traditional relationships between student and faculty. The second, related myth — the Threatened Faculty Myth — is that the technologies threaten not only the traditional role of faculty but their jobs as well. The third myth — the Collegiate Service Station Myth — is that the importance of the campus and of collegiality is in danger of being lost as the institution becomes a kind of academic service station dispensing particular academic services on call throughout the wider community. While the new technologies do involve broadening and changing perspectives in relation to the classroom and the campus, rather than destroying the integrity of either, they place renewed emphasis on the teaching-learning process, on extending the classroom and the campus, and on faculty-student interaction wherever students may be. The role of the instructor is reinforced and enhanced, not just as lecturer but as learning facilitator on and off campus. The new technologies provide a framework for interinstitutional cooperation, coordination, and liaison more effectively to meet the educational needs of the broader society. But to do so, the states have a crucial role to play in ensuring that the technologies are available to smaller and less affluent as well as flagship institutions within their borders. The chapter concludes by exploring the technology component of the Oklahoma project as an important example of an effective statewide telecommunications network.

The final family of myths, discussed in Chapter Eight, involves the interface between business and industry and higher education and the concern that too close a relationship can undermine the independence and integrity of higher education institutions. These concerns tend to rise in three areas: research, instruction, and acceptance of credit. The Business and Industry Interference Myth is related primarily to research and assumes that development of university-industry research liaison activities are likely (1) to undermine university and instructor autonomy and freedom by restricting research to applied research of interest to the company and (2) to lead to conflict of interest and loss of integrity as a result of secrecy and concern for income in contrast to scientific openness and objectivity. The Captive Classroom Myth is related to instruction and the concern that college-business linkages promote vocational training, not education, and end up with business and industry, not the college and its faculty, determining the curriculum. The third myth—the Noncomparability of In-Service Education Myth—involves basic skepticism about the quality and relevance of in-service courses or programs offered by business and industry—the corporate classrooms—to postsecondary or higher education and the danger of diluting or downgrading institutional academic integrity by accepting any such work for transfer credit. While these myths may provide important cautions, the relationships between higher education and business and industry have direct bearing on national economic health and competitiveness, on relevance of work to career in the broad sense as the aim of education, and to our need to move to the point where all students are encouraged and rewarded credentials on the basis of what they know and are capable of doing and not on the basis of structural hurdles that have little to do with the learning process or learning accomplishments.

The final chapter, Chapter Nine, identifies five central themes or perspectives that emerge out of the analysis as particularly relevant for dealing with the realities of the twenty-first century. The first is the recognition that career development extending throughout life is the primary instructional objective of education in general and higher education in particular and provides the key to curricular organization, counseling, and assessment of educational effectiveness. The second calls for the explicit recognition not only of the legitimacy of but of the necessity for a real diversity of postsecondary institutions and programs to meet the variety of appropriate career needs of citizens and the research and public-service needs of society. It also calls attention to the public interest in such diversity as expressed through statewide planning and coordination. The third is the recognition that educational quality needs to be defined in terms of excellence in kind and that one can thus expect excellence from and in all types of institutions and programs, including remedial programs. The fourth calls for the recognition that while access is essential to equity, equity is considerably more than access alone and requires high program and institutional quality. The fifth perspective calls for recognizing the critical importance of bringing nontraditional students and programs into the mainstream of higher education. Finally, the chapter raises the question of whether we can afford the further development of the higher education system to overcome the myths, to accomplish the transition, and to provide the range of opportunity called for. The answer would seem clear. Not to afford it can only lead to national disaster.

Audience for the Book

Today's Myths and Tomorrow's Realities is addressed to the higher education and political communities. It should have direct relevance to administrators of various types, from departmental chairs and admissions officers to institutional presidents and vice-presidents, and to state higher education agency directors and chancellors. Faculty, particularly those responsible for curriculum development, should find it both useful and provocative. It has a considerable amount to say to people involved in institutional and statewide planning and research, to those involved in educational outreach and nontraditional education, and to those concerned with business–industry–higher education linkages and liaisons. It deals with policy issues related to higher education that are highly relevant to current discussion and concerns on state and national levels as reflected not only in individual state activities but through task forces, meetings, and reports by such organizations as the National Governors' Association, the National Conference of State Legislators, the Education Commission of the States, and the State Higher Education Executive Officers. It should be of equal interest to the various national higher education organizations and to those concerned with developing national policy and higher education legislation and thus to congressional staffs and federal departments, particularly the U.S. Department of Education, with interest in and responsibility for carrying out and recommending legislation.

The book also should be of interest to those involved in adult and continuing education. While it is not a book on adult and continuing education per se but is in fact designed to deal with a wide range of postsecondary educational issues, it draws heavily on examples from adult and continuing education, particularly programs funded by the W. K. Kellogg Foundation. The reason for this is that many of the issues and approaches relevant to a critique of the myths and the transition to the twenty-first century have emerged and been dealt with more effectively in the areas of nontraditional and continuing higher education than in many traditional programs. The W. K. Kellogg Foundation in particular has funded a series of programs that, while under the egis of continuing education, have had major implications for and, in many cases, major impact on generic education higher issues. This is particularly the case with the Oklahoma Network for Continuing Higher Education project, which helped provide the challenge and opportunity for developing this book.

Acknowledgments

I owe a special debt to Thurman White for involving me in this project in the first place, for providing insight, information, and inspiration in the process of developing the book, and for his personal support and friendship. I am also indebted to Lynn Luckow for his encouragement and for the suggestion of the myth format. Arlon Elsner has provided information on various projects supported by the W. K. Kellogg Foundation and has opened up contacts with other grant recipients. Through the Oklahoma project, the W. K. Kellogg Foundation has helped provide support for preparation of the manuscript.

In addition to Thurman White, a number of people in Oklahoma deserve special recognition. Chancellor Hans Brisch and, before him, Acting Chancellor Dan Hobbs not only have been supportive but have made available information and contacts throughout Oklahoma. Barbara Gellman-Buzin, associate executive vice-chancellor and successor to Thurman White in helping to bring the Oklahoma project to fruition, has served as my primary contact with people involved in the project, has arranged meetings in Oklahoma, has supplied information as needed, and has read and criticized the section of the manuscript related to the new educational technologies and the Oklahoma technology network. Edward J. Coyle, until his recent retirement from the position of senior vice-president for fiscal affairs of the Oklahoma State Regents for Higher Education, helped arrange for the fiscal and technical support connected with the writing project.

A number of people involved in various modules of the Oklahoma project have been particularly helpful. These include Paul Sharp, president emeritus and Regents Professor at the University of Oklahoma; Clayton Rich, provost and vice-president of the Oklahoma University Health Sciences Center; Huey B. Long, Kellogg Professor of Continuing Higher Education at the University of Oklahoma; and Samuel J. Sackett of Joy Reed Belt & Associates, Inc.

I am also indebted to a number of people at other W. K. Kellogg projects for their time and assistance. These include the following: at the Georgia Center for Continuing Education of the University of Georgia, Edward J. Simpson, Jr. (the director), John E. Azzereto, and their colleagues who hosted me for a series of fascinating days; at the National University Continuing Education Association, Kay Kohl, executive director, and David M. Johnson, director of the Continuing Higher Education Leadership Project; at the Council for Adult and Experiential Education, Morris Keaton; from the Pennsylvania State University, Donna S. Queeny, director of planning studies of the Commonwealth Educational System, and Wayne D. Smutz, head of the Office of Continuing Professional Education; from Ohio State University, Luvern L. Cunningham, Novice G. Fawcett Professor of Educational Administration, and Michael Castro, associate director of the Commission on Interprofessional Education and Practice; from the Intermountain Community Learning and Information Services Project, Glenn Wilde of Utah State University; and from Michigan State University, James C. Votruba. A special thanks is also due to Andrew V. Marusak and Mikki Whitt of the Washington office of the University of Oklahoma for providing encouragement and office space in downtown Washington, D.C., when I needed it.

I am particularly indebted to Alan Knox, consulting editor for Jossey-Bass, for reading the first draft of the manuscript and providing comments, suggestions, and encouragement. Donald R. McNeil of the Academy for Educational Development and Jerry Miller of the American College Testing Program have also read parts of the manuscript and made most helpful suggestions.

I am most grateful to Theresa Branch, my former secretary, for putting the manuscript on a word processor from a combination of my illegible script and tapes.

Finally, without the help and encouragement of my wife, Bernice, including the arduous task of proofreading the original manuscript, this book would not have been possible.

Bethesda, Maryland   Richard M. Millard
June 1991

The Author

RICHARD M. MILLARD is president emeritus of the Council on Post-secondary Accreditation and a consultant in higher education. He received his A.B. degree (1941) in philosophy from DePauw University. He received both his A.M. (1942) and his Ph.D. (1950) degrees in philosophy from Boston University, with some time out for service in World War II. He began teaching philosophy in what was then Hofstra College in 1947. In 1949, he returned to the philosophy department at Boston University as an instructor. He became chair of the Department of Philosophy in 1954, professor of philosophy in 1957, acting dean of the Graduate School in 1960, and dean of the College of Liberal Arts in 1961. While at Boston University, he helped design and put into place one of the first six-year liberal arts–medical programs in the United States.

In 1967, Millard left Boston University to become the first chancellor of the Board of Higher Education of the Commonwealth of Massachusetts. In 1969, he accepted the position of director of higher education services at the Education Commission of the States, headquartered in Denver, Colorado. Among other groups, including governors and legislators, with whom he worked closely while at the Education Commission of the States was the State Higher Education Executive Officers, which in 1978 awarded him its John Dale Russell Distinguished Service Award. He also worked closely with the accrediting community and from 1971 to 1973 served on the Advisory Committee on Accreditation and Institutional Eligibility of the U.S.

Office of Education. In 1981, Millard became president of the Council on Postsecondary Accreditation, a position he held until he retired in 1987. He was subsequently named president emeritus by the board of the council.

Millard has authored numerous articles in philosophy, in higher education, including state higher education relations, and in accreditation. Among his several books and monographs are *Personality and the Good* (1963, with Peter A. Bertocci) and *State Boards of Higher Education* (1976). He has served on numerous boards and commissions and is the recipient of honorary degrees from DePauw University, Southeastern Massachusetts University, Lowell State College, and Wentworth Institute of Technology.

TODAY'S
MYTHS AND
TOMORROW'S
REALITIES

1

Confronting the Myths Impeding Progress in Higher Education

As we move through the last decade of the twentieth century, higher education in America finds itself in a most interesting and critical although not wholly unprecedented situation. It faces something of a dilemma created by its achievements and acceptance, on the one hand, and concerns related to social, economic, and political conditions and expectations, on the other. Its accomplishments, particularly since World War II, are indeed impressive by almost any standards and in contrast to those of most other countries.

Changing Perspectives and Expectations

A relatively small, not politically very important, essentially elite, and predominantly private configuration of institutions prior to World War II, higher education today involves more than twelve and a half million students—5 percent of the total population of the United States (Hauptman and Andersen, 1988, p. 15)—almost four-fifths of them in public institutions. Three-fifths of high school graduates attend college at some time during their lives, and two-thirds participate in some form of post–high school education or training. Further, without national planning or a federal ministry of education but with con-

1

siderable state involvement, the United States has developed a highly diverse system of higher education institutions to meet a wide variety of social and individual higher education needs. This includes the rather remarkable development of what is essentially a wholly new group of two-year institutions closely related to their communities' postsecondary education needs — the community colleges. These now enroll almost a third of all higher education students. What were primarily teachers' colleges and state colleges have expanded into comprehensive regional universities serving a variety of types of students. All of this has been done without compromising the unique functions of highly selective undergraduate colleges or research universities. The extent of this accomplishment has been summarized by Ernest Boyer (1987) as follows: "We have created the world's first system of universal access to higher education. It provides entrance somewhere to virtually all who wish to enroll and offers an almost unlimited choice of subjects to the student. This system of higher education, with its openness, diversity, and scholarly achievement, is the envy of the world. Unencumbered by suffocating ideology, the vitality and integrity of the American college and university are unmatched" (p. 2).

In spite of such achievements, however, higher education is currently subject to extensive criticism and expressed doubts about its continuing ability to serve effectively the changing and developing needs of the nation and to meet national expectations in the twenty-first century. A number of these criticisms have been developed in a series of reports and books from both within and outside the academic community. The most recent set began in 1984 with the National Institute for Education report *Involvement in Learning* (Study Group on the Conditions of Excellence in American Higher Education, 1984) and the National Endowment for the Humanities report *To Reclaim a Legacy*, written by former secretary of education William Bennett (1984). These have been followed by a series of reports from such organizations as the Association of American Colleges, the Southern Regional Education Board, the National Governors' Association, and the Education Commission of the States.

Reports dealing with the need for reform in higher education are not a new phenomenon; they have appeared periodically from the Truman and Eisenhower reports in the 1940s and 1950s through the various Carnegie Commission and Carnegie Council reports of the 1970s. In fact, the history of higher education in the United States is decorated with reports at least from the time of the Yale faculty report of 1828. Regardless, however, of the adequacy or accuracy of the most recent set of reports, they have had and are having an impact on current higher education activities.

Quite apart from the reports, however, it is clear that social, demographic, economic, and structural changes are taking place that have direct bearing on higher education, our expectations of it, and its future effectiveness in meeting societal and national needs in the twenty-first century. First, over the past century or so, we have moved from what was primarily an agricultural and then an industrial society to "an information and service society in which involvement in human resources" (Knox, 1987, p. 22) is becoming progressively important not just in relation to internal social and economic development but in relation to our international competitiveness as well. Howard Sparks (1985) of Virginia Commonwealth University has phrased the matter as follows: "Today . . . the United States is no longer an industrializing nation. The entire world is riding a new wave of historical development, and the new wave is raising a wake of change that is both profound and dramatic. As a result, American goals and priorities are shifting more rapidly and profoundly than they have since the agrarian and republican ideals of the Founding Fathers gave way to the industrial and democratic developments of the nineteenth century" (p. 6).

Second, the nature of the public served—the student body—has changed and is changing. Of the twelve and a half million students enrolled today, fewer than two million are "traditional college students"; that is, eighteen- to twenty-two-year-old full-time campus residents. More than half of the students are over twenty-two years of age; 40 percent are over twenty-five; there are more students over thirty-five than there are eighteen-year-olds in college; two-fifths are enrolled part-time;

and considerably more than a third live off campus. And most of these trends promise to continue. By the year 2000, the adult part-time student is likely to be the new majority, yet most institutions still tend to operate and be structured on the assumption that the traditional student is the norm (Frances, 1989, p. 153; Hauptman and Andersen, 1988, p. 16; Hodgkinson, 1986, p. 6).

Third, while considerable progress was made in the late 1950s and the 1960s in increasing minority enrollments, this trend did not continue in the late 1970s and the 1980s. The black and Hispanic populations are increasing and will constitute a progressively larger portion of the population, including the college-age population, in the future. By the early part of the next century, the minorities in some states — California and Texas, for example — will in fact come close to being the majority (State Higher Education Executive Officers, 1987b, pp. 7–8). Considerably more emphasis on effective advanced and continuing education of minorities seems called for.

Fourth, in spite of what Boyer (1987) correctly cites as our approximation to universal access for all who wish to enroll in higher education, there are still far too many people for whom the "wish" is unrealistic or never comes true. There are still far too many high school dropouts for whom college cannot even be a wish. Of those who go on to colleges, the percentage who persist to the attainment of degrees is far lower than it ought to be. Far too large a segment of the population is considered fundamentally illiterate. The National Commission on the Role and Future of State Colleges and Universities (1986) rightly points out that "In a society in which knowledge is a source of wealth, deprivation of access to higher education is a form of bondage. The social, economic, political, and cultural complexity of contemporary America requires a much higher level of education for everyone than was before envisioned" (p. 14).

There are still barriers of distance, physical conditions, economic deprivation, social position, and age that must be overcome before the Oklahoma Network of Continuing Higher Education's goal of providing a relevant "higher education opportunity to everyone, everywhere, everyday" is anywhere in sight.

On a more modest scale, the goal that the National Commission on the Role and Future of State Colleges and Universities considers essential by the year 2001 if the United States is to maintain its leadership position — 35 percent of American adults with a bachelor's degree — is still a long way off.

Finally, while the percentage of part-time and older students is approaching the majority of those in higher education, many institutions have been slow to refocus attention on this group as a progressively important part of the mainstream of higher education and not simply a passing lucrative periphery, part of the service function rather than part of the central educational function of the institution. This is not to suggest that a shift in function should be carried out in all institutions. It is, however, to recognize that given the spectrum of higher education as it now is — let alone the potential in the year 2000 — with less than one-sixth of the students in the traditional student group, some major refocusing seems clearly called for.

All of this is not to say, as has been suggested in some quarters, that higher education or even undergraduate education has declined, failed, fallen from a previous state of grace, or been unduly unresponsive to changing circumstances. It is, however, to recognize that changing conditions present new challenges that call for new responses and may require altering traditional ways of thinking and acting. It clearly calls for expanding the scope of what we have assumed are the traditional boundaries of higher education. If higher education is to meet its current and future challenges, a number of older assumptions will need to be reassessed, rejected, or modified. The report of the National Commission on the Role and Future of State Colleges and Universities (1986), *To Secure the Blessings of Liberty*, lists some of these: "Assuming that higher education will focus principally on 'traditional students'; assuming that modern technology will have little impact on most of teaching and learning; assuming that . . . colleges and universities will and should return to a condition of 'laissez faire' autonomy; or assuming that it will be impossible to find the resources to respond to these new challenges could halt the effort even before it is attempted" (p. 34). As critical as these are, they constitute only some of the assumptions that it is time to review.

The purpose of this book is not to add another jeremiad on the current sad state of higher education and its "fall from grace." In fact, one of our themes is that it has not "fallen," that it has made remarkable positive progress over the last half century, but that it is facing new challenges that call for examination and possible modification of traditional beliefs and attitudes. These beliefs and attitudes, some of them actually rather recent in origin, could stand in the way of meeting the challenges involved in addressing the higher and postsecondary trends of the twenty-first century.

Challenges and Myths

We have identified seven areas in which modifications of assumptions seem to be imperative if higher and postsecondary education institutions are (1) to meet changing conditions, (2) to provide the contexts that will make possible life-span learning as part of the normal condition of postsecondary education, (3) to meet the social requirements not just of literacy but of adequate advanced education for minorities and the economically disadvantaged, and (4) to help the nation meet the increasing challenges of international competitiveness. The first of these areas involves what might be described as overcoming some of the academy's sacred cows—basic but perhaps outdated assumptions about such issues as the normative character of the past, the nature of college students, the peripheral role of older students and continuing education, and the focus on "the university" as the primary vehicle for higher education. The second area calls for overcoming or diminishing the effect of assumptions that encourage or promulgate turf wars. These include such factors as overemphasis on institutional autonomy and competitiveness and opposition to state-level coordination and planning. The third area involves curriculum and the need to reexamine some of the more confining and even arbitrary assumptions about the nature of the curriculum, the relationship between the arts and sciences and professional and occupational education, and the locus of curricular effectiveness.

A fourth area, one of the major areas of discussion today,

is quality. Involved are a series of limiting assumptions that may have little to do with program effectiveness but create a kind of quality quagmire that needs reevaluation. The issues range from definitions of quality and the conditions of its attainment to programs that are alleged to undermine quality, on the one hand, and to provide a sure means of measuring quality, on the other. Assessment, for example, has become in many quarters, both academic and political, the flag educational concept of the day. Closely related and frequently juxtaposed to quality is the concept of equity. Here a series of assumptions need to be reviewed, particularly if *quality* is not to become a code word for limiting access and equity. Issues range from the relationship between the two to such factors as the role of remedial education and the relevance of the value-added concept.

The sixth area is directly related to the information society and its impact on the academy. It involves the critical issues posed by the explosive development of educational technology, including both computers and telecommunications. These pose what is conceived in a number of quarters as the educational technology threat. Concerns about the sanctity of the classroom, faculty job security, and quality control of long-distance learning all enter into the discussion. Finally, the seventh area involves the impact of relationships between business and industry and the academy and concern that such external influences will dilute and undermine institutional integrity. This concern is sometimes expressed in relation to research liaisons, to instructional linkages between the campus and business, or to acceptance of credit for business in-service education and training.

Within each of these areas, we have identified a set of beliefs and attitudes that constitute myths indigenous to the higher education community. Our list is meant to be illustrative, rather than exhaustive; in addition, any classification of myths is bound to be more than somewhat arbitrary, since some myths tend to fall into more than one category, and the categories themselves may change as contemporary concerns change. Finally, the spectrum of myths itself changes over time; what constitutes a myth at one time may have been an accurate description or reasonable expectation at another time.

Some of these myths are beliefs about the nature of higher education processes or objectives that are sincerely held but that have been only partially tested or have not been tested recently; others are clearly fictions designed to maintain the status quo, protect the particular interests of some group within higher education, or both. Part of what characterizes all of them as myths is that they tend to be held without a clear conception of their implications, without adequate reference to the changing environment or their relevance to the postsecondary educational needs of society, or with emotional rather than rational attachment to what is seen as a comfortable past.

As is often the case with myths, some of these may well have grown out of experience and may contain some valid insights or elements of truth. However, taken at face value, they may simply be false, or they may distort the facts in such a way as to inhibit effective action or misguide the academic community in its attempts to meet current higher education needs. And some of them may contradict each other. While it is not possible to interpret experience without assumptions and hypotheses, it is critical, particularly in periods of rapid transition, to frequently reexamine assumptions to assess their continued relevance as well as their congruity with experience.

Not all of the myths discussed in the following chapters are of equal weight or priority, but any one of them can be a stumbling block to effective change. And taken together, some of the more serious and pervasive myths, particularly if reinforced by political or social groups outside the academy, whether at local, state, or national levels, could become real barriers to achieving quality with equity, expanding the learning society, and meeting the challenge of international competition and leadership, which in our view are basic to maintaining and enhancing America's role in the twenty-first century.

Academic and Social Responsibility and Accountability

We noted earlier some of the social, demographic, and economic changes taking place that have a direct bearing on expectations of higher education and its future effectiveness. The current emphasis on traditional undergraduate education and its assessment, as important as that is, is only part of the picture. All ages and all post–high school levels are involved, including continuing professional education, with its direct relationship to professional practice. One must, of course, add to educational instructional expectations research (both pure and applied) and service expectations.

No institution can provide the full range of educational opportunities required to meet the educational, research, and service needs of society, nor can any one institution be accountable for so doing. Even consortia, which often are linkages of fundamentally similar types of institutions, are limited to the particular common objectives of the institutions in question or to the common objectives that have given rise to the consortium. The responsibility for providing educational opportunity at all levels commensurate with citizen interests and public needs is and has historically and constitutionally been not just an institutional or community responsibility but primarily a state responsibility. There is a clear state and public interest in encouraging and supporting a real diversity of postsecondary educational institutions designed to serve different educational needs. Today, there is also a state interest in establishing and reinforcing, within that diversity, cooperative and complementary activities to make these diverse services readily available to all those who want or require postsecondary education — a far wider population than at one time was even dreamed of. Thus, states and institutions together have a responsibility and an accountability for ensuring that each institution has a clearly defined mission as well as objectives and that the institutions operate within their missions, but the missions must be modifiable to ensure systemwide or statewide adequacy. The state has the additional responsibility of ensuring that the system rather than any single institution is adequate to meet the diversity of higher education needs of the total community.

The state already has the ability to exercise this responsibility in relation to its public institutions. Preferably, it should do so working cooperatively with them through a state higher education board or agency rather than by direct legislative or gubernatorial intervention. In a number of states (New York, Connecticut, Massachusetts, Oklahoma, Pennsylvania, and North Carolina, for example), the state also has some legislative mandate to include the private sector in the planning process. In some states, particularly east of the Mississippi, success in meeting the diversity of needs explicitly depends on involvement and cooperation of both public and private institutions. Such private-sector cooperation is usually provided voluntarily. Where the state makes funds available to private institutions through direct grants, tuition equalization programs, and/or student assistance, some sense of accountability may further enhance private-sector cooperation.

Recognition of the public and statewide role, of the need for a diversity of institutions and programs to meet the variety of communal needs, and of the accountability of the institutions and the state in assuring themselves and the public that the needs are being met does not call for assessment, but assessment that is much more complex than it is characterized in many current discussions. Four kinds of assessment would seem to be essential: assessment of the higher education needs of the citizens on community, statewide, and even interstate and national levels; assessment of the ability of current institutions and programs collectively to meet these needs; assessment of the extent to which the needs are in fact being met by the existing institutions and programs, including where more should be added or some subtracted; and assessment of the effectiveness or quality with which the needs are being met, including the quality of undergraduate programs.

How well the variety of postsecondary educational needs are being met and how planning and implementation to meet them are being carried out vary considerably from state to state and institution to institution; this includes how problems created by or related to the various myths are being dealt with. Nontraditional students and nontraditional programs have been a particular matter of public interest and higher education activity since the period of student unrest of the sixties and early seventies. While a number of programs begun during that period did not survive, a number of others—for example, New York's External Degree Program and Empire State College, New Jersey's Thomas A. Edison College, Minnesota's Metropolitan University, and Washington's Evergreen College—have not only survived but flourished.

The Commission on Non-Traditional Study (the Gould Commission), chaired by Samuel B. Gould, sponsored by the College Entrance Examination Board and the Educational Testing Service, and funded by the Carnegie Foundation, issued its report in 1973. Its first recommendation is as relevant today as it was then: "Full educational opportunity should be realistically available and feasible for all who may benefit from it, whatever their condition of life" (Commission on Non-Traditional Study, 1973, p. 7). In a sense, the Gould Commission at least temporarily placed the imprimatur of the higher education establishment on what was called the "nontraditional movement." In its earlier phases, this nontraditional movement tended to focus primarily (though not wholly) on college-age students. Today, if one accepts the view that traditional students are in general full-time resident eighteen- to twenty-two-year-olds, the nontraditional students far outnumber (by six times at least) the traditional students.

Quite apart from the period of student revolt and considerably antedating it, the adult and continuing higher education movement, as limited as it once was and restricted in some institutions as it still may be, has provided insight, models, and leaders devoted to providing the "full educational opportunity" to nontraditional students of all ages that the Gould Commission called for. While most of the major foundations and the federal Fund for the Improvement of Postsecondary Education have played major roles in support of postsecondary educational innovation, the programs of the W. K. Kellogg Foundation in support of continuing education, lifelong learning, and nontraditional approaches to recognizing and serving the wider community of learners deserve special mention. The W. K. Kellogg Foundation not only has supported institutional developments but has encouraged both institutional and state commitment and action. Beginning in the 1960s by helping to establish and fund adult education centers and programs at a series of institutions around the country (in Oklahoma, Maryland, New Hampshire, and Chicago, for example), during the 1980s it moved into support of state-level experimentation and system development, such as with the Education Commission of the States project on Enhancing the State Role in Lifelong Learning from 1980 to 1983 and the Oklahoma Network of Continuing Higher Education from 1985 to 1988. More recently, the Kellogg Foundation has also funded interstate activities, including an Intermountain Community Learning and Information Services Project involving Utah State University, Montana State University, Colorado State University, and the University of Wyoming to bring postsecondary educational opportunity to isolated communities. In addition, it has provided grants to support projects on continuing professional education at Pennsylvania State University and Ohio State University. Elements of continuing professional education have been included in the more comprehensive grants to Oklahoma and one to the University of Georgia. Like that for Oklahoma, the University of Georgia grant involves a broader approach to a number of aspects of adult continuing education and to institutional and social change. Unlike that for Oklahoma, the Georgia project operates through a single institution, although it clearly has implications for the state as a whole. Another important foundation activity is its support of a major continuing higher education leadership program at the National University Continuing Education Association. Through its foresight, its various grants over recent years, and its support of leadership in the field of continuing higher education, the foundation has had a profound positive effect not only on continuing higher education in a more traditional sense but on higher education in general and its potential ability to deal with what have become key issues in the transition to the twenty-first century.

One further activity of the W. K. Kellogg Foundation aimed at overcoming some of the more traditional myth-related blinders of higher education is its support of the work of Morris Keaton and what is now called the Council for Adult and Experiential Learning (CAEL). CAEL has probably done as much as or more than any other group to help advance the recognition that the crucial issue in education is what a person knows and what his or her skills are, rather than simply time put in in formal classes. It has pioneered the use of portfolio evaluation and has developed criteria of quality control in carrying out such evaluations. It has also been a pioneer in the development of computer-based counseling. Most recently, CAEL has been working with major businesses, industries, and unions in developing Employer Growth and Development Programs utilizing higher education institutions and programs (Gamson, 1988) to expand educational opportunity and ensure not job permanence but work adaptability.

Clearly, then, the continuing higher education movement has many sources of support and inspiration. While it has at times contributed to some of the higher education myths, it can be one of the most seminal areas in enabling higher education to address the central issues of the twenty-first century and help modify many of the myths.

The Oklahoma Experience

The Oklahoma Network of Continuing Higher Education (ONCHE) is one of the recent major projects supported by the W. K. Kellogg Foundation. In many respects, this project is unique; its results have been sufficiently striking and germane to the current challenges to postsecondary education to warrant its use as a key illustration in considering some of these issues. It provides a context in part for counterbalancing, in part for placing in perspective some of the myths that we will consider. While examples or illustrations from other W. K. Kellogg Foundation projects and from higher education in general will be drawn on for illustration, we will utilize the Oklahoma experience as a major point of reference. Even the areas in which it has not quite fulfilled its expectations are instructive.

The uniqueness of the project can be demonstrated in a number of ways. First, the breadth of the project, as stated in its purposes and objectives, is sweeping. It touches directly or indirectly on almost every aspect of higher education in the state. The objectives include the following:

1. To expand the opportunity for relevant higher learning to everyone, everywhere, everyday;
2. To assure quality learning opportunities by integrating continuing education into the academic mainstream;
3. To synergise the educational resources of the state through interinstitutional cooperation and interagency collaboration;
4. To develop a cost-effective delivery system, especially by sharing resources through new educational technologies [White, 1988, p. 4].

To accomplish these objectives, the project was designed to consist of seven major modules involving not only the academic community but important parts of the wider community. Module I was a leadership development program involving regents, trustees, presidents, executive officers, and faculty from the higher education institutions in the state, both public and private. In addition to the major support from the W. K. Kellogg Foundation, this module was also supported by two Oklahoma foundations, the Sarkeys Foundation and the Noble Foundation. More than a thousand people were involved in seminars and workshops and took part in discussions on such issues as the changing student body, the explosion of knowledge, new methods of delivery of instruction, and shifts in the socioeconomic environment. The seminars developed more than two hundred recommendations for improvement of higher education in Oklahoma in nine content and six administrative areas.

The second module was devoted to continuing higher education program development. In addition to the preparation of a major study of the demography of Oklahoma higher education by Dan S. Hobbs, this module involved needs assessment surveys among seven different groups in the state: public library patrons, community leaders, adults with special needs, academic leaders, Native Americans, and black Oklahomans. To assess the needs in continuing professional education, some sixty position papers from representatives of twenty-three professions were prepared. From seventy-three applications, seventeen incentive grants for development of demonstration programs in continuing education have been funded. Noncredit courses have been incorporated into the state unitized data system as an integral part of academic records. Finally, a new challenging statewide Educational Outreach Policy has been adopted by the Oklahoma State Regents, moving continuing higher education clearly into the mainstream of Oklahoma higher education.

The third module, on professional development, has led to the establishment of a research and graduate center on continuing higher education at the University of Oklahoma under the direction of Huey B. Long. A staff has been recruited, a series of Kellogg Fellows have been appointed, and active research and graduate education are under way. In addition, the Oklahoma Center is linked to all the other colleges and universities in the state through a system of Kellogg Associates on the various campuses. Through the fourth module, on adult guidance and counseling, the fifty-two Educational Information Centers in the state have been equipped with computer and guidance software and connected by telecommunications with each other and the regents' office. Thus, a data base for counseling, guidance, and student assistance has been established throughout the state. An effective professional development program for counselors has also been established.

Module V, on telecommunications enhancement, is developing a communications, data, and instructional system encompassing almost the entire state through microwave extension; fiber-optic linkage of Norman, Oklahoma City, Stillwater, and Tulsa; and a televised instruction system linked to the Oklahoma Educational Television Authority, the Oklahoma State University Television Service, and the University of Oklahoma Health Sciences Center. Through the Oklahoma State University Educational Television Service, which is also the home of the National University Teleconferencing Network, the system resources are opened to and reinforced on a national scale. An informal network has been established to ensure partnership and cooperation among the institutions. The president of each of the thirty-one campuses appoints telecommunications coordinators. On most campuses, these coordinators have established their own committees, whose advice has helped to ensure that the network is structured to serve program needs.

An important characteristic of the project is that while telecommunications is a critical part of the glue that holds a number of its aspects together, it is the uses of telecommunications as required by the substantive educational developments that have helped shape the telecommunications system, not vice versa. Thus, the academic community has been involved from the beginning, not called in to use the system after the fact.

The success of the telecommunications module obviously determines to a great extent the effectiveness of not only the guidance and counseling module but also the sixth module, on library collaboration. The model used in developing library collaboration was the Educational Information Centers of Module IV. At least fourteen public libraries are included in the network. Each library has been supplied with appropriate hardware and software for counseling, as well as with facsimile equipment and satellite down-links, thus opening the potential for wide bibliographical search packages. Professional development services for librarians also have been provided. Some of the librarians have set aside special classrooms for teleconferencing and telecommunications instruction in their communities. The participating public libraries have, in fact, become an integral part of the total higher education system.

The final module, Module VII, on interprofessional continuing education, involves particularly health and health-related fields and is carried out primarily by the Oklahoma University Health Sciences Center. As it has developed, it has focused on ethics in the health professions; in addition to a series of seminars on philosophical, legal, and economic aspects of professional ethics in the health fields, it has included appointment of fourteen Kellogg Fellows from the professional fields and the establishment of a professorship in ethics in the University of Oklahoma Health Sciences Center. Of particular significance for the future of health in Oklahoma is the telecommunications network that ties together the Center and various hospitals around the state to provide critical medical information for practitioners.

In addition to its breadth, a second unique aspect of the project is that the first module is by no means confined to adult and traditional continuing education in its scope but covers almost every aspect of the higher education continuum. The more than two hundred recommendations growing out of the module cover almost all facets of higher education in Oklahoma. This, however, is in harmony with the nature of the project as a whole and its concern with continuing higher education as central to higher education as a whole. It involves a recognition of two important issues. The first is that higher continuing education is as relevant to the members of the academic community themselves (regents, trustees, presidents, administrators, faculty) as it is to the larger community and that the form this takes is leadership development. The second is that such continuing education in leadership development can review, renew, and strengthen not only the welfare but the shape of the system. Few aspects of the project underline so clearly as this the essential character of continuing education as an integral part of higher education and the need for "mainstreaming" it. Paul Sharp, former president of the University of Oklahoma and director of Module I, states it as follows: "It is vital to the future of Oklahoma higher education that academic leaders become 'lifelong learners' so that they may respond more readily to change and to new demands. It is they who must devise the plans to deal with change, make the decisions necessary to implement them, and persuade the other faculty and staff to adopt a new way of thinking" (Sharp, 1988, p. 34).

A third striking and unique feature of the project is its recognition that the issues involved are too large for any one institution to handle alone, that dealing with the problems outlined and providing the kind of opportunity described in the objectives require state regent leadership and coordination, interinstitutional cooperation, and common planning and commitment to meeting the higher education needs of the state now and into the twenty-first century. This does not involve a diminishing of the institutional role or responsibility; rather, it means enhancing it by making available to every institution the resources of every other institution in the state to help it to fulfill its own unique function.

If not unique, at least an exemplary characteristic of the project is its effective use of a wide range and combination of internal and external educational leaders, consultants, and experts from the higher education community in implementing the project, in such a way that the leadership and decision making in the project always remain in the Oklahoma system. Thus, the project was an informed exercise in creative planning and implementation to identify and achieve Oklahoma educational objectives. This one aspect of the project clearly increases the applicability of the Oklahoma experience to the rest of the country. Finally, while the various parts of the project are not coequal in funding or in scope and thus might seem to be seven projects rather than one, they do fit together in a total pattern. It is the total pattern that must be kept in mind in assessing the relevance of the Oklahoma experience.

2

The Academy's Sacred Cows

Tradition is clearly central to education, to the preservation and expansion of knowledge, and to evolutionary continuity in education and society. One of the major functions of education is to ensure the transmission and enrichment of tradition. Tradition provides the context and much of the substance of social and personal identity; its loss can result in individual disorientation and social disintegration. Even revolution is only a radical modification of tradition or a substitution of one set of traditions for another.

All of these statements come close to being truisms, yet it is important to recognize at the outset that a critique of assumptions is not a critique of tradition. It is, at least in part, concern about the loss of tradition or too extensive modifications of it that seems to be central to such current negative assessments of higher education as Allan Bloom's (1987) *Closing of the American Mind* and even William Bennett's *To Reclaim a Legacy* (1984). Bloom's concern is with what he takes to be the eclipse of one philosophical tradition, the natural rights doctrine of the Enlightenment, in favor of another, the relativism rooted, according to Bloom, in Nietzsche and Heidegger, which reflects the existentialism of the first half of the century. Bennett is concerned that the traditions of Western (Judeo-Christian) civilization

19

will atrophy by benign neglect as we pursue occupation-related skills and dabble in non-Western cultures.

What is of major concern for the effectiveness of higher education as we attempt to meet the social and economic challenges of this last decade of the twentieth century and move into the twenty-first century is that we utilize traditions, including the unique traditions of the higher education community itself, as points of departure for dealing with these challenges and not as barriers or blinders to action. Unfortunately, traditions can be either platforms for their own transcendence or sclerotic conditions of inaction or retreat.

In the previous chapter, we identified seven areas in which modifications of assumptions seem to be imperative if higher and postsecondary educational institutions (1) are to deal realistically and positively with our rapidly changing world, (2) are to provide the contexts that will make life-span learning part of the recognized central mission of postsecondary education, (3) are to meet the social requirements not just of literacy but of adequate advanced education for minorities and the economically and culturally disadvantaged, and (4) are to help the nation meet the increasing challenges of international economic competition. The first of these areas involves certain persistent traditions that have gained the status of myths. Traditions tend to become myths at the point at which they lose some or all of their current relevance to the world as it is and, if taken at face value, either are false or distort the facts in such a way as to inhibit effective action or to misguide the higher education community in its efforts to meet current higher educational needs.

This first set of myths is made up of what we have described as the academy's sacred cows. While some of these myths are of much more recent origin than others, all of them tend to reinforce a real or imagined higher education status quo. They express what for many are real concerns that recent trends in higher education either have already weakened or are likely to weaken higher education's unique character and contribution to society, may dilute its rigor, or may undermine its quality or commitment. They are sacred cows in the sense that they are rather basic assumptions about the nature and structure of the academic process.

The Golden Era Myth

A major candidate for the position of the most persistent of myths is the myth of the Golden Era—that things were much better in the past. It is by no means unique to higher education. In the Judeo-Christian tradition, for example, it is archetypically embodied in the concepts of the Garden of Eden and the Tower of Babel. It would be most surprising if education in general and higher education in particular did not have its Golden Era interpreters. In part, this myth is a result of the essentially conservative nature of higher education institutions. In 1828, the Yale faculty in its wisdom appeared to close the curriculum for all time against the intrusion of such diverting and nonclassical subjects as modern languages and the natural sciences (Hofstadter and Hardy, 1952, p. 21). Much more recently, the former president of Yale, A. Bartlett Giamatti (1988), commented that "Without constant attempts to redefine and reassert publicly their nature and purpose, universities become frozen in internal methodology, in complacent self-perpetuation. Universities are profoundly conservative institutions, meant to transmit the past, built to remember" (p. B1). It is extraordinarily easy, particularly in periods such as the present, when society is undergoing major change and the effectiveness of higher education is being questioned, to translate this conservatism into the argument that things were better in the good old days and that today we are in a period of decline from some previous golden era.

In part, such a judgment may be due to what is at times perceived as a "promise-performance gap," which has, as Brad Mitchell has pointed out, "encouraged many reformers to call for a return to the 'good old days' when colleges and universities taught the 'best and the brightest' for a reasonable cost" (Mitchell, 1987, p. 124). In part, it may also be due to what Jencks and Riesman (1968, p. 35) suggested some years back is "the human tendency to assume that if things are presently bad, they were once better, rather than realizing that they are likely to be considered bad precisely *because* they are getting better."

Whatever the source, the current prevalence and persistence of the myth is easy enough to document. It appears in some form and as applied to some aspect or aspects of higher education in most of the "reports" on the need for reform in higher education, from the National Institute for Education's study group report *Involvement in Learning* (Study Group on the Conditions of Excellence in American Higher Education, 1984) and the Association of American Colleges (1985) report *Integrity in the College Curriculum* to such general commentaries as Allan Bloom's (1987) *Closing of the American Mind* and E. D. Hirsch, Jr.'s (1987) *Cultural Literacy*. Common to all of the reports and books is the general theme that higher education is in a state of decline and disarray. This theme is developed in different ways and to some extent applied to different aspects of higher education, although all of the reports tend to concentrate on undergraduate, baccalaureate education. While there is rather clearly divergence among them on what constituted the original state of grace from which the decline began, common to all is an assumption of and a nostalgia for an earlier time of academic integrity, wholeness, and effectiveness. Thus, for example, *Integrity in the College Curriculum* harks back to the coherence and integrity of the curriculum in the first two hundred years of American higher education, when "the course of study was shaped by the authority of tradition, seldom challenged and easily accommodating both new learning and changing social conditions" (Association of American Colleges, 1985, p. 35–39). Allan Bloom seems in part to agree when he stresses a period of "a unified view of nature and man's place in it" and of the dominance of reason (Bloom, 1987, pp. 346–347). However, he also cites the fifties, before the student revolt, as "one of the great periods of the American University" (p. 322); and William Bennett (1984), in the National Endowment for the Humanities report *To Reclaim A Legacy,* calls attention to the "steady erosion" of the undergraduate curriculum in "the past twenty years" (p. 19).

In the extreme, Allan Bloom talks about "the collapse of the entire American educational structure" (Bloom, 1987, p. 321) as a result of the student unrest of the 1960s and early 1970s. Other reports, while not going quite so far, echo the theme of decline, of loss of the liberal tradition, of fragmentation, erosion, and decay. Ernest Boyer (1987) regrets the loss of focus by the colleges on "the larger, more transcendent issues" and sees within the academy itself "the fragmentation of knowledge, narrow departmentalization, and an intense vocationalism" (p. 7). *Involvement in Learning* laments the "erosion of liberal learning" (Study Group on the Conditions of Excellence in American Higher Education, 1984, p. 1) and warns that the growing "gaps between the ideal and the actual" as reflected in "the quality of facilities, faculty, morale, and academic standards" are "serious warning signals" (p. 8) of problems ahead. The National Governors' Association Task Force on College Quality (1986) asserts that "evidence of program decline and devaluation, particularly in the humanities, is becoming increasingly prevalent" (p. 155). William Bennett (1984) insists that "teaching and learning in the humanities are not what they should be or can be" and goes on to suggest that "evidence of this decline is compelling" (p. 13). Finally, the Association of American Colleges (1985), in language almost as strident as Bloom's, talks about "the decay in the college course of study and . . . the role of college faculties in creating and nurturing that decay" (p. 1), the "collapse of structure and control" and "the intrusion of ephemeral knowledge developed without concern for the criteria for self-discovery, critical thinking, and exploration of values that were for so long central to the baccalaureate degree" (p. 2). This is more than faintly reminiscent of the Yale faculty of 1828.

The question at this point is not whether greater emphasis should be placed on self-discovery, critical thinking, and values in the college curriculum or whether the humanities and liberal learning should be central to higher education institutional and student objectives. This might conceivably be the case. The crucial questions rather are whether one achieves these or other objectives in a manner relevant to today's challenges by looking or even going backwards and, if one could or did, whether one would find a golden period of coherence, integrity, and appropriate academic devotion that could be reproduced today. Here the answers clearly seem to be no.

Jencks and Riesman's comment that things are likely to be considered bad precisely because they are getting better may be very much to the point. The history of higher education has to be seen in the context of the history of the nation itself; of changing social, political, and even geographical conditions; and of changing and expanding levels of social consciousness or awareness. It is an evolving history. The assumption that the unity or integrity of the curriculum in the first two hundred years of American higher education (even if there were such unity and integrity) is relevant to the complexity and vastly accelerated expansion of knowledge today or to the complexity of current social structure and needs is at best gratuitous. The idea that vocationalism is a modern diversion, that in earlier days students came to get liberal education rather than to prepare for jobs, seems to have little foundation in fact. The early colleges on the whole were established to prepare students primarily for the ministry and law, and the classical curriculum was seen as the best way to do so. However, as early as 1754, agriculture was introduced at King's College (later Columbia). West Point was established in 1862 to provide engineering as well as military education. The first private school of engineering appeared in Maine in 1823. In spite of the faculty report of 1828, Yale added a professorship in agricultural chemistry and animal and vegetable physiology in 1846 (Cheit, 1975, p. 17). These moves were clearly vocational in the contemporary sense. Students were no less concerned with their future careers than they are today. Even the assumption that, because colleges were small, students and faculty had far more intimate contact and mutual respect and understanding does not correspond to the facts (Jencks and Riesman, 1968, pp. 135, 199). As in the schools, the disciplinary role of the professor and the *in loco parentis* role of the college were not necessarily conducive to student-faculty closeness. Although some colonial colleges were concerned about educating Native Americans, and black colleges were created after the Civil War, for most colleges in the first two hundred years, the issues of minorities and the economic and culturally disadvantaged were of minor importance.

The assumption that the 1950s were somehow the golden age to which we should return does not fare much better. While, thanks to the GI Bill, access to higher education had expanded considerably over earlier periods, the broader concern with equity and access growing out of *Brown* v. *Board of Education* (1954) and the impact of the civil rights movement on higher education lay still ahead. The federal funds available to veterans, in addition to enabling them to go to legitimate postsecondary educational institutions, also led to a proliferation of diploma mills and fraudulent correspondence schools, so much so that in the Servicemen's Readjustment Act of 1952, Congress provided for federal utilization of accreditation and state veterans' approval agencies as means of establishing eligibility of institutions to receive federal funds. Concerns about growing vocationalism, the splintered curriculum, conflict of special interests, and the weakening of the central role of the liberal arts, along with what was described as student apathy, were in many quarters the order of the day. The Truman Commission in 1947 cited as a grave concern "the failure to provide any core of unity in the essential diversity of higher education." It went on to comment, "Some community of values, ideas and attitudes is essential to a cohesive force in this age of minute division of labor and intense conflict of special interests" (Education Commission of the States, 1986, p. 11).

In the late 1950s, I was one among others who were writing and talking about the crisis in the liberal arts (Millard, 1964). In some respects, the fifties were the lull before the double crises of rapidly increasing enrollments and student unrest of the 1960s and early 1970s. From the standpoint of enrollments, expenditures, and federal reinforcement, the 1960s might better be considered a golden era. Enrollments increased from 3,789,000 in 1960 to 8,498,117 in 1970. Expenditures rose from $5.6 billion in 1960 to $22.7 billion in 1970. Community college enrollments, which had been relatively small in 1950, reached 2.2 million in 1970, with almost a 40 percent increase in enrollment between 1969 and 1970 alone (Millard and Berve, 1970, pp. 311, 313; 1972, pp. 318–319). More than twice as much federal legislation was passed in support of various aspects of higher education during the decade of the sixties than in the entire previous history of the country. This included the landmark Higher Education Act of 1965, with its focus on federal student assistance.

Yet, by the end of the decade, Earl Cheit (1971) was talking about *The New Depression in Higher Education,* and the period of student unrest was approaching its climax. That unrest was so pervasive that it not only shook the academic community but weakened public and political confidence in higher education as well. Allan Bloom's experiences at Cornell undoubtedly had something to do with his concern about "the closing of the American mind." For Bloom (1987), this was the period of the collapse of the American educational structure, a period he described as one "of dogmatic answers and trivial facts" (p. 322). Others, including many who lived through it, considered it a period of increased awareness and social concern. While Bloom's assessment seems overly negative, it seems clear that the late sixties and early seventies were an uncomfortable period for many higher education faculty, administrators, or students — and thus for higher education institutions.

And so it goes: Any time one looks more closely at a so-called golden age, like the pot of gold at the end of the rainbow, it tends to disappear. This is not to suggest in any way that the past is unimportant or is not in fact crucial to understanding the present and planning for the future. It may, however, raise questions about the reasonableness and appropriateness of establishing a new "National Association of Scholars" dedicated to "reclaiming the academy" and overcoming such "radicalization" of American higher education as its active involvement in affirmative action (Mooney, 1988, pp. A1, A11). And it does recognize the evolutionary nature of higher education, the fact that while there are continuities and continuing objectives of higher education, its objectives not only are legitimately diverse but are subject to modification in the light of changing social and cultural conditions and educational needs. If they are to remain "eternal," the "eternal verities" must be adaptable and relevant to current and changing conditions. The element of truth in the Golden Era Myth, and what makes it so appealing, is the recognition of the relevance of the past to the present: how we got here, what we are, and our potential for continued development. The point at which it becomes an inhibiting myth is where the past or a particular section of the past is taken as normative, binding, and restrictive in relation to present change and future development.

In contrast to the nostalgia of a golden-era approach to stimulating concern and actions within the educational community, the first module of the Oklahoma Network of Continuing Higher Education project (see Chapter One) can be cited as an approach to creating awareness and stimulating change that uses the past to analyze the present and to project the future. This leadership development module was in many respects central to the project as a whole. It did not involve continuing education in a restricted or traditional sense but rather focused on the overall leadership of higher education in Oklahoma. It was based on the premise that if higher education in Oklahoma is not only to meet and deal with changing conditions but to be an active participant in helping to inform and guide those changes, all of higher education leadership needs to be informed and involved — needs to continue its own education for educational effectiveness. Thus, the project included trustees and regents, administrators, and faculty from across the state at both public and private institutions in what in effect was a three-year analysis of five themes: (1) current issues in higher education, (2) our changing students, (3) the expanding knowledge base, (4) new educational technologies, and, out of these, (5) recommendations for change and future plans for higher education in Oklahoma. The participants were and are the leaders in higher education who will play a crucial role in shaping its future. The program was carried out in a series of workshops, seminars, and discussion groups. The thirty-three seminars involved some 3,700 participants, and more than one hundred national and state leaders in higher education served as keynoters, panelists, and discussion leaders. People such as Clark Kerr, Howard Bowen, Bryce Jordan, Patricia Cross, Ernest Boyer, Michael O'Keefe, and Ann Reynolds helped set the national context.

The emphasis throughout was on quality improvement: for trustees and regents, on quality of policy formulation and effectiveness of governance; for administrators, on quality of planning and decision making; and for faculty, on quality of teaching, research, and leadership, particularly at the departmental level. Working through committees and task forces in a series of fifteen subjects (for example, humanities, agriculture) and operational areas (such as research, fiscal affairs, and academic leadership), participants in the series of seminars developed more than two hundred recommendations to the chancellor and board of regents for the strengthening of higher education in Oklahoma in the future. These are currently being reviewed and utilized as appropriate in the Oklahoma planning process.

This Oklahoma program involved using and borrowing from the past, analyzing the current environmental issues and problems, nationally as well as locally, and developing recommendations for the future, not looking back to a golden era but focusing on the continuity of development in improving higher education in the state. Given the scope of the program, it is unlikely that it could have been carried out by one institution or without the stimulus and help of an outside agency — in this case, the regents and the W. K. Kellogg Foundation.

The Reform from Within Myth

While the Golden Era Myth involves looking to the past for guidance as to what higher education ought to be in the future, the Reform from Within Myth assumes that effective academic reform originates primarily from within the academy. Part of the academy's common wisdom is that through research, social criticism, and effective teaching, the colleges and particularly the universities bring about changes and reform in society and affect both national and global events. This common wisdom may indeed describe the impact that higher education has had in many spheres in the twentieth century. Few would challenge the claim that many, perhaps most, of the major advances in knowledge and technology have had their origin in university research and scholarship. In recent years, our knowledge base and its technical applications have expanded in almost a geometric progression. While this has not necessarily led to a better world, it clearly has led to a far more complex world in which the universities have also supplied the requisite new professionals, technicians, and fields of investigation essential to its operation, and the end is nowhere in sight. Higher education has also been seen by much of the public as a primary avenue to social mobility. It can, with some justification, claim to be one of the major sources of social reform.

It is far too easy, however, to move from the proposition that the academy has a major impact on societal change and reform to the assumption that it provides the primary impetus for its own reform. This is not to deny that, given external impetus, higher education has carried through essential reforms and shaped these to meet societal needs for higher education. Nor is it to say that in some areas, such as graduate education in the second half of the nineteenth century, higher education has not in fact taken the lead in its own development. It is, however, to recognize both the inherent conservatism of the academy, as noted by Giamatti (1988), and the historical impact of external events and actors in effecting major changes and reforms in higher education and its directions of development.

Thus, in the 1820s and 1830s, it was public concern led by Horace Mann and Henry Barnard about schoolteachers, not the colleges, that brought about the establishment of normal schools for teacher preparation (Rosencrance, 1962, p. 47). In contrast to the Yale faculty action of 1828, it was the federal government that through the Morrill Land Grant Act of 1862 opened the curriculum not only to modern languages and natural sciences but to the agricultural and mechanical arts as well. While its full impact was not felt until later in the nineteenth century, Earl Cheit calls it "the key element" in bringing about "the growth of 'applied' subjects mixed with 'pure' subjects [that] became one of the special characteristics of higher education in the United States" (Cheit, 1975, p. 26; see also Moos, 1981, pp. 3-8). It specifically called for extending access to the children of farmers and laborers. The Cooperative Extension (Smith-Lever) Act of 1914 anticipated adult and continuing education through agricultural extension. In the World War I period, the federal government supported the development of vocational education and rehabilitation for veterans through the Smith-Hughes Act of 1917, the Vocational Rehabilitation Act of 1918, and the Smith-Bankhead Act of 1920.

During World War II, through the Servicemen's Readjustment Act of 1944, or GI Bill, the federal government provided the primary impetus not only for increased enrollments but also for expanding recognition of the range and types of students who could benefit from higher education. While some people within the academic world were concerned that the influx of veterans would lead to a lowering of academic standards, exactly the opposite turned out to be the case. The seriousness and commitment that the veterans exhibited tended to offset what they may have lacked in previous motivation, background, or educational experience. In some respects, while few recognized it at the time, the experience with the GI Bill helped to set a major part of the national agenda for higher education for the next three decades. It demonstrated (1) that it is feasible to provide financial support for large numbers of students, (2) that extending access does not necessarily lead to a diminution in quality, and (3) that a far larger portion of the population can benefit from higher education than the academy or the public had traditionally assumed.

The launching of *Sputnik* in 1957 and the National Defense Education Act of 1958 brought about an increased emphasis on science and technology and university research to support technological supremacy. We have already noted the radical increase in federal higher education legislation from 1958 on. While under the reserve clause of the U.S. Constitution, education, including higher education, has been primarily a state responsibility, it would not be incorrect to say that from 1958 at least until 1982, the federal government has played a major role through higher education legislation in defining the parameters and directions of the development of higher education. The federal programs emphasizing student assistance rather than direct institutional support; support of research through the National Science Foundation, the armed forces, and the National Institutes of Health; support of education of health professionals; vocational education (at postsecondary as well as secondary levels); adult and continuing education; and educational opportunity for minorities and students from low-income families — all of these and more illustrate the federal initiative in bringing about higher education change. Among the most important federal initiatives have been the various measures related to civil rights, equal opportunity, and affirmative action. To be sure, many of these, perhaps most, were supported and in some cases even initiated by people and organizations from higher education, but the primary impetus for change in these areas has been through legislation regarding institutions rather than internally through institutions themselves.

The states have played an even more important role, though frequently it has received less national attention. The states provide the major nontuition funding to higher education. It was primarily the states that financed the radical expansion of higher education in the 1960s and 1970s so that, while not all students were able to go to the institutions of their choice during this period, few if any qualified students were turned away from higher education altogether. Before World War II, private institutions accounted for approximately half of the students in higher education. Today, public institutions accommodate almost five times as many students as private institutions, although the enrollments of private institutions have also increased. With very few exceptions, the states have developed statewide governing or coordinating boards for their public institutions, charged in most cases with planning, program review or approval, and budget review; in some instances, this even extends to fund allocation. Over the past three decades, the states have become increasingly concerned with the accountability of higher education institutions and recently more specifically with quality improvement and assessment of educational effectiveness. Finally, the courts have also played a significant role in setting boundaries and providing initiatives for reform, particularly in such areas as civil rights and affirmative action. Clearly, behind all of these federal, state, and legal boundaries and initiatives for change and reform are the political and social movements that have brought them about.

What all this points to is simply the obvious fact that higher education is integral to social, governmental, and legal contexts and that initiatives for change and reform of higher education, while they may in some cases come from within the academy, much more frequently and insistently come from these wider contexts. Through a fascinating and unintended reciprocal arrangement, many of the initiatives for change and reform in society come from the academy, while many of the major initiatives for change and reform in the academy come from the wider society. Further, in many higher education institutions, there appear to be indigenous conditions that, if not militating against change, at least inhibit some institutions (and the academic community) from being the major initiators of their own reform.

One of these conditions seems to be what was underlined in the Golden Era Myth: the tendency exemplified by Bennett, Hirsch, and Bloom to look back to the Judeo-Christian and European philosophical traditions, not just as exemplifying our historical roots but as the only foundation on which a common cultural heritage can rest. This comes close to constituting what Carol E. Schorske (1988) of Princeton calls "the new fundamentalism of Western Culture" (p. B1), a fundamentalism that overlooks the wider multicultural world of which we clearly are a part. The Bennett position tends to be an appeal to ethnocentrism, to the past, and to resistance to change. In contrast, in a forum funded by the W. K. Kellogg Foundation and sponsored by the National University Continuing Education Association, David Hayes-Bautista (1988), the director of Chicano studies at the University of California, Los Angeles, insisted that what we are dealing with is "the fundamental question of intellectual development even if that development means growth in directions that make us uncomfortable. This is crucial both to deal with a changing society at home and to compete economically and intellectually with the Pacific Basin world in which we live" (p. 6). To recognize this is not to abandon or downgrade the Western tradition but to expand our horizons by placing it within an intercultural context.

A second factor frequently inhibiting internal initiatives to change in some universities is the complexity of universities themselves. In the report of the Kellogg Interdisciplinary Task Force on Governance at the University of Georgia, Lief Carter (1988), the task force chair, argues that "the very recommendations for university reform do not consistently address how a complex organization that rewards teachers primarily for research accomplishments can even choose a clear model of desired behavior" (p. 50). According to William Vandament, this complexity is exacerbated by the fact that in most colleges and universities there are at least three rather distinct governance structures that are related to each other but not necessarily coordinated or consistent. The first is the administrative hierarchy, which moves from faculty members through department chairs, deans, and vice-presidents to the president and trustees. The second is a faculty senate or council (or in some cases a faculty union), which bypasses the intermediate levels in dealing with the president. The third is "the shadow governments of the academic disciplines" (Vandament, 1988, A52), headed by leaders and mentors in specialty fields. The likely result is that internal reform is dissipated through governance complexities and even rivalries within the institutions themselves.

A third inhibiting factor is what Alexander Astin has described as a combination of faculty skepticism and inertia resulting from three related characteristics: the faculty's "jealous protection of its own autonomy"; an inherent "mistrust and contempt for administration," including administrator attempts to bring about reform; and the "tendency to be critical of new ideas and to display . . . critical skills at any possible opportunity," where critical skills means "detecting flaws in the views of others" (Astin, 1986, pp. 28–29). While Astin's characterization does not necessarily apply to all faculty members, it helps to describe a reluctance in many institutions to initiate or carry out reforms without some reinforcement and appropriate outside stimuli.

None of this means that higher education institutions in general are incapable of change or that initiative for change and reform is impossible from within. Rather, it points to the need in many institutions for more careful attention to the environment: political, social, and economic. It calls for the development of faculty, administration, and trustee leadership that is increasingly aware of and willing to deal positively with changing environmental conditions without sacrificing the essential missions and integrity of the higher education enterprise. This is easier said than done; however, one step in this direction might be wider development of an environmental scanning process not unlike that used in some parts of the corporate world as a foundation for strategic planning. This currently is being done at the University of Georgia Center for Continuing Education (Simpson, McGinty, and Morrison, 1987), which is sharing the results with the wider University of Georgia community. A final word of advice on this issue comes from Robert Birnbaum (1988): "Those who wish to influence campus administrators should probably direct some of their energy to influencing the external political and bureaucratic leaders to which campus administrators are responsive" (p. 453).

The Traditional College Student Myth

The persistence of the Traditional College Student Myth is a rather striking example of a failure in some institutions and some parts of the academic community not only to engage in environmental analysis but, more fundamentally, to engage in effective analysis of their own current student distribution and characteristics. The Traditional College Student Myth involves the assumption that the "real" college students are the eighteen-to twenty-two-year-old full-time resident students. While there are a good many other students around, they tend to be considered peripheral to the central administrative function of higher education and not where primary attention should be focused. In fact, the primary function of higher education for many institutions is still perceived to be preparing the young to enter contemporary society.

While preparing the young to enter adult contemporary society is an important function of higher education, it clearly is not the only one today, and it can at least be questioned whether it is the primary function or one among a number of related primary functions. There obviously will and should always be a place for institutions or parts of institutions focused primarily on resident, full-time, eighteen- to twenty-two-year-old students. They are a critical and integral part of the higher education system. But even these institutions have had to recognize increases in the number of older students within their residential full-time student bodies. These institutions clearly do not account for or accommodate the majority of students today, nor are they or should they be designed to deal with the variety of students and participants in higher education projected for the twenty-first century.

As already noted, of the 12.5 million students in higher education today, fewer than a sixth (2 million) fit the traditional college student description. More than half of the students are over age twenty-two. Forty percent are over twenty-five. Well over a third live off campus. By the year 2000, adult part-time students are likely to constitute the new majority (Hauptman and Andersen, 1988, p. 16; Hodgkinson, 1986, p. 6). Some additional relevant statistics and projections in relation to the current students and projected future ones are perhaps in order. By 1995, the sixteen- to twenty-year-old population is expected to have fallen by 20 percent from its 1980 numbers (Grant Commission, 1988, p. 29). The U.S. Department of Education estimates that enrollments will continue to increase until 1991 and thereafter to see minor decreases through 1997 (Evangelauf, 1988, p. A34). However, given the shifting student population, these decreases may not occur any more than did the major enrollment losses predicted for the 1980s by a number of sources that dealt primarily with decreases in the eighteen- to twenty-four-year-old age group (Breneman, 1982).

While the overall population of sixteen- to twenty-four-year-olds will continue to decrease, within this group, as in the population in general, the percentage and number of blacks and Hispanics will increase. By the early part of the next century, minorities are expected to become the majority in states such as California and perhaps even Texas. The Population Reference Bureau projects that by the year 2080, more than half of all Americans will be Hispanic, Asian, or black. A more concerted effort to involve college-age and adult minorities in higher education would seem essential for the future economy and welfare of the country. This may help offset the overall eighteen- to twenty-two-year-old decline (State Higher Education Executive Officers, 1987, pp. 7–8).

Although some decrease in the number of twenty-two-to thirty-four-year-old students is expected by 1997, the over-thirty-five age group will increase from 16 percent to 21 percent of the student body (Department of Education, 1988). Women currently constitute the majority of college students and will continue to do so. Of the women currently enrolled, 40 percent are over twenty-five. By the early 1990s, those over twenty-five will constitute half or more of the women enrolled. Added to all of this is the increasing involvement of higher education institutions and systems with continuing professional education, with education in cooperation with business and industry, and with providing education for such groups as union members. All of this gives a perspective on the students enrolled in the real world of higher education that is considerably different from the traditional perspective.

Presumably speaking for the academic community, the Commission on National Challenges in Higher Education (1988) of the American Council on Education argues in the *Memorandum to the 41st President of the United States* that "Colleges and universities must recognize that they have a host of new constituents whom they must serve more effectively. These include part-time and mid-career students, displaced workers, the unemployed and underemployed and those who lack the skills to compete in tomorrow's labor market" (p. 3).

While many institutions have become aware of the new and changing student body, of the inadequacy and even short-sightedness in terms of self-interest for most institutions of concentrating primarily on the "traditional college-age student," and are in fact moving toward a far broader conception of service, the Traditional College Student Myth tends to persist in a great many institutions and is even encouraged in some cases by state agencies and accrediting bodies. In line with such an emphasis on traditional students, Allan Bloom (1987) while recognizing that there are other types of students with different needs, would have us focus on the advantaged students at the twenty or thirty most selective and prestigious institutions in the country, for these are the students who will have the "greatest moral and intellectual effect upon the nation" (p. 22). As he sees it, they are the ones who "most need education, inasmuch as the greatest talents are most difficult to perfect." While his suggestion that we need (as in the post-*Sputnik* period) "better education for the best people" (p. 49) may well be true, to assume that this is where our primary efforts in higher education as a nation should focus seems to disregard both the extent and the depth of current higher education needs and social and national priorities. At best, such an approach would seem to reinforce what Ernest Boyer (1987) has described as "a parochialism that seems to penetrate many higher learning institutions, an intellectual and social isolation that reduces the effectiveness of college and limits the vision of the student" (p. 6).

In preparation for the 1988 issue of the American Council on Education publication *Campus Trends,* college administrators were asked to name the three most important issues facing their institutions over the next five years. As might be expected, these turned out to be finance, enrollment, and quality, with quality leading the list (El-Khawas, 1988, p. 13). In the area of enrollments, the primary concern seemed to be maintaining or increasing them. What is somewhat surprising is that "serving new needs and new populations" appeared as a subcategory under quality rather than under enrollments and was listed as an issue by only 19 percent of the responding administrators. As might be expected, it was recognized as considerably more of an issue for public community colleges (33 percent) than for public four-year institutions (17 percent) or independent institutions (10 percent) and was of least concern for doctorate-granting institutions (8 percent). In fact, the major enrollment challenge for doctorate-granting institutions was how to recruit academically strong students despite demographic changes.

Failure to take into account changing student demographics is seen on the state level as well. While Oklahoma as a matter of state policy has attempted to expand the horizon of higher education's central mission to include all adults capable of benefiting from it wherever they may be, utilizing whatever instructional and learning methods are appropriate, some states, such as Texas and Connecticut, have attempted to limit the amount of off-campus and experiential learning credit that can be applied

toward a degree. Unfortunately, this is reinforced by some accrediting bodies. The Western Association Accrediting Commission for Senior Colleges and Universities (1988, pp.
45–46), for example, restricts the number of experiential learning credits
that can be accepted, the methods by which such credit is to
be established, and the levels at which it can be applied. Even
in Oklahoma, the respondents to surveys of six different groups,
varying from higher education leaders to employers and library
patrons, indicated the highest confidence and preference for
traditional classes in on-campus classrooms at regular school
hours (Belt and Sackett, 1987, p. 5).

It seems clear that we still have a long way to go to leave
behind what George Johnson, the president of George Mason
University, has described as the factory model of higher education designed for eighteen-year-olds in the nineteenth and first
part of the twentieth centuries. "The process was serial, in-
cremental, lock step, synchronized by class hours, standardized
in credits and ordered by semesters . . . . The full-time 18–21
year old undergraduate is not and has not for a decade been
a majority representative of our enterprise, and the factory model
is no longer even in factories. Yet the academy I know keeps
a death grip on outworn conventions" (Johnson, 1985, p. 8).
And Lynton and Elman (1987) point to the importance of recognizing that even the distinction between continuing education
and what is called "regular education" not only is no longer clear
but is ceasing to exist: "At least half of all undergraduate students interrupt their studies for the minimum of one year. . . .
The proportion of part-time students is steadily increasing . . . .
The average age of college students in our urban, commuter
campuses is now twenty-seven or twenty-eight. The non-traditional student is becoming the norm" (p. 97).

What all this points to is not that the eighteen- to twenty-
two-year-olds are less important or even that there is not a place
for institutions primarily aimed at their education. Preparing
youth for entry into society and the world of work and even,
as Bloom (1987) suggests, socializing the advantaged, are legitimate aims of education and may constitute the missions of specific institutions. What is important, however, is to recognize
that the "traditional student" is no longer the norm, that the

"mainstream" students in the twenty-first century will include all post–high school learners in a variety of types of programs in a diversity of institutions designed to meet their multiple higher education needs. Of the major types of higher education institutions, community colleges have generally come closest to recognizing this expanded universe. At this point, a great many four-year and even doctorate-granting institutions need to reassess not only who their students are but whether their structures and services are designed to serve both current and future students.

One example of a college that seems to have recognized who and where the "new" students are and that has adapted its program to serve them in the inner city is the School of New Resources of the College of New Rochelle. It has established six branches in various parts of New York City, such as the South Bronx, Harlem, and Brooklyn, in which it currently has more than 4,000 students. According to Dean Bessie Blake, "We take the program to the community rather than saying to the community, 'you come to us'" (Collison, 1988, p. A40). Not only are these branches in the neighborhoods where people live; the classes are offered at times convenient for the students, and the staff members make themselves available during evenings. The courses are offered not in lectures but primarily in informal seminars. Each campus has the requisite support services, including libraries and academic and financial aid counselors. Unlike its home campus, the School of New Resources is coeducational. Most of its students are older. Many have been out of school for twenty years or more. They come from a variety of backgrounds, though all inner city. The effectiveness of the programs is indicated by the fact that 52 percent of the graduates to date have gone on to some form of graduate education. This is a highly respectable number for any college. For the School of New Resources, the nontraditional student has indeed become the norm.

The Centrality of the University Myth

The term *university* has been so broadened in the last twenty-five years by everything from state legislative action to individual institutional name change as to include types of institutions from complex research universities (Carnegie Research Universities I) to some baccalaureate institutions with only one college and little if any graduate work and, in at least one case, what in fact is a community college. It is not our intent to try to redefine "the university." We have no real quarrel with this broad and amorphous use of the term. Our concern, rather, is with a family of related assumptions that tend to persist. The first is that research universities constitute the model to which all higher educational institutions should aspire. The second is that (using even the broadest sense of the term) universities constitute the major and most important part of higher education and should be, if not the only source of higher education support and concern, at least the center of it. The third is that colleges whose primary purpose is to prepare students for graduate and professional schools, whether they are part of complex universities or freestanding, constitute the norm for undergraduate colleges—what Jencks and Riesman (1968) more than twenty years ago called the university colleges (p. 24).

First, it is obviously not the case that, even if one includes all institutions that call themselves universities and all the "university colleges," one has included even the majority of postsecondary institutions or of students. Not only does this not include a number of four-year colleges not in "the university colleges" group; it leaves out community and other two-year colleges, almost all special-purpose colleges, the entire proprietary sector, and what the Carnegie classification lists as corporate colleges and universities. Community and two-year colleges alone enroll 45 percent of the students in public institutions and 37 percent of students at public and private institutions. One of the criticisms directed at some of the reform reports such as *Involvement in Learning* and *Integrity in the College Curriculum* is that they tend to overlook or disregard the community colleges and their role. Even Ernest Lynton and Sandra Elman (1987) address their fascinating book on new higher education priorities to universities without recognizing that a number of their suggestions are in fact close to if not fully operational in some community colleges and community college systems.

Second, while research universities are critically important in the higher education spectrum, are at the frontiers of
the creation of new knowledge, and are vital in providing the
research essential to national welfare and international competitiveness, to consider them as normative for all higher education or even for all "universities" is neither in their best interests
nor in the interests of other institutions, of students, of the states,
or of the nation. The National Governors' Association Task
Force on College Quality (1986) recognizes particularly the
danger posed to undergraduate education by the use of research
universities as a model: "The predominant model to which most
colleges and universities currently aspire is that of the research
university. Current reward structures for promotion and tenure
in American higher education often encourage faculty to concentrate their efforts on research-oriented tasks. This can lead
to a loss of enthusiasm for undergraduate instruction" (p. 161).
The problem, however, is considerably more pervasive than just
a diminution in enthusiasm for undergraduate instruction. It
involves perception of mission, effectiveness, quality, and prestige. In fact, it directly and adversely limits the possibility of
a diverse system of higher education to meet the variety of postsecondary educational needs in the nation.

In *Choosing Quality,* Frank Newman (1987) recognizes both
the negative impact and part of the continuing source of the
tendency to use the research university as the norm: "A major
cause of the difficulty over mission is the single pyramid of institutional prestige. Despite the assumption of different goals,
the greatest prestige and merit awards accrue to the research
university. It is understandably hard to convince those at regional universities, state colleges and community colleges that
they should be happy with second class status" (p. 45). The
faculty at these institutions, Newman points out, have been educated in the graduate schools of the research universities and
unfortunately are not necessarily reeducated to the importance
of the different missions of the schools at which they are teaching. Thus, their interests seem to them to lie in making their
institutions as much like the research universities as possible.
This attitude tends, sometimes inadvertently, to be reinforced

on the state level through state magnification of the differences in status and prestige. Thus, "there is internally and externally generated pressure driving institutions to move from teachers' colleges to state colleges to state university to research university" (p. 45). In some cases, the pressure starts in two-year community colleges as well.

In many respects, the undergraduate counterpart exemplified in the "university college" phenomenon is an extension of the research university model but is tied particularly to success of students in admission to the most prestigious research university graduate schools. While Jencks and Riesman's (1968) *The Academic Revolution* is in many respects outdated (see Thelin, Casteen, and Bailey, 1988), the tendency they noted of some institutions to succumb to the lure of moving upward by copying parts of the research universities and their feeder institutions has not entirely disappeared. Even the period of student revolt, while it may have modified some of its directions, did not stop this movement, in part because this was also the period of higher education expansion.

While this "upward" movement might be described in some quarters as a concern with continuity and tradition, it is perhaps more accurately described as an example of a tendency of some institutions under market pressures to move toward imitation and homogenization. There are too many examples of good community colleges aspiring to become four-year institutions, of good four-year colleges, including state teachers' colleges, becoming universities by adding questionable graduate programs, and so on. The end result in too many instances is giving up uniqueness for mediocrity. It was this tendency, among other factors, that led a number of states to develop statewide governing or coordinating boards charged with responsibility for planning and assurance of a real diversity to meet the variety of state higher education needs.

The use of the research universities and the highly selective colleges as the norm and prestige base for all of higher education is clearly related to the conservatism of institutions noted by Bartlett Giamatti (1988) and to the persistence of the Golden Era and the Traditional Student Myths. Such a practice has a number of interesting but not necessarily salutary results and side effects. One is that it helps account for and is fed by the fascination of institutions and the public with various reports of institutional and program ratings, almost regardless of their accuracy. In most of these, including the *U.S. News and World Report* special report ("America's Best Colleges," 1988), the research universities and university colleges tend to dominate. Community colleges are not included. Institutions "take pride in" and strive for placement in the ratings, and the public view that the prestige colleges and universities are what higher education is really all about is reinforced.

A second effect is that it leads to what can only be described as false assumptions about price and costs of higher education as a whole that result from considering primarily the research universities and selective colleges. This is the case even with people who should know better. Thus, Chester Finn (1988), currently professor at Vanderbilt University and formerly Assistant Secretary of Education for Educational Research and Improvement, notes that some illustrious colleges and universities now charge $20,000 per year and that the $100,000 bachelor's degree is not far off. He argues that what we need is a low-cost, no-frills university that would counteract the high-cost tendency, do away with "frills and furbelows," and provide a strong quality education. While it is the case, as the president of one private college admits, that raising costs to students in some people's minds raises prestige, this applies to a relatively narrow group of institutions. It may be that new "no-frills universities" are desirable, but a good many of what approximate such universities now exist in every state. What both Finn and former secretary Bennett overlook, perhaps intentionally, is that higher education is considerably broader than research universities and prestige university colleges.

Third, this use of the research university and selective college model has at least contributed to reluctance to accept nontraditional forms of learning and evidence of student accomplishment, to inhibiting effective use of new techniques in some instances, and generally to hindering movement toward what Lynton and Elman (1987) have called "the extended university"

(p. 4). Specifically in relation to regional universities, Lynton and Elman point out that "A major barrier threatening the potential of regional universities is partially self-imposed. *All* universities adopt the goals and measures appropriate to the few larger institutions with ample research funding . . . . The internal hierarchy of values, the measures of academic respectability, and the faculty reward system are astonishingly — and distressingly — uniform" (p. 11). In contrast, these regional universities, for the sake of their own uniqueness and service to the public as no- or few-frills institutions, should follow different but "well established traditions for their scholarly as well as teaching functions, one that places as much value on the interpretation and dissemination of knowledge as on its creation, and that pays as much attention to providing opportunities for life long and recurrent education as to the instruction of the young" (p. 7). From the standpoint of the range and types of current and future students, the societal and individual needs for post–high school education, and the different types of programs and institutions essential to a vital, productive, and renewed internationally competitive America, even Lynton and Elman's description may be too restrictive.

Under the dominance of the research university model, the academic community has been historically reluctant to recognize or encourage its own expansion of types of institutions and the legitimacy of its emerging components. It should be remembered that it was only with reservations that in the 1960s baccalaureate institutions and universities accepted community colleges as legitimate parts of the higher education community. Some still resist accepting community college credits. Today, the proprietary sector is accepted by only very few other institutions as part of the club (see Chapter Three). This is in spite of the fact that it was in 1972 that the U.S. Congress, in amendments to the Higher Education Act of 1965, recognized that even *higher education* is too confining a term for the types of institutions and opportunities that need to be available to post–high school citizens. Accordingly, it adopted the term *postsecondary education,* which is considerably more inclusive. The need for such inclusiveness seems even more evident today than it did in 1972.

All of this is not to downgrade universities in general or the research universities in particular. Nor is it to suggest that research on the range of postsecondary education and initiatives for its improvement are not part of the legitimate activities of investigators and theoreticians in the universities. It is, however, to recognize (1) that postsecondary education in this country has legitimate complexity, (2) that in talking about the university, whether it be the research universities, the range of institutions called universities, or even the "university colleges" — or all of them together — one is talking about only one sector of postsecondary education, as important as that sector is, and (3) that the research university model in particular is not an appropriate model for all postsecondary education. Far too frequently, university faculties, departments, and even planners have condescended to study, develop programs for, and even plan for other segments of higher education without effectively working with them with a common concern for meeting the needs and improving the quality of postsecondary education across the board. It is this lack of recognition of the community of postsecondary education and complementary functions of its various parts that needs to be reassessed as we approach the new century.

The next three myths in interesting ways tend to be variations on themes closely related to the Centrality of the University Myth.

The Transfer of Credit Myth

The issue of transfer of academic credit is a thorny one that has been around for a long time and has a number of different aspects. It was one of the issues that gave rise to the regional organizations of schools and colleges that became institutional accrediting bodies in the latter part of the nineteenth and the early part of the twentieth centuries. For them, the questions were essentially articulation questions — articulation between secondary schools and colleges (including defining at what level college begins), among colleges, and between colleges and graduate schools. The questions of whom to admit, what credits to accept, and on what basis to accept them have tended to be jealously guarded prerogatives of the institutions themselves and are considered among the cornerstones of institutional autonomy. Since prestige is frequently related to selectivity, admission and transfer of credit are areas in which the tendency to imitate the research universities and university colleges is likely to be high. Among public institutions in states where law or custom requires admission of all resident high school graduates who apply, there may not be as much control over general admissions as in independent institutions, but there may be considerably more control over admission of transfer students and acceptance of credit by the receiving institution.

It is clear that there ought to be some reasonable basis for accepting credits. In a "Joint Policy Statement on Transfer and Award of Academic Credit," the Council on Postsecondary Accreditation, the American Council on Education, and the American Association of Collegiate Registrars and Admissions Officers list three basic considerations that should be taken into account. First is the educational quality of the institution or program from which the student is transferring. This condition is usually assumed to be met if the institution is accredited by an accrediting body recognized by the Council on Postsecondary Accreditation. The second is the comparability of the nature, content, and level of credit offered for transfer. The third is the appropriateness and applicability of the credit earned to the program offered at receiving institutions in the light of the student's educational goals (Council on Postsecondary Accreditation, 1990, p. 1). While the spirit of the joint statement and the three considerations make good sense if liberally interpreted, part of the problem — and what gives rise to the Transfer of Credit Myth — is an overly narrow concept of comparability. The Transfer of Credit Myth involves the assumption that comparable content means content that is identical (or very nearly identical) to the content and even structure of courses at the receiving institutions. Implied in a good many instances is the view that the institution from which the student is transferring should be as close to a clone of the receiving institution as possible.

While the joint statement on transfer of credit obviously addresses primarily the transfer of credit among higher education institutions, the issue involved is in fact broader than interinstitutional transfer, as important as that is, and extends to acceptance of and evaluation of credit from non–higher educational institutions and nontraditional sources, including credit for experiential learning. The statement affirms that one factor relevant to interinstitutional transfer of credits is the accreditation status of the institution from which the student comes. Accreditation helps ensure that the institution meets at least minimal conditions or standards related to educational quality. Accreditation by itself is clearly not enough to establish transferability, but where it applies, it is a relevant condition and should mean that a student should be given reasonable consideration in assessing the credits that he or she wishes to transfer.

Beyond this minimal (and external) condition are the far more critical issues of the student and his or her educational objectives, the relationship of these to the objectives of the institution into which he or she is transferring, and the relevance and adequacy of the course work being transferred to both. And yet it is exactly these factors that tend to be downplayed or lost in reliance on the Transfer of Credit Myth. Institutional structure, which may be completely irrelevant to the educational value of particular courses or programs, too often gets in the way of achieving either the students' or the institutions' educational program objectives.

This rigidity of credit transfer and utilization in some cases is actually found within and among the parts of complex institutions themselves. At one point when the author was dean of the College of Liberal Arts at Boston University, the college faculty engaged in an extended debate as to whether to accept courses in transfer from its own evening program toward its bachelor of arts degree. What made this particularly ironic was that the courses in question were being taught in most instances by the same faculty, using the same textbooks, making the same assignments, and, while the schedule was arranged somewhat differently, requiring the same hours of classwork as in the "regular" program during the day. Even when the instructors were different, they were all departmentally approved and appointed. While the opponents of accepting evening credits were not able to carry the day, they were able to restrict the number of evening credits that could be counted toward the degree.

This is not an isolated or wholly unusual situation. In some institutions, a rather sharp distinction is drawn between credits earned in their continuing education, outreach programs, and community service units, on the one hand, and their traditional colleges of arts and sciences, on the other. Transfer of credit is by no means automatic. Thus, for example, in one major east coast university, the adult and continuing education unit is set up as a separate college even though it is located on the parent university campus. Its credits are considered for transfer as though it were an external institution by the college of arts and sciences of the parent university. In some institutions, such as the University of California, off-campus and adult education courses give "extension credit," which is not considered equivalent to regular credit normally counted toward regular university degrees. In contrast, to avoid any designation of first- and second-class credits, the Oklahoma State Regents for Higher Education in February 1988 adopted an Educational Outreach General Policy that eliminates internal credit distinctions: "Credit awarded for completion of approved courses at off-campus locations or offered through approved electronic media and non-traditional methodologies shall be equal to that for courses offered on the main campus of the credit granting institutions, and shall be fully applicable towards the satisfaction of requirement for academic degrees and certificates" (Oklahoma State Regents, 1988, pt. IIA, p. 2).

The transfer-of-credit situation as it involves the relationships between community colleges and four-year institutions has improved considerably in recent years. However, in the earlier days of the rapid development of community colleges, a number of senior institutions were highly reluctant to accept community college students or their credits. Now that two-year institutions enroll more than a third of all college students, senior institutions are much more interested in encouraging community college transfer students to continue their education than was once the case. On the whole, accommodation has been made to substantive equivalence in transfer rather than formal equivalence. It is particularly crucial that transfer policy of senior institutions toward community colleges be both liberal and clear, since community colleges constitute one of the key avenues of access to institutions of higher education in general. Thirty-nine percent of all black students, 53 percent of Hispanic students, and 43 percent of Asian students enter higher education through the community college system (Cohen, 1988, p. 383). It is essential that this avenue of access be kept open and that minority students in community colleges be encouraged to continue in advanced education. If this is to occur, senior and community colleges have an obligation to work closely together to encourage continuity in transfer to senior institutions.

Not all senior institutions even today have been equally amenable to acceptance of community college transfer of credit. In this area as in a number of others, it has in many cases taken external pressure, usually from the states, to bring about effective articulation. A number of states with developed community college systems, through legislative action, action by a statewide governing or coordinating board, the report of a special planning commission, or a combination of these, have developed articulation agreements between the senior colleges and the community colleges. In some cases, articulation agreements have been worked out by direct interinstitutional consultation between one or more community colleges and senior colleges on a voluntary basis. Regardless of the source, such agreements do at least provide both assurance of continuity in transfer and procedures for carrying it out.

Unfortunately, on the undergraduate baccalaureate level, articulation agreements between four-year institutions are relatively rare. Among the exceptions to this are a number of consortia designed to provide wider resources through intercollegiate registration, such as the five-college consortium in central and western Massachusetts (Smith, Holyoke, Amherst, University of Massachusetts, and Hampshire). Where neither consortia nor articulation agreements exist, the transfer-of-credit situation is close to laissez-faire. This applies to lateral transfer among two-year and graduate institutions as well as baccalaureate institutions. Theoretically, the joint statement on transfer of credit furnishes guidelines, but even when institutions are aware of it, it is often more honored in the breach or in rigid interpretation of some parts of it than it is accepted as providing operating procedures. Far too frequently, formal structural issues take over, and student accomplishments get lost.

For example, accreditation of an institution by a recognized accrediting body should serve as a starting point or base for consideration of transfer of credit between institutions and open up for review other relevant factors, such as student accomplishments and institutional educational objectives. What tends to take place in many institutions, however, is that the institution, by explicit policy or historical precedent, will consider only credits from other regionally accredited institutions (and sometimes not all of them). Among these, it usually accepts without question (assuming acceptable grades) transfer of credits from what it considers to be its "peer" group institutions. But this leaves out students and credits from institutions accredited by other recognized national (rather than regional) institutional accrediting bodies, such as the American Association of Bible Colleges, the Association of Independent Colleges and Schools, and the National Association of Trade and Technical Schools. It may well be the case that some types of courses from some of these institutions, as also from some regionally accredited institutions, are not relevant to the programs and objectives of the would-be receiving institution and should not be transferred. But a good many of them in business, arts and sciences, and even certain technical fields may be not only relevant but in some cases more effectively taught than at some "peer" institutions. To refuse to consider such work for transfer would seem both arbitrary and unwarranted. This is not to argue that any courses or students from any institution even where articulation agreements exist should be accepted without review. It is, however, to suggest that arbitrary refusal to review students and course work from institutions on the basis of type of accreditation alone is not in anybody's best interest and is particularly unjust to students.

And yet this practice of excluding certain accredited schools and their students from consideration for transfer of credits, although not officially sanctioned, tends at least to be institutionalized by the American Association of Collegiate Registrars and Admissions Officers (1988), one of the signatories of the joint statement, through publication of a biennial guide called *Transfer Credit Practices of Designated Educational Institutions* (*TCP*). *TCP* is a report by the registrars or admissions officers at what are usually the flagship public universities in each state. The report includes the name of each institution, its accrediting body, the institutions within the state from which it accepts credit, those from which it does not, and those from which it accepts credit only under limited conditions. Institutions accredited by national institutional accrediting bodies usually are either not listed or listed with a notation that credit is not normally accepted. *TCP* does state that it is a voluntary exchange of information among member institutions and adds: "No implication is intended, that the practices of the reporting institutions must be followed by other institutions. Each institution should determine its own policy for acceptance of credit. The use of this publication should be limited to transfer credit practice" (1988, cover page). The problem is that it is indeed used for "transfer credit practices," not just by public flagship institutions, where there might be some relevance to the listings, but by a great variety of other institutions and even by certain foundations and funding agencies, such as businesses and industries that provide tuition benefits or matching gifts for employees. By noninclusion or inclusion with negative listing, this comes remarkably close, whether intended or not, to being a system of institutional blackballing that hurts not only other institutions but also their students.

Most of the institutions accredited by the Association of Independent Colleges and Schools, the National Association of Trade and Technical Schools, and the National Home Study Council, for example, are proprietary schools, but to exclude them and their students from consideration of transfer of credit on this basis is to assume that quality is a function of governance and ownership rather than of accomplishing educational objectives. This would be extraordinarily difficult to prove. Nell Eurich (1985) has pointed out that "it would be short-sighted to think that proprietary status per se has any direct bearing on the quality of academic work given" (p. 116). To shut out either the proprietary sector or the Bible college sector from consideration in transfer of credit at the very least is contrary to recognizing the positive role of diversity in American postsecondary education in meeting current educational needs and at worst is a form of dogmatic exclusionism.

The impact of the Transfer of Credit Myth extends to at least two other, related areas. The first of these involves accepting credits for comparable academic work taken in what Eurich has called the corporate classrooms. While not all in-house training programs in business and industry are relevant to continuing postsecondary or higher education, many of them are. Some, in fact, are offered jointly by business and industry in cooperation with colleges and universities. Others, including the ones involved here, are developed and carried out within businesses and industries themselves. Both the University of the State of New York and the American Council on Education, first working together and then separately, have developed Programs on Noncollegiate Sponsored Instruction (PONSI) to evaluate specific corporate courses and recommend academic credit at appropriate levels. The evaluations are carried out by experts from the academic world. This has been valuable not only to students but to the corporations and higher education institutions as well. Yet even here there is reluctance on the part of many institutions to accept the recommended transfer credit. An executive of Consolidated Edison points out that "Most of our management courses have been approved for college credit, but we have had great difficulty in obtaining cooperation from local institutions to grant such credit. This seems to be a continuing problem which both discourages the students from attempting to gain credit and discourages our staff from having the course qualify for credit" (Eurich, 1985, p. 82).

A second area, which technically does not involve transfer of credit but tends to be negatively affected by the Transfer of Credit Myth, is credit for experiential learning. This is an area that can be subject to abuse, particularly by less scrupulous and fraudulent institutions. To be effective and legitimate, it requires expert and careful evaluation of experiential accomplishments. And yet if higher education is concerned not just with class time and tuition income but with educational accomplishments, with knowledge attained and utilized, and with the continuity of education for people within our society, then evaluation of experiential learning and inclusion of it as part of the process seem essential. The Council for Adult and Experiential Learning (CAEL) under the leadership of Morris Keaton has performed over the last fourteen years an extraordinarily important function both in underlining the importance and legitimacy of experiential learning and in developing effective means of assessing it, including portfolio preparation and evaluation. A large part of the higher education community now recognizes that prior experiential learning is here to stay and is an integral part of the higher education picture. And yet Zelda Gamson (1988) in a historical review and assessment of CAEL and its contribution, points out that "CAEL did not penetrate the academic establishment — the selective private colleges, the research universities, and the disciplinary departments in many colleges and universities. . . . The core is not easy to penetrate. Change is much more likely to occur through the addition of parallel structures" (p. 240).

Some institutions either do not accept validated credit for prior experiential learning or strictly prescribe the amount of such credit, no matter how much the student knows. Unfortunately, this rigidity is reinforced in parts of the accrediting community. The Commission for Senior Colleges and Universities of the Western Association of Schools and Colleges includes a special policy on credit for prior experiential learning in its *Handbook for Accreditation.* This policy restricts acceptance of such credit to undergraduate education. Even on the undergraduate level, it will allow no more than thirty portfolio-based credits toward the baccalaureate degree (Western Association of Schools and Colleges, 1988, p. 45). With all due respect to the commission and its many accomplishments, this appears to be an arbitrary restriction on the structure of the baccalaureate degree with very little relevance to student accomplishments and institutional educational creativity and autonomy. Much more relevant for today's world and the next century is the following pasage from *Assessing Learning: A CAEL Handbook for Faculty:* "In recognizing the college-level learning acquired by adults outside the formal classroom, we are fostering the growth and self-confidence of individuals and the academic flexibility and efficiency of our educational institutions and . . . in the end the real benefit to be gained by more flexible and responsive educational providers is a society better able to accommodate itself to the pressures and demands of an increasingly complex world" (Simosko and Associates, 1988, p. xi).

Our concern with calling for the reassessment of the Transfer of Credit Myth is not with undermining responsible and effective assessment of student knowledge, competencies, or progress, nor is it to urge in any way that transfer credit or credit from experience should not be related to the institutions' and the students' educational goals. It is not to suggest that all or any institutions accept credit solely on the basis of accreditation or other external factors. Rather, it is to recognize that the real and fundamental task is to provide both the rigor and the flexibility that will allow each student, regardless of age, full- or part-time status, or on- or off-campus location, to be assessed in the light of what he or she knows substantively and is capable of doing, not on the basis of structural hurdles that have very little to do with the learning process.

The Older Student Myth

With the influx of veterans after the passage of the GI Bill in 1944, as already noted, there was real concern in some quarters of the academic community about the impact on quality of the presence of so many older students, students for whom the continuity of formal education had been interrupted by the war, students whose attention had been focused on issues far removed from the classroom and the library. This concern turned out to be unfounded. The veterans on the whole equaled or outperformed traditional students and made up for any gaps by increased motivation, clearer conceptions of educational objectives, and maturity lacking in many traditional college students. Veterans entered not just part-time or evening courses or continuing education courses but regular degree programs at undergraduate and graduate levels, where many of them excelled and from which many went on to become the national and educational leaders of the next decades.

From the experience with veterans, it would seem that the academic community should have learned once and for all that except at the extremes, age per se is not a primary determinant of academic ability or adaptability in educational accomplishment even in traditional classrooms and that intervening experience can and usually does not only widen perspective but also enhance motivation toward academic accomplishment for those who continue their education. Quite apart from the postwar experience with veterans, the current demography of college students, as reviewed above, seems to undermine any assumption of a unique educability and contribution to quality of traditional college-age students in contrast to older students. The academic profession itself is built, at least partially, on the assumption that even college professors continue to learn, to contribute to knowledge, and then to share their continued learning with others.

The idea that education is an ongoing affair that should continue throughout life has been around since Plato, as Cyril Houle (1984, p. 8) has pointed out, and has had exemplars throughout the ages. Adult education as a movement, however, seems to date from the 1920s and until relatively recently has been considered in most academic quarters as legitimate but as apart from the regular curriculum and central thrust, particularly of the undergraduate college. Graduate education, in contrast, always has been recognized as primarily for adults but has not been considered as "adult education."

Adult education, in contrast to regular undergraduate education, frequently has been looked at as something for which one made special provision. In a sense, the Older Student Myth is the obverse side of the Traditional College Student Myth. In effect, it involves the assumption that older students are unique, that while it is both a public service and frequently profitable to provide educational opportunity for older people, this should be done separately and specifically under adult or continuing education auspices. In some instances, this has led to the development of a separate adult degree or degrees called by various names. Under such separate auspices, it is argued, the unique educational needs of adults can be met while avoiding or keeping to a minimum the dilution of regular classes and the undergraduate curriculum by older students who, if they are to maintain the pace, will require special attention. It is this implicit assumption, seldom today made explicit, that also leads to and reinforces the Continuing Education Myth and makes the issue of mainstreaming of adult and continuing education a central and critical issue today.

None of this should be taken to suggest that all advocates of separate continuing educational structures within higher educational institutions subscribe to the Older Student Myth. In many cases, departments, divisions, and centers of adult and continuing education have been established to provide more flexible and appropriate curricula and time frames adapted to adult needs and concerns and to provide more effective administrative coordination and support services for adults from various parts of the college or university structure. The critical questions involve (1) administration and faculty attitudes toward such "continuing" or "adult" education programs and students, (2) the degree to which adults are also welcomed into other programs of the college or university, and (3) the degree to which the continuity of education throughout life is recognized in institutional mission and objectives. We will return to this shortly when we consider the Continuing Education Myth. It is important to recognize here, however, that to the extent that either faculty or administration considers continuing education programs, regardless of what they are called, not as integral to the central functions of the college or university but as add-ons with part-time and second-class faculty, as primarily sources of additional income for the institution or faculty, or even as public-service activities essentially separate from other central college or university objectives, the Older Student Myth is at work. The degree and kind of separateness are key. It should be recognized, however, that some adult educators have perhaps unintentionally aided and abetted continuation of the myth by overemphasis on the separateness and uniqueness of "adult education."

The key to overcoming this myth where vestiges of it remain would seem to lie in an emphasis on educational continuity and explicit recognition of the current scope of higher education clients. As Alan Knox (1987) points out, one of the major transformations in current society is the transformation "from higher education for the young to higher education institutions in which adult, part-time students are becoming the new majority" (p. 22). It is thus essential, as we suggested earlier, for institutions to recognize and reassess the relevance of their educational programs to the range of their students.

This emphasis on continuity should not be taken as a failure to recognize that various teaching and learning methodologies may be more appropriate for some purposes, in some situations, and for some students than others. It is, however, to suggest that the factors that determine appropriateness are the educational purposes, the situations, and the students' interests and backgrounds, not their age per se. From this standpoint even the attempt to distinguish andragogy, the art of teaching adults, from pedagogy (Knowles and Associates, 1984) is somewhat artificial, as both Jerold Apps (1988, p. 43) and Leonard Freedman (1987, p. 62) have pointed out — particularly if the line between the applicability of the two concepts is drawn between undergraduate and adult education. The various methods of instruction, including the traditional lecture method (Freedman, 1987, p. 70), are as relevant for adults twenty-five and over as they are for undergraduates given particular educational purposes and situations.

What all this seems to indicate is that more and more the question of age, of older student versus younger student, is close to irrelevant. Students of all post–high school ages are involved in most phases of postsecondary and higher education, whether it is undergraduate, graduate, professional, continuing professional, recurrent, or communal education. There obviously are differences in educational functions and needs of different students and different parts of society. The relevant question today may well be whether institutions or systems of institutions are willing to review and if necessary recast postsecondary education to perform the variety of functions and meet the corresponding needs posed by a learning society of people of all ages. The nature of the challenge facing higher education in the light of this is well stated by Harriet Cabell and Jerry Hickerson (1988): "Today, the challenge for colleges to change in response to the increasing diversity of those needing higher education comes from many quarters. . . . Allan Tucker states that a 'deliberate development effort' should be undertaken to help faculty work with the increasing number of learners with wide ranges of abilities and interests, and life experiences — who 'may have more experience than the instructor and be as knowledgeable in some subjects . . . , [who] often challenge time-tested traditional ways of perceiving how knowledge is organized . . . [and may] wish to be involved in educational decision-making processes, such as needs assessment, goal setting, selection of content and method, and evaluation.'" (p. 132).

Removal of assumed age restrictions has obviously accentuated the fact that for meeting some types of postsecondary or higher education needs, the traditional campus is no longer the primary locus of learning or even the appropriate place for it to occur. The inner city poses one set of problems, which are being dealt with in unique ways by institutions such as the College of New Rochelle. Rural isolation poses a different set of problems, which are being approached in a number of places by use of educational technologies in conjunction with libraries. This is taking place in Oklahoma and in the Intermountain Community Learning and Information Services Project funded by the W. K. Kellogg Foundation involving Utah State University, Montana State University, Colorado State University, and the University of Wyoming. The needs of workers and union members in major corporations for education not only for advancement but for flexibility in the labor market are being addressed by such programs as the College and University Option Program (United Automobile Workers and Ford Motor Company) and the Pathways to the Future (Mountain-Bell and Communications Workers of America) with the help of the Council for Adult and Experiential Learning. The needs of professionals for continuing professional education are being dealt with in Module VII of the Oklahoma Project on Interprofessional Continuing Education and by special programs at Ohio State University, Pennsylvania State University, and the University of Georgia under W. K. Kellogg Foundation sponsorship. These constitute only a small illustrative sample of the expanded universe of postsecondary activities involving older students both on campus and in various nontraditional higher education settings.

The challenges presented by older students are not challenges related to diluted program quality or loss of institutional integrity. If anything, they are challenges to greater innovation, creativity, and quality attainment that can be applied across the board to students of any age. The Older Student Myth may have had some foundation in the desire to meet the unique needs and even time requirements of older students. However, in its form as a myth — that is, as the assumption that older students are not really of the caliber of college-age students and should be dealt with separately — it fairly clearly is a matter of prejudice. And yet it tends to persist in forms that are sometimes not so subtle but that may not be recognized even by the people involved. It is reflected in the administration and faculty pecking order, where, with the notable exception of graduate education, people primarily involved with older students fall rather far down the scale. It is reflected in the faculty reward system, where little credit may be given to teaching in general and even less to working with adult students and groups. As already noted, it sometimes is reflected by restrictions on transfer of credit even within the offering institutions. Finally, it tends to be reflected in organizational structures that relegate education to something approximating an auxiliary enterprise rather than recognizing it as a central function integral to the institutional mission.

The Continuing Education Myth

We are at a point in history that Alan Knox (1987) describes as "the emergence of an educative society in which lifelong learning is essential for social, political and economic well-being and progress for individuals and society" (p. 22). If this is the case, then it would seem that continuing education and concern with lifelong learning should be part of the central function, if not the central function itself, of most systems of postsecondary and higher education (Knox, 1987; Niebuhr, 1984). In 1973, the presidents of Notre Dame University, Michigan

State University, and Rochester Institute of Technology were calling for recognition of the unity of education, including "formal and informal education [and] . . . one time and continuing education" (Hesburgh, Miller, and Wharton, 1973, p. xvi). They talked about the importance of "the Lifelong University" (pp. 57–61). It is significant that the discussions leading to these recommendations were supported by the W. K. Kellogg Foundation and that the foundation has recently provided a major grant to Michigan State to try to translate the concept into practice.

In spite of this emphasis on the continuity of education and the centrality of continuing education, in far too many cases the Continuing Education Myth persists. This myth involves the assumption that adult and continuing education are not part of the central functions of colleges and universities but rather are closer to auxiliary enterprises that should be kept separate, both administratively and academically, from the mainstream teaching and research functions of the institution. As a result, the landscape is dotted with separate adult education schools, departments, centers, and units with, in many cases, minimal connection to the central operations and commitments of the institutions themselves. Even in Oklahoma, the 1985 prospectus for the Oklahoma Network of Continuing Higher Education project described the situation as of that time as follows: "Throughout the Oklahoma System of Higher Education, continuing education programs are operated in splendid isolation from the rest of the establishment" (Oklahoma State Regents, 1985, p. 6). This has changed dramatically in the last few years.

In a great many cases, adult education units were and still are expected not only to be self-sufficient but to provide additional income for the rest of the institution. For public institutions in some states, the situation is exacerbated by explicit legislative prohibitions against using state funds in support of adult continuing education (where it is so labeled) or by legislative refusal to allocate funds for such purposes. In at least one state (Massachusetts), until relatively recently there were periodic attempts to require that any excess funds gained through continuing education be returned to the state general fund. Other factors not unrelated to the financial situation both indicate the prevalence of the myth and help reinforce it. One is the tendency of continuing education programs to rely heavily on part-time and adjunct faculty, who usually are considered less expensive and in many cases less experienced than their full-time counterparts. Closely related is the tendency when full-time faculty are used to extend their teaching functions on an overload basis. This further underlines the perceived marginality of the activity and precludes its consideration in the normal institutional reward and recognition system. All of this leads to an attitude described — but not subscribed to — by the president of George Mason University as follows: "Now we all know that *status* and *continuing education* are mutually contradictory terms within the academic vocabulary" (Johnson, 1985, p. 6).

The end result for those institutions trapped in the myth tends to be not only a devaluing of the educational importance of adult and continuing education in contrast to its fiscal importance but the developing of marketing appeals and approaches aimed primarily at the easy-to-reach, more affluent, and already educated clientele at the expense of attempting to reach those for whom continuing education is of equal or more importance and whose education may be most crucial to the future of the country, such as the blue-collar work force, minorities, and the economically disadvantaged. Further, it reinforces a status quo in which, as Cabell and Hickerson (1988) point out, "many colleges . . . still seem to lack incentive to reorganize to serve persons who would bring disparate backgrounds, variable attendance patterns, and various preferred ways to learn" (p. 133).

The perpetuation of the Continuing Education Myth where it exists and the attitudes and practices connected with it seem particularly shortsighted for many institutions today. As already noted, the statistics about students point to the artificiality of sharp distinctions between "regular" students and programs, on the one hand, and "continuing education" students and programs, on the other. Over the last several years, younger students have been tending more and more to delay or interrupt their studies, so that both the timing and the former "normal" sequences are becoming less typical. At the same time, older students and adult educators have taken on new dimensions, bringing older and part-time students into the traditional class-rooms. Thus, Lynton and Elman (1987) point out that "Both trends . . . are part of the same phenomenon: a change in the pattern of advanced study that constitutes a fundamental change in the characteristics of higher education. Instead of being full time and continuous, it is becoming spread out, recurrent and increasingly part-time" (p. 87).

The issue today for most colleges and universities is not how to build or preserve separate programs for traditional students and for adults. Both the adults and the younger students are already in traditional as well as nontraditional programs. The question quickly becomes how to adapt the institution's mission, objectives, and structures most effectively to provide educational opportunity commensurate with the institution's unique strengths to appropriate students at various stages of their life-span learning. While modified adult education structures may be part of the answer, they will not suffice if the adult programs remain isolated from the core of the institution's operations and commitments.

Cyril Houle (1984, p. 225) has pointed out that even though community colleges are not involved in baccalaureate and graduate education, they have on the whole been the most successful institutions to date in incorporating lifelong education into their curricula, at least in part because of their close relationships to their communities. The American Association of State Colleges and Universities' Commission on the Future, chaired by Terrel Bell, has recognized the acute need for a change in perspective and structure of many of the state colleges and regional universities. The Commission argues that "state colleges and universities should restructure their modes of delivery of instruction and services to give adult and part-time students full access to undergraduate and graduate programs" (National Commission on the Role and Future of State Colleges and Universities, 1986, p. 24). This should include taking the campus into the workplace through utilization of new technologies as well as work-study, internships, and other forms of campus-community liaison. We already have noted the concern expressed in 1973 by Theodore Hesburgh of the University of Notre Dame and Clifford Wharton, then president of Michigan State University, with integrating lifelong learning into the central functions of complex universities (Hesburgh, Miller, and Wharton, 1973). The former president of the University of Oklahoma, Frank Horton, insisted at the outset of the Oklahoma project that a major issue for the university was "how to integrate the expertise which has been acquired over the past twenty years about non-traditional students into the traditional organizational structure and curriculum of universities" (Horton, 1986).

The Continuing Education Myth is at best anachronistic and needs to be scrapped. We can no longer afford to treat continuing education as an addendum, as a lucrative sideline, or as something that serious faculty members should look askance at (even on an overload basis) as interfering with their academic advancement—in other words, as the preserve of the part-time and the less distinguished members of the faculty. On the contrary, continuing education is sufficiently central to the role of higher education in meeting the educational needs of the twenty-first century that for most institutions it should become—in fact, may have to become—far more central to institutional operations. For many institutions, it may well become the central function. To accomplish such objectives will require utilization of first-rate faculty. Any invidious distinction between regular faculty and faculty for continuing education will have to disappear and be replaced by the concept of one faculty carrying out different functions. It will also require reaching out to develop effective partnerships not just with business and industry but with the professions, government, community services, and other providers, as well as users. For many institutions, it will require restructuring. And, as the Oklahoma experience suggests, to be fully effective, it will require coordination and support at the state level.

While all of this calls for moving continuing education into the mainstream of institutions and thus of higher education in general, it does not necessarily mean dissipation of continuing education awareness and planning or dismantling of continuing education centers and other such units. It may well mean decentralization of academic functions involving program development to departments and schools within complex institutions, but, as Alan Knox (1987, p. 26) suggests, it may also mean retaining and strengthening administrative centralization to prevent loss of commitment and coordination of activities essential to serving the wider clientele. There is a real danger of dissipation through fragmentation. Administrative and planning responsibility probably should rest as close to the president, chancellor, or chief executive officer of the system as possible. However, our concern here is not to outline or recommend specific structures but rather to underline the fact that the "new world" requires a central substantive and not a peripheral position for continuing education in institutional system organization and planning in the years ahead. This may mean, in some cases, restructuring the institution itself on what has been the continuing education model.

Summary

This chapter has dealt with a series of assumptions that perhaps can best be described as sacred cows of some of the more traditional circles in higher education. These are basic assumptions that, if not carefully reexamined and modified, could seriously inhibit the effective role that higher education can and should play in meeting the social, economic, and even international challenges that our nation and the world face as we move into the twenty-first century. They constitute a kind of orthodoxy that comes close to resisting the world of higher education as it is today and would substitute for the current directions of higher education evolution a move backward from the rather remarkable progress that has been made by higher education over the last thirty years.

It appears that if higher education is to meet its current and future challenges, it is important that as many people within the academic community as possible recognize the following realities:

1. There is no golden era of higher education to which we can return or that can or should serve as normative for the present.

2. Higher education reform is usually a product of interaction between the external environment, including governments, and the higher education community and is frequently initiated by forces and movements external to the academy, and frankly recognizing this interactive and reactive context may itself be an important source of reform.

3. While traditional college students constitute an important minority of students involved in higher education today, the academic community has an obligation not only to recognize the current demography of higher education but also to focus far more clearly on how to more effectively meet the higher education needs of the new students now and in the years to come.

4. While "universities" in general and research universities in particular have crucial roles to play in the increase of knowledge and in meeting community, national, and international needs (including international competitiveness), the universities do not constitute all of postsecondary or higher education, and effective strategic planning for higher and postsecondary education for the future must address the full range of the postsecondary educational community.

5. Given student mobility and the range of postsecondary opportunities available, transfer of credit should be based not on formal institutional peer-group equivalence but on substantive knowledge and competency attained and should be assessed in the light of student and institutional objectives in the program into which the student is transferring.

6. Age per se is not and should not be a criterion of academic capabilities.

7. Given the changing student clientele, adult and continuing education, far from being a peripheral, primarily income-producing activity, should for many institutions become a central part of institutional mission and the basis for restructuring to deal with not only future but also current higher educational realities.

3

Territoriality and Turf Wars

Beyond the sacred cow myths and assumptions but reinforced by them are what would have to be described as the turf war assumptions. These involve heightened concern with turf, territoriality, and competitiveness. They frequently are justified or rationalized under the heading of institutional autonomy. They exemplify essentially a laissez-faire attitude and market orientation to higher education. They tend to be atomistic and to focus on individual institutions and their achievements and aggrandizement rather than on the communal aspects of higher education as these are related to the diversity of higher education needs. They become the basis for downplaying formal cooperation, system planning, and state or governmental concern about and involvement in institutional affairs. Among public institutions, this does not, of course, imply lack of concern about state appropriations and their increase. However, such public institutions usually prefer to have as little state involvement in how the funds are spent as possible.

Concern with turf is not limited to the interinstitutional level but in complex universities often manifests itself in interschool or intercollege rivalry, departmental confrontations, program conflicts, and even confrontations among faculty members within the same department. Turfdom may manifest itself

66

in attempts to preserve the pecking order both within and among institutions. It clearly can become a major issue among and between institutions in off-campus outreach and continuing education activities. It also manifests itself at times in concern for "ownership" and control of technologies that facilitate educational opportunity and service to the wider community. As is the case with a good many other myths, the turf war myths are exaggerations or, perhaps more dangerously, action patterns based on extraordinarily important principles that in their exaggerated forms come close to being self-destructive. In the light of their pervasiveness, of the elements of truth in them, and of what in many cases is their negative impact on the wider educational and political communities, the turf myths and assumptions need careful review and reassessment.

The Autonomy Myth

If the Golden Era Myth is one of the most persistent, the Autonomy Myth is undoubtedly one of the most deep-seated and emotionally embedded of the higher education myths — a crucial principle that has been pushed or has drifted to extremes. Essentially, the myth involves the assumption that because some degree of autonomy is essential to the teaching, learning, and research processes and their effectiveness, the college or university, to be effective, must be as fully autonomous as possible. This means in effect that the higher education institution considers itself self-defining and self-completing and in its definition and completion believes that it serves a society that should support it and that should be grateful that it exists. To paraphrase the old cliché attributed to a former president of General Motors, what is good for our institution is good for higher education. While few college presidents today would formulate the assumption in quite this way, in practice it comes close to describing the way some institutions and some parts of institutions operate.

The uniqueness and the autonomy of individual institutions are in many ways built into the higher education system and can be one of its strengths. On the ability of institutions to maintain and foster their freedom from external noneducational interference depend both higher education's integrity and the genius of higher education's contributions to the nation and society at large. Such freedom must apply to the teaching-learning process, the search for knowledge, and the capacity of faculties not only to develop knowledge and provide information but to criticize and propose changes in the society in which they exist. Maintaining such integrity and autonomy requires commitment to the institution, its mission, and its objectives and to realizing its potential. In *The Control of the Campus*, the essential nature of such freedom is described by Ernest Boyer (1982) as follows: "The university is a unique institution, a repository of our cultural heritage and a source of the nation's future intellectual and economic growth. Therefore, the academy must be free to direct, without outside interference, those functions that may, from time to time, challenge, but ultimately will enrich, the culture they sustain" (p. 4).

We hire college and university presidents to strengthen their institutions. In each institution, the president is expected to work toward the reinforcement of its mission, its uniqueness, its financial health, its further development, and its contribution to society. It thus should not be surprising if the interests, objectives, and activities of an individual institution and its president are internally institutionally focused and not necessarily the same as or complementary to those of other institutions or the public at large as represented through state or federal governments. Ironically, the difference and conflict in objectives may themselves be due to the similarity or even identity of objectives of various institutions as they are related to achievement of conditions or resources that either are in limited supply or are redundant in meeting educational needs. The difference in objectives then focuses on locus of their attainability.

John Millett (1984) has pointed out that "An institution often wants to enhance its stature, to grow in size, and to assure itself of constantly expanding financial support, regardless of the activities of other universities and colleges, regardless of desirable patterns of collaboration, and regardless of costs and the economic circumstances of state government" (p. 6). While such institutional interests are natural and understandable, they become or create problems when the "regardless of's" become predominant.

In many respects, however, the Autonomy Myth, with its overemphasis on institutional independence and self-interest, is a matter of degree. Few if any people would argue that colleges and universities should be completely autonomous even if such a state were possible. In 1973, the Carnegie Commission on Higher Education, under the direction of Clark Kerr, pointed out in *Governance of Higher Education* that "It is customary to speak of campus 'autonomy,' but there is no such thing in any full sense of the word . . . . Autonomy, in the sense of full self-government, does not now exist for American higher education, nor has it existed for a very long time — if ever. Autonomy is limited by law, by the necessary influences and control that goes along with financial support, and by public policy in areas of substantial public concern. Autonomy in these areas is neither possible nor generally desirable" (Kerr, 1973, p. 17). Almost ten years later, the Carnegie Foundation for the Advancement of Teaching echoed essentially the same position in *The Control of the Campus:* "We do not suggest that colleges and universities can carry on their work in isolation. There is, in the strict sense, no such thing as autonomy on campus. Both public and private institutions are socially engaged. They are answerable to the people who support them and cannot be excused from explaining, and perhaps defending, what they do" (Boyer, 1982, p. 4).

The central question is neither whether higher educational institutions should be fully autonomous or independent nor whether accountability should be carried to the point of major external control. The first is impossible, and the second would reduce higher education to structured training. The question rather is where and how legitimate concern with independence becomes confrontational turfdom and what impact this has. Frank Newman (1987) has suggested part of the answer: "Although a significant degree of independence is essential, a constructive relationship recognizes the need for checks and balances. Left totally to its own, the university will evolve toward self-interest rather than public interest" (p. 8).

To this the staff of the Oklahoma Network of Continuing Higher Education (1987c), in a paper on interinstitutional
cooperation in Oklahoma, adds that concern with independence
and autonomy "has some of the characteristics of nationalism,
and the voluntary yield of turf or proud position is an extraordinarily difficult act by powerful leaders" (p. 29). Whatever the
causes, the impact of overemphasis on autonomy and institutional independence as exemplified in the Autonomy Myth can
be extensive and has a number of different forms. At one end
of the spectrum, it reinforces institutional conservatism, satisfaction with things as they are, and resistance to change. This,
as Nell Eurich (1985, p. 122f) suggests, may take the form of
institutional resistance to new fields (shades of the Yale faculty
of 1828), resistance to accepting or working with new providers
of postsecondary education such as business and industry, or
resistance to new methodologies. It may reinforce the inertia
of complex institutions against undertaking significant change
(Carter, 1988, pp. 49–51), particularly when such change threatens what appear to be successful traditional or conventional ways
of doing things (Cabell and Hickerson, 1988, pp. 133–134). It may
reinforce resistance to nontraditional instructional approaches
ranging from individual study to long-distance learning by new
technologies. Closely related, as might be expected, is the whole
issue discussed earlier of resistance to transfer of credit and particularly to acceptance of validated experiential learning (Gamson, 1988, pp. 125–127).

On the surface, it might seem that this essentially conservative aspect of the Autonomy Myth would be counterproductive to ensuring institutional strength and survival in light of
the changed and changing student clientele, particularly in
periods and areas where fiscal retrenchment seems called for.
In the long run, this may well be the case. However, if some
significant portion of the public can be persuaded that the old
way (that is, continuation of the current way) is best, and such
institutions continue to draw or increase their share of students,
then the dislocations and costs of change to meet changing conditions may at least temporarily be offset and the change delayed.
The difficulty with this, however, is that by the time conditions

make the changes essential, both the costs and the dislocations involved in the changes are likely to have increased considerably.

At the opposite end of the spectrum is what might be described as the confrontational turfdom that constitutes genuine turf warfare. We will return to this overt confrontation in discussing the myth of Competition. However, at this point, it should be noted that such overt confrontation, even if it does not go as far as competing advertising campaigns and mutual public criticism, as has happened in some cases (Newman, 1987, p. 46), can undermine public confidence and invite legislative intrusion rather than reinforce institutional independence. This quickly becomes counterproductive.

One characteristic of the autonomy mentality is the tendency — perhaps *intent* would be a more accurate way to describe it — to circumvent normal procedures and communal expectations even when these procedures have been developed to benefit or advance important higher education objectives. Such circumventions constitute "end runs." They obviously can and do occur within institutions, among institutions where agreements or arrangements for consultation are sidestepped, in state agencies, including the legislature and the governor, and even in the federal government.

On the federal level, one of the most striking examples of end runs has been the growth of pork-barrel congressional funding of research at individual institutions. This enables institutions to avoid peer review and assessment of merit — the usual means used by various government agencies for funding research and research facilities — by obtaining direct individual congressional appropriations for specific research activities or facilities. While there are exceptions, such appropriations are usually obtained through direct institutional arrangements with or lobbying of their own congressional delegations. For 1989, the funds involved in such pork-barrel activities amounted to some $289 million (Cordes, 1989). Such practice has been deplored by the research universities' own organization, the Association of American Universities, and its director, Robert Rosenzweig. And yet only one university president — Frank Rhodes of Cornell — had the courage at one point to refuse on principle to accept such direct congressional largess. According to *The Chronicle of Higher Education* (Cordes, 1989), the lobbying firm of Cassidy and Associates, which specializes in trying to obtain earmarked funds for its client universities, has been highly successful. In the same issue, the assistant dean for research at the College of Engineering of Arizona State University is quoted as justifying receipt of such federal funds as follows: "My need is to have a building . . . . I really don't care if it's state funds or federal funds or private funds, as long as we get the money" (p. A20).

Similar end-run operations occur on the state level when the institutions within a system, instead of operating through the system with its appropriate mechanisms for review related to system concerns and common planning, appeal directly to the legislature or the governor for special funding as part of either the operating budget or the capital funds budget. This may call for shifting of priorities at the expense of other institutions. In some instances, end runs may even be attempted by a school — such as law, engineering, or nursing — within a university around its central administration to the system governing board, a state coordinating board, or even the legislature itself. Unfortunately, the latter sometimes may be aided and abetted by a professional accrediting body. What is more likely to be the case, however, is the misuse of the accrediting report or of the name of the accrediting body without its sanction or in some instances even its knowledge. Such procedures on the part of a component school, however, are likely to confuse immediate gain and long-range advantage within the institution itself and can very easily be self-defeating.

One major approach to help ameliorate, if not overcome, the overemphasis on institutional autonomy and independence of the Autonomy Myth was exemplified in the leadership development module (Module I) of the Oklahoma Kellogg project described in Chapter Two in connection with the Golden Era Myth. As noted there, it created awareness and stimulated change by taking into account the relevance of the past but utilizing it to analyze the present and to project and plan for the future. It helped Oklahoma institutions to move beyond the Autonomy Myth through involving as wide a spectrum of the academic community as possible from the institutions in the state. It included regents and trustees, presidents and various types of administrators, department chairs, and faculty representing all types of public and private institutions. Together with the help of state and national leaders, the participants explored over a three-year period issues facing higher education nationally and in Oklahoma. In planning sessions, task forces, committees, and working groups, they developed recommendations for the improvement of higher education in Oklahoma.

Clearly, the leadership development module in Oklahoma did not solve or remove all the turf problems or substantially reduce concerns about institutional prerogatives. However, it did help create a sense of community and a recognition that the issues involved in meeting the higher education needs of all citizens in Oklahoma now and in the next century are too large for any one institution to handle alone. It stressed the community of higher education and its institutional obligations to the present and future rather than conflict and atomism. A highly positive estimation of the impact of the module on overcoming institutional insularity is contained in the 1986–87 annual report to the W. K. Kellogg Foundation (Oklahoma Network of Continuing Higher Education, 1987a, vol. 3, p. 37): "An encouraging sign of future benefit to higher education has been the apparent enthusiasm on the part of those attending the conferences to cooperate, collaborate, and have dialogue with their colleagues in other types of institutions and disciplines. Apparently these conferences have helped to generate an awareness that the turf protection attitude is fast becoming an anachronism, given the restriction of resources and increase in demands." On the kind of attention now given in Oklahoma to the recommendations growing out of the meetings by the regents may well depend the continuation of that sense of community and the fostering of further inclusive, rather than exclusive and conflicting, institutional perspectives.

While it probably is not feasible to replicate the Oklahoma experience in every state, the Oklahoma experience at least suggests how essential creating a common awareness of the higher education issues and developing a communal as well as an individual institutional commitment to their solution are in helping to overcome the negative aspect of the Autonomy Myth. It seems clear that unless an institution is able to expand its conception of its own uniqueness and best interests to include a commitment to positive interaction with other institutions in meeting the higher education needs of the wider society, the alternative is likely to be, if not self-destruction, at least crippling competition and isolation.

The Competition Myth

As long as students, faculties, and funds are in limited supply, higher education institutions are bound to be in competition with each other. Much competition is in fact healthy and benefits not only students but the institutions themselves and society. The Competition Myth, however, involves the assumption or assertion that competition not only is normal but is the only or at least the primary mode of interinstitutional interaction and that to rely on cooperation except as a temporary measure to attain comparative advantage is not in the best interests of the institution and its survival and growth. In fact, it may be argued that in the long run, such primary emphasis on competition best serves not only the institution but its students and the public.

This extreme emphasis on competition obviously is closely related to and to a large extent grows out of the Autonomy Myth. Much of the discussion of that myth is equally relevant here. One factor that makes discussion of the Competition Myth difficult is that where one draws the line between the kinds of competition that enhance positive institutional development and strengthen the educational community and destructive or divisive competition is not all that clear and may vary considerably from issue to issue.

Competition to achieve educational and research effectiveness or educational quality within the context of institutional missions would seem to be to everyone's advantage. Thus, a number of states have developed incentive grant programs to encourage and support quality improvement, grants for which institutions and programs compete. New Jersey, Tennessee, Florida, Virginia, and Ohio are cases in point. For example, Ohio has developed a series of six types of challenge grants to support, encourage, and reward superior academic and research achievements within the framework of institutional missions. One, called Program Excellence, is aimed at undergraduate programs in two- and four-year public colleges and universities and awards one-time program-enrichment grants on a competitive basis. A second, the Independent College Challenge Program, rewards the best "showcase" liberal arts programs at Ohio independent colleges. The Academic Challenge Grant Program provides supplementary funds for developing centers of institutional excellence to strengthen good programs clearly related to institutional mission. The Research Challenge Program reinforces research programs relevant to business, industry, and government. The Productivity Improvement Challenge Program reinforces two-year college job training and retraining programs and programs to encourage high school students to pursue degrees. Finally, the Ohio Eminent Scholars Program provides matching funds to particularly strong programs to enable them to add outstanding scholars to the faculty as a means of raising the programs to national prominence (Ohio Board of Regents, 1988, vol. 1, pp. 20–21). These competitive programs have made a major difference in strengthening Ohio institutions since 1982 and promise to have more impact in the future. Interestingly enough, in a number of cases the competitive grants have actually led to or reinforced institutional cooperation. One of the criteria in judging applicants is the extent to which other Ohio programs and institutions will be involved in and affected by the program.

On a considerably more limited scale, under Module II (program development) of the Oklahoma Network of Continuing Higher Education program, Oklahoma institutions were invited to compete to carry out demonstration projects in continuing higher education related to (1) the goals of continuing higher education in the state, (2) the mission of the institutions, and (3) exploration of new approaches to meeting identified continuing education needs in the state. For seventeen grants with a total of $350,000 available from the W. K. Kellogg Foundation, seventy-three applications were submitted, with requests in excess of $2.7 million. Thus, the level of interest was extraordinarily high. Seventeen grants were awarded, ranging in program areas from Economic Development in Small Communities (Cameron University) to Multiple Learning Opportunities Educational Delivery System (Rogers State College) and a Health-Related Information Management System at the University of Oklahoma Health Sciences Center. Through such a competitive program, not only the institutions receiving grants but also those that developed proposals but did not receive grants were able to explore and develop new complementary and, in many cases, cooperative programs directly relevant to meeting the continuing educational needs of the state as a whole (see Belt and Sackett, 1987).

The problem, thus, is not just competition but the form that the competition takes and the assumptions underlying it. One key factor, illustrated in both the Ohio and the Oklahoma examples of healthy and positive competition, is the role of the missions of the various institutions in relation to each other. The competitive situation is aggravated and the competition is much more likely to become destructive where institutional missions are not clearly delineated or where they obviously overlap. The importance of the identification of missions as a factor in ameliorating excessive competition is stressed by Frank Newman (1987), who points to factors that lead to legislative intervention or intrusion: "Unless mission can be differentiated and multiple pyramids of prestige created, the natural ambitions of the campus cannot become means for channelling campus entrepreneurship into useful purpose. Instead, the result is often that the entrepreneurial drive essential for institutional quality is often directed into competition among institutions for prestige and resources" (p. 45).

In one case reported by Newman, a state legislature established a special commission to study what was described as the escalating warfare among its public colleges. While the committee's description of what it found may involve some exaggerations, it is probably not too far off the mark. It charged that the institutions in that state were engaged in "such uncoordinated and inappropriate competition as lowering admission standards to attract more students, pressing for new facilities and opening up new programs when the prime purpose was not to serve the public but to compete with each other, lowering tuition charges for courses offered, conducting extensive advertising campaigns, opening storefront classrooms and publicly criticizing each other" (p. 46). This particular combination of factors may be rare and some of them impossible in states where tuition and admissions standards at public institutions are centrally determined. However, the general pattern of interinstitutional confrontation is far from rare. Such confrontation, for example, is one of the factors that has led to replacement of coordinating boards by governing boards in states such as Massachusetts and North Carolina.

Such competition clearly fosters public skepticism about the integrity and the intent of higher education institutions. It obviously does invite governmental intrusion. It is usually characterized by considerably greater concern for immediate advantage than for long-range commitment to principle and to meeting public educational and research needs. This is exemplified in a number of ways. First is the end-run phenomenon described in the previous section. Such end runs involve circumventing or playing outside the rules even when the rules are geared to the department's, the institution's, or the system's long-range advantage. Second, many of the current and continuing athletic scandals illustrate this all too well. Third, in more extreme cases where income is based primarily on tuition or on student full-time equivalence, it has led to encouraging high-risk students to take student loans when the probability of repayment is low to nonexistent. As a result, in too many instances (particularly among some proprietary schools but not restricted to them), this has led to exceeedingly high (50 percent or more) default rates (Wilson, 1988, p. A21). This further helps to undermine the public confidence, and such undermining has a tendency to be generalized from some institutions to higher education as a whole. Fourth, at the other end of the spectrum of institutions, it has led to what appears to be excessive tuition charges among some prestigious private institutions, which, while perhaps justified in some cases, in others ironically seem to have been based on the competitive desire to maintain public perception of exclusiveness. While former secretary of education Bennett's criticism of tuition increases have been far too sweeping (Jaschik, 1988, p. A22), they are clearly applicable to such institutions, as is Chester Finn's (1988) call for "no-frills" universities. Both overlook a wide range of public institutions, in particular, where tuition increases have not been excessive by any means. Again, however, the Bennett and Finn criticisms, with their broad, unqualified generalizations, further illustrate the negative impact that such competitiveness can have.

In contrast to such reliance on more extreme and disruptive forms of competition, the American Association of State Colleges and Universities' Commission on the Future Role of State Colleges and Universities suggests that the days of rugged competition, of the frontier spirit in higher education are over. The challenge to leadership now lies in the direction of cooperative endeavor to meet the nation's higher education needs. "The bottom line outcome of education is improving students' competence, knowledge and skills. Strengthening an institution's educational effectiveness, then, is to be found in its *cooperative* dimension. Where an institution sees itself as competing for students and resources, it is hindered in developing productive consortia, sharing institutional strategies, and mounting joint research ventures" (National Commission on the Role and Future of State Colleges and Universities, 1986, pp. 36–37). The report adds, "Cooperation—not competition: This is the new challenge for leadership in higher education" (p. 37).

The importance not of eliminating competition but of emphasizing cooperation, of placing competition within a cooperative framework of planning and action aimed at meeting society's higher education needs, seems particularly crucial today. To do this involves overcoming or transcending institutional atomism and replacing it with a sense of membership in the educational community. This community obviously includes a wide variety of types of institutions, with different but complementary missions and with tasks following from these missions, competing to achieve their own educational objectives but together attempting to meet what will be the variety of educational demands and needs of the twenty-first century. The community also includes not just traditional educational institutions but the wide variety of nontraditional education providers within our complex society. Although Alan Knox (1987) was addressing primarily continuing higher education in Oklahoma, among his recommendations to policy makers in a 1987 paper was the following, which could be taken as applicable to higher education nationwide: "Promote cooperative relations among various types of providers, based on an emphasis on distinctive contributions, which can be beneficial regarding referrals, co-sponsorship, and mutual assistance" (p. 47). It is at this point that the statewide perspective becomes particularly important.

The State Board Myth

Clearly, there is such a thing as what Frank Newman (1987, p. 39) calls inappropriate intrusion of the state into the internal affairs of higher education institutions, particularly public ones. In fact, as Newman points out, the ability to intrude by state legislators, governors, and various state agencies and officers has increased tremendously over the past few years. Legislative and executive staffs in some cases have grown exponentially in the last twenty years. In many cases, the legislative and executive staffs are highly educated and capable people. Their ability to gather and analyze information about and from institutions has been vastly augmented by the use of computers. The fact that some nine state legislatures now meet year-round has not reduced their concern with or interest in higher education. When one adds to what might be described as clearly educational concerns of various state groups and agencies the wider range of other legislative and agency concerns only peripherally related to education but affecting it, the hands of bureaucracy can seem to be very heavy indeed. These additional concerns range from building authorities to waste disposal, auditing procedures, and personnel policies.

It is little wonder that many higher education institutions and administrators not only have felt but continue to feel that any state agency or board designed to deal with higher education is inherently repressive and intrusive and likely further to undermine institutional autonomy and integrity. Such intrusion tends to be much more frequent and extensive in the public sector than in the private sector — and for good reason. The states spend some $30 billion annually in support of public higher education, and it would be surprising if they did not hold the institutions accountable for the use of public funds (Hauptman and Andersen, 1988, p. 17). However, the private sector is not without its concerns about state intrusion also.

Citing cases of unreasonable intrusion and overregulation is not very difficult. As recently as 1985, a special Independent Commission on the Future of the State University of New York (1985), appointed by its then chancellor, Clifton Wharton, to review the extent of state regulation of the State University of New York (SUNY), reported that "The Commission finds that SUNY is the most over regulated university in the nation. Given the vast array of laws and practices that govern New York state agencies, a fundamental and basic change in SUNY's structure is required to allow the university to carry out the function for which it was created" (1985, p. 2). It is important to note that most of the regulations cited were not regulations by SUNY or by the New York Board of Regents but regulations applied to SUNY by various other agencies in the state. As a result of the report, the legislature took action to considerably increase the responsibility and autonomy of the SUNY administration and trustees and decrease the authority of outside noneducational agencies.

Some legislators have the tendency to act as school boards for higher education even to the point of mandating courses and examinations and restricting fund transfers in line-item budgets. Some coordinating boards, such as that in Texas, have set what appears to be arbitrary limits on types of transfer credit, scope of off-campus operations, and fees for adult and continuing education students, regardless of need (Cross and McCartin, 1984, p. 50). Some legislatures (Ohio and West Virginia) have mandated medical schools over the objections not only of the institutions but in one case of the coordinating board and in the other of the governing board of the systems. The Nebraska legislature until very recently restricted associate degree in nursing programs at public institutions to the University of Nebraska, even though the University of Nebraska had given up its associate degree program, and the need for associate degree nurses was acute (Nebraska state law 890, 1988). And the examples could go on.

The crucial question, however, is not whether state legislators, governors, and state agencies, including higher education agencies, have at times been overly regulative or intrusive. This must be conceded. The states do, however, have the primary responsibility for ensuring that the higher education needs of their citizens are met. The question then becomes how the state can most effectively carry out this responsibility working with and through the educational resources of the wider educational community, including higher education institutions and programs, which, as far as the public institutions are concerned, the states have to a large extent created and now support. While recognition that this is the pertinent question does not justify excessive regulation of or intrusion into higher education institutions by states, it does put a somewhat different light on the issue. A series of additional questions follow: (1) How can the states and the higher education institutions, given the changing social and economic conditions, work most effectively together to meet state needs? (2) Are there areas that institutions separately cannot effectively deal with? (3) Are there or should there be self-imposed conditions on the part of the states and the institutions essential to meeting communal higher education objectives? (4) What should be the role of statewide higher education boards or agencies, and what form should such boards or agencies take? To try to answer all or any of these questions adequately would be well beyond what is possible or desirable here. Rather, our concern is with challenging the assumption or myth that state higher education boards or agencies — particularly coordinating boards — are the enemy, bent somehow on undermining the uniqueness and autonomy particularly of public higher education institutions. To this end a number of comments are in order.

To most of the questions listed above there are almost as many answers as there are states and territories. This is not surprising, for each state and territory has developed an indigenous statewide board or agency related to its history and its perception of its problems. These vary tremendously in responsibilities and structure. Currently, all states, with the possible exception of Michigan, have some form of statewide higher education board or agency responsible for some type of oversight of higher education institutions. Even in Michigan, the board of education has some very limited advisory functions. Such boards vary in scope of institutions included, from the New York Board of Regents, which is responsible for all education in the state and as the University of the State of New York includes all postsecondary education institutions, public and private, to consolidated governing boards in seven states responsible for senior public higher education institutions only.

The boards also vary in powers and responsibilities, from those with limited advisory roles only, such as Delaware, Vermont, and possibly Michigan, to consolidated governing boards for all of public higher education. Fifteen states have such governing boards, although in four cases there is also an advisory board with some responsibilities for both public and private institutions. Seven states have governing boards for senior institutions only. Altogether, twenty-two states have some form of statewide governing boards, and thirty-two states have statewide coordinating boards.

Coordinating boards differ from each other considerably more than do governing boards. Unlike the powers of governing boards, their powers do not include personnel decisions or internal fiscal operations and control. They range from boards with weak advisory powers only (advisory to the institutions and to state government) to the Oklahoma State Regents for Higher Education, which, in addition to planning, program approval, and budgetary review, actually allocates funds to the institutions. Most coordinating boards, however, have some responsibility for planning, for program review or approval, and for budgetary review and recommendation to the executive and legislative branches of state government (Berdahl, 1971; Millard,

1976; Education Commission of the States, 1980; Folger and McGuinness, 1984; Hines, 1988).

In all three of their primary functions, statewide boards can find themselves in conflict with the Autonomy and Competition Myths and subject to the State Board Myth. It is the function of such boards, however, to try to develop a systematic and complementary approach to utilizing the resources of the state and the various state institutions to meet the wider educational needs and interests of the state as a whole. The charge that the New York state legislature in 1787 gave to the first coordinating board — the New York Board of Regents — was "to mold the several institutions [in the state] into a unity that would serve the best interests of the people of the state as a whole" (Abbott, 1958, p. 14). While seventeen states developed centralized higher education agencies prior to World War II, the major development, particularly of coordinating boards, came during the 1960s and 1970s, the period of the most rapid expansion of higher education in the history of the nation.

These boards were established to accomplish a number of objectives. The first was to ensure the orderly growth and development of higher education in the state through effective planning. A second objective was, through such planning and its implementation in cooperation with the institution, to clarify the role and mission of the various institutions and to ensure the diversity of types of institutions and programs commensurate with the postsecondary educational needs of the states and nation. A third, growing out of and part of the rationale for the first and second, was to ensure access for all interested and qualified citizens of the state to types of postsecondary education commensurate with their interests and needs. A fourth was to avoid unnecessary duplication and to increase the accountability of the institutions separately and the community of postsecondary education collectively to the state, the citizens, and their students. A fifth was to develop and provide the information essential to continued planning on state and institutional levels to meet changing conditions and needs.

Given the differences in scope, powers, and structures, some state boards stressed some of these objectives more than others; most had other objectives in addition to these five rather basic ones, and they obviously varied considerably in the extent to which they were able to achieve their objectives. While the first objective today needs to be modified in many states to stress conservation of resources and further development to achieve the states' educational objectives rather than growth, the objectives remain largely the same, although with changing applications. One fascinating part of the picture is that while there have been numerous studies in the various states and considerable modifications in boards over the years, with two possible exceptions (the Oregon Coordinating Board and the West Virginia Board of Regents), states have tended to move in the direction of continuing and strengthening such boards, rather than weakening or doing away with them.

Even given the variety of boards and their powers, the range of their objectives, their relative successes and failures, what perhaps most needs to be recognized is that their development and evolution have resulted from recognized public and institutional higher education concerns, that their purpose has never been to undermine institutional diversity and integrity, and that, particularly in larger, more complex states, they help provide a perspective and direction for ensuring that higher education needs and concerns do not fall between the cracks, something that no one institution alone could do. In addition, they help provide an important buffer against direct political interference in the internal affairs of institutions.

This does not mean that state boards are not in some instances part of the problem rather than the solution, but it does mean that the myth that they are inherently repressive and intrusive is both contrary to the facts and dangerously counterproductive for the long-range benefit of the higher education community itself and the country. What is clear is that they are not going to go away. Not only for the twenty-first century but for the last decade of the twentieth century, the nature and scope of the problem and challenges facing higher education in most states far transcend what any one institution is capable of accomplishing. These are problems and challenges that require statewide perspective, planning, and informed action, reinforced, on the one hand, by the cooperation and commitment of the higher education community and, on the other, by the support and backing of the legislative and executive branches of government.

The issues to be dealt with involve the range of postsecondary educational institutions in the state — public, private, proprietary — and frequently various providers not ordinarily thought of as part of the higher education system — business, industry, community organization, and national associations. Among such issues in most states are likely to be the following:

1. Ensuring a diversity of educational institutions and programs within the state adequate to meet the variety of postsecondary educational needs of the citizens of the state
2. Meeting the challenge of the changed and changing student clientele through appropriate modifications in missions and structures of institutions and programs
3. Providing and ensuring access to appropriate higher education programs for all citizens of the state of all ages who could benefit from it
4. Working toward effective coordination and complementation of the various collegiate and noncollegiate providers of educational services
5. Ensuring the continuity and quality of life-span learning from preschool through adult continuing education, including continuing professional education
6. Fostering the development of more effective partnerships between higher education institutions and business and industry in the development both of human capital and of applied research to strengthen our economic base and state and national competitiveness
7. Developing effective statewide telecommunications networks to serve the wider postsecondary educational community, including students both on and off campus and in remote locations, higher education institutions, and other learning resources, such as libraries, business and industry, and service organizations

These obviously are exemplary rather than exhaustive, but they do underline the kinds of critical problems that must be dealt with on a statewide level and the roles that state higher education boards or agencies can, do, and are intended to play, not in competition or in negative interference with but in complementation and enhancement of higher education institutions and programs. The state boards, in other words, are in the unique position of being able to develop perspectives and deal with matters that involve but transcend the scope and abilities of particular institutions.

Specific examples of such comprehensive and complementary state board activities could be chosen from a good many different areas. We will simply cite a few from the area of life-span learning as cases in point. Obviously, the Oklahoma Network of Continuing Higher Education project as a whole is a striking case in point. It is significant that the W. K. Kellogg Foundation grant was made not to an institution but to the Oklahoma Regents for Higher Education, which had the ability to draw on all of the higher education resources of the state. Six of the seven modules required statewide interinstitutional, intersegmental, and even interagency commitment. Representatives from all of the public and independent institutions in the state were involved in the first module, on leadership development. Module V, on telecommunications, not only tied together existing telecommunications and computer networks within the state but involved their extension to the state as a whole and, through the National University Teleconferencing Network at Oklahoma State University and the various library networks, to the nation as a whole. Through the telecommunications network, Module VI, on library collaboration, and Module IV, on education guidance and counseling, brought together public libraries, college libraries, and state libraries and educational information centers throughout the state in an effective interconnected system not just to share information but to provide counseling to students (actually post–high school students of all ages) throughout the state. One spinoff of Module IV was the development of a voluntary coalition of educational information officers at the various state institutions and military bases to reinforce and continue the work of this module. The module on program development not only identified general and, particularly, continuing and professional education needs with the help of the professional associations, schools, and practitioners in the fields but provided a series of grants to institutions to develop pilot programs to meet at least some of these needs. Finally, Module III, on professional development, while located at the University of Oklahoma, created a network of Kellogg Associates made up of the people responsible for continuing education at all of the public institutions in the state. The scope of the project would not have been possible without the involvement of the Regents.

Two of the states involved in the W. K. Kellogg Foundation–funded project by the Education Commission of the States (ECS) on Enhancing the State Role in Lifelong Learning (Cross and Hilton, 1983) should be mentioned. Through the ECS project, the Ohio Board of Regents undertook the role of catalyst in bringing the needs of employers, learners, and state government together with the resources of higher education. As a result of a series of studies, the regents established Regional Work and Learning Councils in various parts of the state for continuous sharing of information and planning for job training and opportunities for learners (Cross and McCartin, 1984, pp. 23–24). Partly with the help of the same ECS project, the New York Board of Regents developed a statement of eight goals for adult learning services to be accomplished by the year 2000 and defined the strategies for their accomplishment (New York State Department of Education, 1981). It should also be noted that with the help of another W. K. Kellogg grant, New York was able to expand its educational career information centers through the public library systems, as has more recently been done in Oklahoma (Cross and McCartin, 1984, p. 46).

In addition to six pilot states (California, Colorado, Kansas, Illinois, New York, and Ohio), the ECS project involved twenty-seven "associate" states that shared information and concerns related to lifelong learning. What the ECS project perhaps best succeeded in doing was highlighting state interests and obligations related to life-span or lifelong learning. At least partially as a result of the project, Cross and McCartin (1984) identified a series of what might be considered statewide or state board obligations transcending individual institutional obligations in lifelong learning. These included (1) ensuring access to equal education and job opportunities, (2) monitoring quality and ensuring consumer protection against exaggerated and poor educational quality, (3) ensuring that the state is in a competitive position to attract industry to the state through development of the necessary human capital, and (4) avoiding "wasteful over-lap and destructive competition" and through "communication and coordination mak[ing] a more effective system for providers and learners" (pp. 7–8).

The intent of this section on the State Board Myth is not to downplay what are inevitably tensions that exist between institutions and statewide boards. Some such tensions may in fact be fruitful. It is, however, to point out that, some institutions and presidents to the contrary not withstanding, these boards are not inherently the enemy. Rather, whether they are consolidated governing boards or coordinating boards, they are integral parts of the higher education scene, designed to ensure that higher education, public policy, and societal needs coalesce. As such, even given their variety from state to state and the fact that their existence does help define a more restrictive context for institutional autonomy, they today constitute a positive condition of the overall effectiveness of higher education in, among other things, overcoming its own turf wars.

Summary

In this chapter on overcoming turf wars, we have looked at what might be described as the roots of turfdom in the Autonomy Myth, at its more negative aspects in the Competition Myth, and at the resistance to systems in the State Board Myth. In each case, the myths incorporated but exaggerated some issues of fundamental and positive importance for higher education. Thus, the Autonomy Myth is based on the recognition of the importance of sufficient institutional autonomy for an institution to carry out its educational, research, and service functions in accordance with its mission, free of undue external interference or control. The Competition Myth is based on the legitimate institutional concern for achieving its mission and objectives as fully and uniquely as possible. And the State Board

Myth underlines the necessity of clearly defined areas of institutional responsibility, on the one hand, and state board responsibility, on the other. What this discussion indicates is that the position of rugged institutionalism is no longer adequate for dealing with the changing environment and higher education's responsibility to society. Such rugged institutionalism can only lead to chaos. Paul Sharp's (1988) comment seems particularly pertinent. We need more than ever to "generate an awareness that the turf-protection attitude is fast becoming an anachronism" (p. 7), and the sooner we overcome it, the better for higher education and the country.

4

Curricular Myopia

Curricula constitute the substantive content of the educational part of higher education. It is to matters of curricula that most of the recent higher education reports are addressed. The Association of American Colleges' (1985) report is entitled *Integrity in the College Curriculum*. *To Reclaim a Legacy* (Bennett, 1984) is concerned with both the nature of the humanities and their place in the college curriculum, as is the more recent *Humanities in America*, the report of the current chair of the National Endowment for the Humanities, Lynne V. Cheney (1988), and "Speaking for the Humanities," the report of the American Council of Learned Societies (1989). The latter is addressed to current critics of the substance of the humanities, including, among others, Bennett, Cheney, and Allan Bloom. *Involvement in Learning* wants "to restore liberal education to its critical role in undergraduate education" (Study Group on the Conditions of Excellence in American Higher Education, 1984, p. 10). The ECS report, *Transforming the State Role in Undergraduate Education* (Education Commission of the States, 1986, p. 12), calls for restoring the curricular balance between specialized training and general education. Allan Bloom (1987) seems to think that "the only serious solution" to revitalizing the college curriculum is "the good old Great Books approach" (p. 344).

In spite of the critical nature of curricula in higher and postsecondary education and the expressed concern of the various reports about them, if one looks carefully, one finds that the term *curriculum* itself is slippery and frequently ill defined or undefined. Even in *Integrity in the College Curriculum*, there are a series of different definitions or implied definitions, ranging from "a course of study" (Association of American Colleges, 1985, p. 2) through a "program of study" (p. 15) and from "methods and processes, modes of access to understanding and judgment, that should inform all study" (p. 15) to "criteria and objectives that should define the learning of every college undergraduate" (p. 24). Joan Stark and Malcolm Lowther (1986) identify six different and not necessarily compatible definitions of curriculum currently in use: "The term *curriculum* is used to mean (1) a college's or program's mission, purpose or collective expression of what is important for students to know; (2) a set of experiences that some authorities believe all students should have; (3) the set of courses offered to students; (4) the set of courses students actually elect from those available; (5) the content of a specific discipline; and (6) the time and credit frame in which college provides education" (pp. 4–5). Stark and Lowther themselves define a curriculum as an academic plan that includes most of these plus other factors relevant to actualization and assessment of the results of the plan (pp. 5–6). They also comment that much of the discussion of curricular issues, as of the purposes of college education, seems to be rooted more in rhetoric than in research—and judging by the language of the various reports, this indeed seems to be the case.

Our purpose in this chapter is not to try to offer either a research or a rhetorical definition of what the term *curriculum* means, nor is it to propose *an* ideal curriculum. In fact, given the variety of higher and postsecondary institutions and programs, the variety of legitimate educational objectives that they are designed (theoretically) to meet, and the complexity of post–high school educational needs in our society, the probability that there could be a single or common curriculum, regardless of the particular definition—even for baccalaureate programs—does not seem very high. Rather, our concern is with types of assumptions related to curricula that seem to be overly confining or even arbitrary about (1) the substance of curricula, (2) the relationship of the arts and sciences to professional and occupational education, and (3) what might be described as the locus of curriculum effectiveness. From this standpoint, any and all of the definitions cited by Stark and Lowther have some relevance to the discussion.

At the heart of the discussion is the age-old tension between the liberal arts, particularly that part of the liberal arts frequently designated as general education, and specialized, professional, occupational, and vocational education. However, even this distinction is far from clear-cut. The liberal arts obviously include a multitude of subject fields or disciplines, and the tension between breadth and specialization can be as acute within liberal arts programs as between liberal arts and undergraduate professional areas. Further, even the canon of what constitutes the liberal arts or liberal arts subjects not only has changed radically over the years but continues to change today. In the 1880s, the Wharton School of Business at the University of Pennsylvania was established in part, at least, to make it possible for students to major in history and social sciences, majors that at that time were not accepted by the liberal arts faculty (Cheit, 1975, p. 85). It is interesting to speculate how the Yale faculty of 1828 and the Pennsylvania faculty of 1880 would react to inclusion of computer science today as an arts and sciences subject. Further, while the arts and sciences subject areas have multiplied in the current century, this is minor compared to the number of emerging professions and occupations that have developed in the same period reflecting the growing complexity of knowledge, of society, and of technological change. To cite only one example, under the general heading of allied health professions, some twenty-three new fields or occupations have emerged since 1920 and have developed to the point where the educational programs to prepare practitioners in these fields now undergo accreditation by recognized specialized accrediting agencies. These fields are in addition to the traditional health professions, such as medicine, nursing, and dentistry (Council on Postsecondary Accreditation, 1986).

In spite of and in part because of what would appear to be the dynamic and continuously emerging and changing nature of the curricular substance of postsecondary education, it is not surprising that there is concern that the higher education curricular landscape is changing too rapidly, that older values are being lost, and that the broader purposes of higher education are being subverted through the very complexity of the developments taking place. This has led to a series of assumptions that need careful review if they are not to become myths inhibiting curricular development.

The Liberal Arts Contamination Myth

While enrollments have not decreased as anticipated over the last decade, and have, in fact, increased by more than a million and a half students between 1977 and 1988, the distribution of students by academic field and primary interest in coming to college has changed rather substantially. Interest in college as a means to a better position and to increased income has never been of negligible concern to students. However, in the fall of 1988, 82 percent of the entering freshmen listed getting a better job as a very important reason for attending college. Some 72.6 percent listed making more money as a major reason. The latter contrasts with 63.4 percent in 1980 and 49.9 percent in 1971. Somewhat offsetting this is the fact that 73.8 percent included learning more about things as very important, but this is not incompatible either with getting a better job or with making more money. In contrast to the concern with jobs and money, obtaining a general education dropped as very important from 70.9 percent in 1977 to 60 percent in 1988. Only 35.4 percent included becoming a cultured person as a matter of much importance in 1988 (Astin and others, 1988, pp. 7, 59). The majority of students are frankly and primarily interested in better and more lucrative jobs. Among older and part-time students, the interest in career and job enhancement and career change, as might be expected, is also pronounced. Although the proportion of adults is not as high as that of entering freshmen, about two-thirds of adults are enrolled for job-related reasons.

Among students thirty-five to fifty-four years of age, the proportion exceeds three-quarters (Center for Education Statistics, 1987, p. 251).

The distribution of students by intended field of major also has changed considerably over recent years. Between 1975 and 1985, the number of freshmen planning to major in business increased from 19 to 27 percent, thus constituting more than a quarter of all entering freshmen. The percentage of prospective engineering majors also increased, but much more modestly — from 8 to 12 percent. On the other hand, between 1970 and 1985, the percentage of freshmen intending to major in arts and humanities dropped from 21 to 8 percent, in the physical sciences from 6 to 2 percent, in the biological sciences from 4 to 3 percent, and in the social sciences from 9 to 8 percent (Ottinger, 1987, p. 41; Boyer, 1987, p. 105; Astin and others, 1985, pp. 48–49).

While freshman indication of majors in some cases may be more wishful thinking than actual commitment, the figures on graduations or degrees received tell the same story and are even more striking. Between 1979 and 1984 alone, the number of business and management degrees increased by 36 percent. Degrees in computer and information sciences increased by 32 percent. However, degrees in the social sciences dropped by 13 percent and in the humanities by close to 27 percent. During this period, the total increase in number of bachelor's degrees awarded was only 4 percent (Ottinger, 1987, p. 45). Obviously, this shift in student attitudes and choices has resulted in considerable dislocation in a great many colleges and universities and their departments.

As might be expected, this shift has produced concern about the role and future of the arts and sciences in general and the humanities in particular. It has also led to serious questions in a good many quarters as to whether students in these shifts to occupational-oriented major and undergraduate professional schools are not losing much of the perspective that the arts and sciences could give them, on the one hand, and whether the liberal arts themselves are not being overly professionalized or contaminated by "careerism," on the other. Ernest Boyer (1987) suggests that colleges today face a basic crisis involving confusion over goals: "scrambling for students and driven by market place demands, many undergraduate colleges have lost their sense of mission." Integral to this loss of mission, he suggests, "is the conflict between careerism and liberal arts. Today's students worry about jobs. Narrow vocationalism, with its emphasis on skills training, dominates the campus. Several institutions we visited are virtually torn apart as new majors battle old" (p. 3). Boyer points out that the *College Blue Book* now "lists more than six thousand different majors and the number is rapidly expanding. From the Sun Belt colleges to universities in the Ivy League, careerism dominates the campus" (p. 102).

The AAC report complains that "At a time when the major as it has developed should be under critical review and evaluation, majors have instead been proliferating, especially in the vocational and technical fields, where the appeal of jobs has blinded institutions and students to the ephemeral nature of much that is contained in the new majors. In the meantime students are being short changed" (Association of American Colleges, 1985, p. 27). The question, however, is not just or perhaps even primarily a matter of majors, as important as these may be, but rather what is expected of an educated person and more specifically of a college graduate. The issue then becomes whether students are obtaining a sufficiently liberal education not only to understand and operate effectively in but to appreciate the world in which we live, including, as Bennett, Cheney, Bloom, and a number of others would insist, the Western cultural tradition of which they are a part. This obviously involves questions of the broad objectives of general education and of graduation requirements. If one looks at such general education requirements in terms of required courses, including interdisciplinary courses, or even distribution requirements, then, as Cheney and Bennett point out, the results do not appear impressive, particularly in the humanities and humanities-related fields. According to Cheney (1988, p. 5), one can graduate from any of 80 percent of the four-year colleges in the country without a course in Western civilization and/or without a course in American history. In 37 percent of the colleges, no history at all is needed. No foreign language is required in 77 percent of the colleges and no American or English literature in 45 percent.

To the extent that these figures are indicative, it is not surprising that Bennett (1984) insists that "there has been a steady erosion in the place of the humanities in the undergraduate curriculum" (p. 19) or that at one of the leadership development sessions in Oklahoma, Bryce Jordan (1987), the president of Pennsylvania State University, should point to "the national decline of public concern for those disciplines which attempt to study our value systems and our cultural heritage, namely, the liberal arts" (p. 8). Even the National Governors' Association Task Force on College Quality (1986) laments the "evidence of program decline and devaluation particularly in the humanities" (p. 155).

The movement toward general education through required courses and distribution requirements after World War II was inspired in part by the Harvard Committee report *General Education in a Free Society* (1945) (which was never adopted at Harvard). During the late sixties and the early seventies, in response to student unrest, this movement was pretty well undermined in the name of a truncated view of "relevance" as immediate and specific rather than long-range and encompassing (Gray, 1981, pp. 16-17). To some extent, at least, the reform reports of the eighties involved a legitimate attempt to refocus attention on the common objectives of a college education — and thus on general education or liberal education in the broad sense. From the standpoint of helping to create curricular movement on the part of college faculties, they seem to have been successful. In *Campus Trends, 1988,* Elaine El-Khawas (1988, pp. 11-12) reports that nine out of ten colleges and universities either are engaging or have recently engaged in curricular change and that nine out of ten now require course work in general education. She also reports, as might be expected, that there is considerable variation in how this is done.

What is important but not surprising is that the recommendations of the various reports and books vary considerably as to what should be done to reinstate the centrality of liberal education. As noted, Bloom (1987) suggests that "the only serious solution" is to go back to "the good old Great Books approach" (p. 334), but he recognizes that such a return is not likely. Bennett and Cheney come close to recommending required courses in Western civilization, as does Jacob Neusner (1989). In spite of his opposition to changes at Stanford, Bennett (1984, p. 30) does agree that "the college curriculum must take the non-western world into account." The NIE study group calls for "at least two full years of liberal education" (Study Group on the Conditions of Excellence in American Higher Education, 1984, p. 41) in the hope that this will develop "capacities of analysis, problem solving, communication, and synthesis," including integration of knowledge from various disciplines (p. 43). There is no specification as to how this might be done, although there is a recognition that in professional fields this may require a five-year rather than a four-year baccalaureate.

Interestingly enough, neither *Integrity in the College Curriculum* (Association of American Colleges, 1985) nor Ernest Boyer (1987) in *College: The Undergraduate Experience in America* proposes a specific set of courses. Back in 1959, Earl McGrath (1959) had pointed out "that no particular curricular pattern any longer exists that can be exclusively identified as liberal education" (p. 16). He went on to suggest that the courses in the liberal arts in many cases tend to be every bit as if not more specialized and preprofessional in character than those in professional sequences and schools (p. 57). Almost echoing McGrath, the 1988 AAC report points out somewhat plaintively that "One major obstacle to making general education work is the attempt to offer general education through a conglomerate of courses conceived along specialized disciplinary lines. The problem is that most of us who teach undergraduates do not ourselves engage in the sort of integrative learning that we expect of our students" (Association of American Colleges, 1988, p. 48). If this is the case, it is a bit difficult to see just how the liberal arts have been contaminated by "narrow vocationalism."

Instead of proposing a curriculum in the sense of a series of courses, Boyer (1987, p. 92) proposes what he calls common themes that constitute an academic framework in general education. These include:

- Language: The Crucial Cornerstone
- Art: The Aesthetic Experience

- Heritage: The Living Past
- Institutions: The Social Web
- Nature: The Ecology of the Planet
- Work: The Value of Vocation
- Identity: The Search for Meaning

The AAC report lists a series of "nine experiences . . . we think . . . are basic to a coherent undergraduate education" (Association of American Colleges, 1988, p. 15). They involve an interesting combination of skills, awareness, activities, and, in a broad sense, subjects:

1. Inquiry, abstract logical thinking, critical analysis
2. Literacy: writing, reading, speaking, listening
3. Understanding numerical data
4. Historical consciousness
5. Science
6. Values
7. Art
8. International and multicultural experiences
9. Study in depth

What is significant about both lists is (1) that they are process-oriented, (2) that they do not specify particular courses, and (3) that, while the presumptions may be that they or at least part of them will be available through the arts and sciences, in neither case is it specified that they are or should be offered only by a liberal arts college. Thus, at least in theory, the opportunities for their achievement could be provided in any baccalaureate program.

It would seem particularly important, then, to distinguish rather carefully between a liberal education and the arts and sciences as departments, disciplines, or courses in a college of liberal arts or of arts and sciences. The assumption that the latter are not overly specialized or vocational, that they are necessarily the hallmarks of liberal education, may indeed be contrary to fact. In far too many cases, even introductory courses in the arts and sciences tend to be organized and taught as though everyone in the class were planning to concentrate in and go on to graduate school in the field in question. Earl McGrath's (1959) comments are particularly pertinent: Frequently "professional students who must select studies in liberal arts colleges find themselves in courses often more specialized and fragmented than the instruction in their own schools" (p. 16). To a remarkable extent, by implication, at least, Boyer, the AAC report, and even Bennett and Cheney agree. If this is the case, then the problem would not seem to be, as so frequently stated, that the liberal arts have been contaminated by vocationalism and professional education but rather "that the growth of new knowledge in academic fields, and not the intrusion of vocational subject matter . . . disintegrated the traditional pattern of liberal education in this country" (McGrath, 1959, p. 16).

Much of the cognitive as well as affective content of what needs to be integrated into the "coherent undergraduate education" of the AAC report or of Boyer's academic framework for undergraduate education may indeed come through the arts and sciences, but it may also come through technical and even professional education. What we are struggling for, however, is a paradigm or an interpretive concept whereby liberal general education gains significance or meaning as an integral part of the developing and continuing education of individuals in undergraduate college and beyond — a concept relevant to the range of life-span learning and experience.

Such a unifying or integrating concept, I would suggest, is readily available and has been around since the time of Plato. It is expressed by Whitehead (1932) in his definition of education as "the acquisition of the art of the utilization of knowledge" (p. 6) and particularly in his insistence that "the antithesis between a technical and a liberal education is fallacious. There can be no adequate technical education which is not liberal, and no liberal education which does not impart both technique and intellectual vision" (p. 74). The concept is suggested by Boyer (1987) through his inclusion of "Work: The Value of Vocation" in his list of common themes of general education and indirectly by the AAC report's claim that its "curriculum" will enable "the American people to live responsibly and joyfully, fulfilling their promise as individual humans and their objectives as democratic citizens" (Association of American Colleges, 1988, p. 15). The issue and the concept were particularly well identified by Hannah Gray (1981) in her David Henry Lecture *The Liberal Arts Revisited:* "It is interesting that we have chosen this term [*vocation*] to connote something confined and external rather than to express what might in fact be the outcome of liberal learning. The consequences of breadth, of liberality, of seeing professional training in a wider context would be to arouse a sense of vocation" (pp. 13–14).

The unifying concept suggested in all of this might well be described as career or vocation in the broad sense. Career so conceived is clearly far more than just a job. In its broadest sense, career or vocation includes not only preparation for but continuous involvement in life work, life plan, and life-style. It includes, as Whitehead suggested, not just acquisition of knowledge but the art of the utilization of knowledge. Viewed as the primary aim of education (Millard, 1973), it becomes the organizing principle and the culmination of liberal education itself. For the individual, it provides a sense of direction that makes it possible to compare and choose among competing values not only in his or her more formal educational development but in other areas of experience as well. Further, it provides a lifelong or life-span context, for career so considered is not something static but is developing, constantly changing with new experiential content and shifting social contexts throughout life.

It is unfortunate that too many liberal arts colleges and faculties have tended to promulgate the myth that liberal arts and concern with career are conflicting concepts. It would have been far more helpful to students, to the common concern of the educational community, and to the arts and sciences colleges themselves, if they had co-opted the concept of career rather than considering "careerism" as the enemy and stressed the essential role that the arts and sciences, including the humanities, can and should play in adequate (let alone satisfying) career development. Instead of lamenting increased student interest in jobs, even in making money, they should have welcomed it and placed their emphasis on helping students to discover or recognize that career or vocation, while it includes work, includes much more.

The liberalizing task then becomes helping students to identify the career components that extend considerably beyond work in the restricted sense but that also give work meaning and place it in a life-span perspective. Such a concept gives relevance to general education throughout life and not just or primarily in the first two years of college. It gives meaning and substance to Boyer's academic framework and the AAC conditions of coherent education by providing for them definitions and integration in terms of individual people's career objectives. Implicit in it is the recognition of the organic relationship of various careers or vocations to each other in society. Careerism in this sense, far from contaminating the liberal arts, could actually inform and strengthen them, and career becomes the viable concept for their integration into the lives of individuals and the community.

Making career development and enhancement the aim of education has a number of further implications. It calls, for example, for the kind of diversifiied educational system that will in fact provide the range of opportunities commensurate with human interests, needs, and societal demands. It recognizes the diversity of individuals; their interests, abilities, and backgrounds; and capitalizes on the relevance of education, including the arts and sciences, to personal and social development through career preparation, enrichment, and change. It places the emphasis not on terminal education but on the continuity of education throughout life, on articulation between various levels of education, and on the relevance of education to work and other phases of individual and communal life.

The Liberal Arts Contamination Myth does reflect a long-standing real and justified concern that if we are not careful, any education focused primarily on technical preparation for particular jobs, including overspecialization in one academic field, very quickly shortchanges students by becoming training rather than education. When this occurs, not only are the students deprived of the vision essential to understanding themselves and the world in which they live, but they also are likely to have little perspective or understanding of the work in which they are engaged. The myth serves as a warning against overspecialization in any field. However, the antidote to such overspecialization and technical preparation would seem to lie not in a series of required courses in the liberal arts per se, or in insisting somehow that concern with careers is contrary to the spirit of liberal education, but rather in recognizing that the concept of career, even vocation, in the broad sense is what education is all about. Thus, a major function of liberal education and particularly general education is to enrich, widen, and provide the perspective that constitutes an essential part of the substance of people's careers. As guides to career development, recommendations such as those of Boyer and the AAC report make excellent sense. Apart from the concept of career, they tend to be abstractions and to lack a unifying base.

On affirmation of the career development and enrichment function of higher education in general and liberal and general education in particular may well depend not just the continued relevance and thus the future of higher education but the ability of the country to meet its internal and international challenges, including competitiveness in the twenty-first century.

The Professional Education Exclusion Myth

Whereas the Liberal Arts Contamination Myth involves the assertion that the arts and sciences have been weakened or contaminated by shifts in student interests to more vocational subjects, on the one hand, and overspecialization even within the arts and sciences themselves, on the other, the Professional Education Exclusion Myth focuses on the undergraduate professional schools or departments and, to some extent, graduate professional schools as they affect the undergraduate curriculum through prerequisite structures. The claim is that, by consistently increasing technical professional requirements, undergraduate professional schools (or departments) have squeezed out or narrowed the possibility of taking liberal arts courses and thus receiving the kind of general or liberal education essential to the breadth and perspective of a truly educated person. Implicit in this argument is the assumption that professional courses have no liberal redeeming qualities. Part of the argument frequently involves the assertion that rigidity and narrowness in professional programs are aided and abetted, if not required, by professional accrediting bodies.

That there has been a continuing explosion of knowledge and information in most areas of specialization and in professional fields would be hard to deny. Further, that there is pressure from some faculty and specialists in particular fields to add specialized courses and prerequisites at the expense of breadth — of general education or liberal studies — would also be hard to deny. As already noted, this tends to be as much the case in many arts and sciences concentrations or majors as in professional fields. Among the factors, however, that highlight the issue as it relates to the professions is, first, the immediate perception or identification of the professional sequence or curriculum, particularly when it exists in or as a separate school, as indeed "separate" from the arts and sciences core of the college or university. By virtue of this separation, the burden of proof that its graduates are both technically and liberally educated rests with the professional school. The initial presumption is frequently that they are not, particularly if its students are not obviously in a wide range of arts and sciences courses.

A second factor is the close relationship between the professional sequences as preparation for practice in the field and the professional field itself, including its practitioners. Such perception of professional relatedness is reinforced by the existence in most professional fields of strong professional associations concerned with the status of the field, with the relevance of preparation to practice, with the quality of professional preparation, and, in health-related fields, with the impact of the field on public health and welfare. A number of these associations have developed accrediting bodies that set standards for educational programs and schools related to educational content, faculty preparation, and educational outcomes. In a number of fields, the accrediting activities are further reinforced by state licensing bodies, which frequently require graduation from an accredited program as a condition for taking the licensure examination. Thus, the presumption is further strengthened that professional education is dominated by the professions and their external organizations, that their primary concern is technical professional proficiency and professional aggrandizement, and that the arts and sciences and general education, if present, are there by sufferance. Since the professional associations also play a major role in professional continuing education, it is assumed that, if anything, such continuing education is even more restricted and practice-oriented.

There are a number of aspects of this scenario that need to be challenged. It must be admitted at the outset that there is considerable difference among the professions in professional education, as much or more so than among the arts and sciences disciplines. Thus, generalizations about "professional education" are as dangerous as generalizations about "arts and sciences" or even "liberal" education. There are, however, some general comments that can be made and that have some relevance to the concern for the liberal education of professionals, particularly at the undergraduate level.

In challenging this scenario, one can first ask whether it is the case that on the whole professional education has been moving in the direction of excluding or limiting liberal education, general education, or even arts and sciences education from undergraduate professional sequences. Is it, in other words, moving in the direction of job training rather than career development? If this is the case, is this the result of or is it encouraged by the accrediting activities sponsored by professional associations? While there are and have been tensions between arts and sciences and professional faculties and while, in some instances, accrediting bodies have not helped and may in fact have aggravated the situation, the answer on the whole to both parts of the question would seem to be no.

Historically, the movement in this country of professional preparation in such fields as medicine, law, nursing, dentistry, and engineering from apprenticeships to college and university settings at least in part involved recognition of the broader resources available within the collegiate setting. This includes scientific foundations in fields where professional education takes place primarily at the graduate level, as well as the ability to rely on undergraduate preparation in the humanities and social sciences (McGrath, 1959, p. 31). Where professional preparation takes place at the undergraduate level, as in nursing and engineering, the direct availability of arts and sciences subjects for inclusion in the program has not been an inconsiderable factor in the movement into the academy. Admittedly, other factors, such as prestige, influenced the migration, but, to a large extent, the prestige itself followed from the expanded career preparation involved.

Interestingly enough, in one area, business administration, some of the first schools—Wharton (1881) and Stanford (1898), for example—were established at least in part to provide a more liberal course of study for future businessmen than their founders believed could be obtained from their own arts and sciences colleges (Cheit, 1975, 85–86). The specialized or professional accreditation issue seems, however, to be a continuing one. The concern about what are claimed to be curricular restrictions imposed by accrediting agencies is very much alive. The 1982 report of the Carnegie Foundation for the Advancement of Teaching, *The Control of the Campus* (Boyer, 1982), concentrated primarily on what it considered administrative intrusion, but it sharply raised the issue of the relationship of specialized accreditation to the larger purposes of the campus (p. 78). In *Involvement in Learning,* the NIE study group is far more explicit. Specifically, it charges that "Accreditation and standards for undergraduate professional programs often stand as barriers to the broad understanding we associate with liberal learning. . . . While depth of study in any area has great value, the guidelines laid down by many professional accrediting bodies distort students' expectations and close off their future options. The result is that the college curriculum has become excessively vocational in its orientation, and the bachelor's degree has lost its potential to foster the shared values and knowledge that bind us together as a society" (Study Group on the Conditions of Excellence in American Higher Education, 1984, p. 10).

The NIE report notwithstanding, the question still is relevant as to whether in fact the professional or specialized accrediting bodies do place a straitjacket on the general aspects of the curriculum. In 1985, the Council on Postsecondary Accreditation (1985) undertook an analysis of the standards of the twenty specialized accrediting agencies it recognizes that accredit twenty-six undergraduate professional programs to determine how they provide for inclusion of liberal arts and general education programs. It found that fourteen of the twenty-six do specify minimum requirements in the liberal arts (including the natural sciences). Among these, "the average requirement of the general education component is 45% of the total course of study, and the average requirement for the course of professional studies is 41% of the total curriculum" (p. 1). The other 14 percent provides for electives. Twelve of the twenty-six do not specify numbers or percentages, but "almost all of them developed statements of objectives which emphasize a major importance of the arts and sciences in education for the professions" (p. 1). Of those specifying percentages, the professional degrees in fine arts and music such as the B.F.A. and B.M. degrees (in contrast to the liberal arts music and fine arts degrees), tended to be among those requiring a higher percentage of professional studies (60 to 65 percent), with journalism requiring the least (25 percent). Engineering, which is frequently cited as one of the more rigid fields, actually requires only forty-eight semester hours in engineering courses. Sixteen semester hours must be in the humanities and social sciences and thirty-two in the natural sciences and mathematics. The rest may be in electives. In some fields, engineering included, the accrediting bodies have insisted on maintaining a major role for the arts and sciences, in contrast and sometimes in opposition to some local faculties that have pushed for higher professional course content.

All of this is not to say that specialized accreditation has not been in some cases a constraining influence on curricular breadth, nor is it to fail to recognize that in a good many cases accreditation may have been misused at the local level in illiberal ways not consistent with either the letter or the intent of the accrediting body. It is, however, to suggest that the claim that the specialized accrediting bodies or their standards "stand as barriers to the broad understanding we associate with liberal learning" as a generalization is not borne out by the facts.

A note must be added about the impact of one graduate professional field on the curriculum. Whether correctly or not, medicine has been considered one of the fields in which the scientific prerequisites for admittance to medical school — or perhaps more accurately for doing well on the Medical College Admission Test (MCAT) — tend for many students to crowd out or limit broader involvement in the humanities and social sciences. The Association of American Medical Colleges in March 1989 announced a revision in the MCAT, to go into effect in 1991, that will place considerably greater emphasis on thinking and writing skills and less on accumulation of technical scientific information (Spector, 1989; Magner, 1989b).

It may well be the case, however, that to focus on the number of hours or the percentage of time devoted to the arts and sciences and to the professional sequence is to miss the point and to substitute form for substance. It would seem to reinstitute the problem involved in the Liberal Arts Contamination Myth. If the key to liberal education lies not in a prescribed series of courses but in the characteristics, skills, experiences, and expectations of an educated person, in the development of continuing coherent careers in the broad sense, then the number or percentage of hours spent in various liberal arts subjects is, in fact, close to irrelevant. Further, it may well mean that the professional courses themselves can become in many instances an integral part of liberal education. If this is the case, then, as Stark and Lowther (1988) point out, the issue is not one of restoring or creating a balance between specialized training and general education as recommended by the Education Commission of the States (1986, p. 12) report and even the NIE report. "While such a goal is well intentioned, the assumption that education for life and career are distinct and the idea of 'restoring balance' requires close examination" (Stark and Lowther, 1988, p. 8). The real challenge is integration, not balance. Again according to Stark and Lowther, "the crux of today's educational problem is how to integrate liberal and professional study effectively, building upon the best that each has to offer" (p. 8).

It was such a concept of integration that Eric Ashby (1966) was aiming at when he suggested that "the path to culture should

be through a man's specialization, not by by-passing it . . . .
A student who can weave his technology into the fabric of society can claim to have a liberal education; a student who cannot . . . cannot claim even to be a good technologist" (p. 84).
To some extent, even the Association of American Colleges
report, as well as the Boyer report, tends to support such a view.
For example, the AAC report recognizes that "education in a
professional or vocational field may . . . also provide a strong
enriching force of study in depth" (Association of American Colleges, 1985, p. 30). Boyer calls for the integration of "the liberal
and useful arts" (Boyer, 1987, p. 115) and suggests that such
integration depends as much on people as on programs. There
is rather strong evidence that a substantial number of educators in the professional fields also would agree on the importance of such integration of results.

   In 1983, a conference on "Integrating Liberal and Professional Education" was held, jointly sponsored by the Association of American Colleges and the Council on Postsecondary
Accreditation. The participants included representatives of professional education, accrediting bodies, and the liberal arts. The
representatives of professional programs made clear that their
understanding of "professional" included far more than technical learning—that it extended to "skills, abilities, and habits of
thinking commonly believed to be acquired through the liberal
arts" (Schulman, 1983, p. 1). They also agreed with their counterparts from the arts and sciences that these characteristics are
generic and cannot be assumed to be automatically inculcated
by the arts and sciences any more than by specialty fields but
rather must be developed by attitudes and processes ideally characteristic of both.

   One of the most enlightening and important projects in
this area was carried out from 1983 to 1988 by Joan Stark and
Malcolm Lowther at the University of Michigan with the help
of the Fund for the Improvement of Postsecondary Education
and the Spencer Foundation. This project has dealt with the
liberal outcomes of professional education. Examining primarily eight professional fields, all of which involve undergraduate
programs (architecture, business administration, education, en-

gineering, journalism, nursing, pharmacy, and social work), the project identified a series of what might be described as desired generic outcomes of professional education. These were refined through the Professional Preparation Network, which included educators and practitioners from each of the professions plus counterparts in the arts and sciences. In the process of the study, the members of the network developed, with varying degrees of success, integrated professional–liberal arts programs on their various home campuses.

What is important for this discussion is the outcomes identified and developed through the project. These are stated in terms of a series of competencies. Four of them are classified as specific professional competencies: conceptual competence (theoretical foundation of the profession), technical competence (skills required by the profession), integrative competence (integration of concepts and skills in practice), and career marketability. An additional ten competencies are recognized as outcomes in common with liberal education (Stark and Lowther, 1988, pp. 21, 23–25): communicative competence, critical thinking, contextual competence (understanding the societal context in which the profession is practiced), esthetic sensibility, professional identity (improving the knowledge, skills, and values of the profession), professional ethics, adaptive competence, leadership competence, scholarly concern for improvement, and motivation for continuing learning. One striking aspect of the list is its similarity to the nine essential undergraduate experiences of the AAC and the six common themes of Boyer. These competencies, however, were arrived at independently through analysis of objectives of the professional fields themselves, supplemented by further suggestions from the network.

The real challenge would seem to be to move beyond curricular turfdom as evidenced either by the arts and sciences or by professional programs or schools to the kind of integration that recognizes the common characteristics of truly professional education in contrast to training and of effective liberal or general education in the arts and sciences in contrast to narrow specialization at the undergraduate level. But it also involves an integration that takes into account the importance of depth or specialization of professional, technical, and conceptual competence as developed for each student in the broad context of his or her career.

In the introduction to *Strengthening the Ties That Bind* (Stark and Lowther, 1988), Frank Rhodes describes rather nicely the competent and professionally committed citizens that should be the product of such integrated education: "Regardless of their specific field or professional area, all college graduates should be skilled communicators and critical thinkers. They should have an understanding of the social goals their profession promotes and the ethical standards it demands. They should appreciate the aesthetic elements of experience as means to both their personal enrichment and the improvement of their professional practice. And they should be committed to improving their skills and refining their values through life long learning and reflection" (p. i). This comes very close to describing the broad career paradigm we discussed earlier. Career becomes the organizing principle for the skills, experiences, and knowledge content drawn from the arts and sciences and the professional fields that should be characteristic of active, informed, and educated people. It provides for the diversity and relatedness of careers and professions and for the uniqueness of each person's educational program to meet his or her needs within a broader framework. It should do away with invidious comparisons between the arts and sciences and the professions. As Earl McGrath (1959) has suggested, "higher education could then be recognized, as it should be, as having certain universal functions which should be common to all curricula regardless of the administrative devices which for convenience now separate undergraduate students in terms of their vocational objectives" (p. 62). Finally, what should be involved is the clearer recognition that the liberalizing aspects of college education can and should be as much available through courses or programs in professional fields as through those in the arts and sciences.

It was the recognition of the importance of knowledge of technical fields in the liberal education of arts and sciences students that led the Sloan Foundation in the mid-1980s to develop its "New Liberal Arts Program" (Koerner, 1985). The foundation provided funds to more than forty liberal arts colleges across the country to develop and incorporate courses in technology, based in many instances in engineering and related professional programs, into the liberal arts colleges themselves as part of "general education." The rationale is described by Barrett Hazeltine (1985) of the Division of Engineering at Brown as follows: "No one can understand the world about him/her without some understanding and appreciation of technology. Democracy implies informed citizens. Graduates in any field will have to deal repeatedly with technological options and devices. The engineering approach to problem-solving . . . offers much to decision-makers. The insights and aesthetic appreciation offered by the study of technology are as valid as those offered by other approaches" (p. 1). It seems evident that we have passed the point at which the old divisions between the arts and sciences and professional education make much sense either as a basis for distinguishing liberal and "nonliberal" education or as a basis for dealing with the complexities of the current and emerging world. This is not to fail to recognize the differences between bodies of knowledge and ways of knowing. It is, however, to recognize that liberal education should be equally characteristic of professional and of arts and sciences education (and frequently it has not been characteristic of either). The key for people, regardless of specialization, to incorporating liberal education, including appropriate skills, awareness, experiences, and bodies of knowledge, into effective learning and service lies in career development, whether that career is in anthropology, nursing, engineering, philosophy, or the ministry.

Curricular Absolutes Myth

The claim is sometimes made that curricular standards were lost during the period of student unrest. As a result of the academy's surrender to an immediate and relativistic conception of relevance, curricular structure and integrity disappeared with the result that today's undergraduate curriculum is both capricious and mediocre (Mitchell, 1987, p. 124). Thus, if integrity is to be restored to the curriculum, we must rediscover and reinstate those curricular components, particularly courses, that are essential to the education of all students. With his nostalgic call for a return to Great Books as the most desirable option, Allan Bloom (1987, p. 344) epitomizes this position. But close behind is William Bennett (1984), both in the rhetoric of *To Reclaim a Legacy* and in his attack on the Stanford move to modify its general éducation curriculum by shifting primary emphasis from Western civilization to world cultures.

Admittedly, Bloom (1987) recognizes that the Great Books approach has itself tended to become a cult and as such is marked by "amateurishness," "encourages self-assurance without competence," and engenders a "spurious intimacy with greatness" (p. 344). However, when the Great Books constitute a central part of the curriculum, students "are excited" and feel that they are "getting something from the university they cannot get elsewhere" (p. 314). Bloom is far from optimistic about a return to the Great Books approach, but he strongly suggests that without it, truly liberal education is not really possible. "Liberal education flourished when it prepared the way for discussion of a unified way of nature and man's place in it, while the best minds debated on the highest level" (p. 347). This, he argues, no longer takes place.

Part of the problem lies in determining what constitutes the canon of Great Books or, to extend the concept to courses, what constitutes the canon of courses that make up the irreducible core or the absolutes essential to the development of truly educated people. Thus, recognizing that there is some value in becoming acquainted with other cultures, Bennett (1984) insists in *To Reclaim a Legacy* that the irreducible core should be Western culture. "The core of the American college curriculum — its heart and soul — should be the civilization of the West, source of the most powerful and pervasive influence on America and all its people" (p. 30).

It should have come as no surprise when Bennett expressed his displeasure at Stanford University's adoption of a new core course on "Culture, Ideas, and Values" to replace a core course in Western civilization. Essentially, the debate at Stanford, according to Carl Schorske (1988), was not about excluding Western texts but about including "the cultures of those heretofore regarded as the others — the outsiders — and to make exposure to their ideas part of the way all Americans will define themselves" (p. B2). It is in this context that Schorske described Bennett "and his allies . . . as the new fundamentalists of Western Culture."

    Fundamentalism is indeed an appropriate term and is the matter at issue. By definition, fundamentalists have "the truth," and anyone who disagrees is in error. This seems to be the posture not only of Bloom and Bennett but, more frighteningly, of the new National Association of Scholars. In its opposition not only to taking affirmative action into account in faculty procurement but to demands by feminist scholars for recognition and to "replacement of Western Civilization programs . . . by 'oppression studies' . . . and 'radical egalitarianism,'" if the *Chronicle of Higher Education* report of November 23, 1988 (Mooney, 1988), is even partially correct, we are in for renewal and acceleration of the insistence on curricular absolutes.

    At this point, the question is not the importance or relevance of the Great Books or of courses in Western civilization or world cultures to curricula appropriate for the liberal education of undergraduate students regardless of age. They clearly are relevant. But so are a wide range of other courses and subjects — social sciences, physical sciences, mathematics, literature, philosophy, the "new liberal arts" technology courses of the Sloan Foundation program, and professional courses designed to develop liberal outcomes. There is nothing wrong with a core curriculum, particularly if its objectives are made clear to students at the outset. There are indeed some courses that provide more of a liberal perspective in career development than others. Interdisciplinary courses can undoubtedly provide additional perspective, particularly if they involve not only the arts and sciences but professional perspectives and content as well.

    Nor is the question, as Bloom would have us believe, a reduction today of everything to relativism. To recognize the importance of relevance as it relates to career development, personal and communal awareness, and the search for truth is not relativism. One can hold a probabilistic view of knowledge of truth without subscribing to the view that all statements are equally true. Much of the discussion in relation to the Liberal Arts Contamination Myth and the Professional Education Exclusion Myth is also relevant in relation to the Curricular Absolutes Myth. It became obvious in considerations of these that liberal education in the arts and sciences and in professional fields cannot be defined in terms of a set of prescribed courses or curricular absolutes. In relation to Bloom, to Bennett, and to Cheney, the American Council of Learned Societies (1989) report "Speaking for the Humanities" seems right on target. "A national core curriculum or a national list of books would be not only a recipe for unimaginative teaching, but a restriction of fundamental intellectual liberties" (p. A22). Rather, liberal education needs to be seen in terms of a series of objectives related to careers that include developing certain skills, attitudes, awareness, and means of dealing with the world. Here, as indicated, while the statements and even the lists of objectives of various reports, studies, and people differ in details, there is something approximating agreement in the recognition of liberal curricular objectives as characteristics, skills, and experiences rather than courses or content absolutes. Hannah Gray (1981) has summarized these objectives of liberal education for students as developed in most of the reports extraordinarily well: "To equip them to cope with complexity itself; to equip them to see the relatedness of things; to equip them to find ways of coming to judgment and of coming to understand the nature of choices that may lie before them, and others to whom they relate, in a way that makes sense, that has some logic, that has some coherence, and at the same time makes them responsible" (p. 20). If this is the case, then it is undoubtedly true that some particular courses in the arts and sciences and the professions may be more relevant to achieving these objectives than others, but it would be extraordinarily difficult to make the case that any one course or set of courses is an absolute condition of their attainment. If there are any absolutes, the objectives of liberal education rather than particular courses would come close to embodying them. However, as our discussion has indicated, these objectives are capable of alternative related but not identical formulations; and perhaps more strikingly, if one is talking about skills as objectives, modification and additions even in skills in the light of changing academic and societal conditions do occur.

To take only one example, today computer literacy is emerging as an important skill objective essential to much educational and career accomplishment. This is a concept that would have had little meaning twenty-five or thirty years ago. And yet we can cite three current examples from W. K. Kellogg Foundation–funded projects. First, in the Oklahoma project, in addition to Module V (telecommunications), which has involved developing a computer telecommunications network for the state as a whole, Module IV (educational guidance and counseling), Module VI (library collaboration), and a number of the demonstration projects under Module II (program development) depend on computer literacy as fundamental to their operation and success. Second, in the University of Georgia program, the Personal Adult Learning Laboratory, a major and exciting individual counseling and guidance system, is a computer-based operation available to students of all ages. Third, the Intermountain Community Learning and Information Services Project in Colorado, Wyoming, Utah, and Montana is designed specifically to utilize computers (and computer literacy) in extending educational opportunity to remote communities.

We seem to be at a point in the history of higher education and the country where the last thing we need is a renewed "educational fundamentalism" dedicated to curricular absolutes and maintaining the higher educational status quo or reaffirming by implication the Golden Era Myth. The changing student body, the state of technology, the changing economy, the concerns for international competitiveness, the changing work force, and the need to incorporate all citizens and particularly the growing minority populations as active participants in a productive learning society all point in a different direction. Lynton and Elman (1987) have described the direction in terms of achieving competence: "We believe that education aimed at the achievement and the maintenance of competence constitutes the essence of true liberal education . . . the purposes of general and liberal education as basically utilitarian and instrumental" (p. 57).

A somewhat different and more inclusive way of phrasing it might be to talk about the objective of liberal education as providing for enriched and continuing career development in an increasingly complex society.

The Feet of the Master Myth

Like the Golden Era Myth and the Autonomy Myth, the Feet of the Master Myth is one of the persistent, almost classical myths in higher education. It is closely related to the Traditional College Student Myth and in fact tends to rest at least in part on the assumption that the primary function of higher education is to prepare the young to take their appropriate places in society, particularly those young people with time and funds to spend the appropriate time on campus. *Appropriate* here is defined in terms of time to attain the degree in question. The myth rests on the recognition of the essential role of the scholar-teacher-professor in shaping academic policy, maintaining academic standards, and providing instruction. It places a high premium on student-faculty contact, particularly when that contact takes place in the context of the transmission of knowledge through lectures and seminar techniques.

Historically, the roots of the myth go back to the beginning of higher education itself. The importance of the teacher-pupil relationship has been recognized at least since the time of Plato's portrait of Socrates. While not all teachers fit the Socratic mold, the master teacher-scholar with his or her students has been the dominant feature of higher education from the emergence of the university during the Middle Ages until today and promises to remain so in the future. Although contemporary postsecondary institutions are made up of considerably more than faculty — even faculty and students — the faculty remains the centerpiece, the academic capital, and to a large extent the basis of both the uniqueness and the reputation of the institutions themselves. While there are examples today of institutions and programs, such as the New York External Degree Program and the New Jersey Thomas A. Edison College, where faculty as such do not teach, these are exceptions, and even with these, faculty, whether their own or from other institutions, still play a basic role in test development, setting of standards for assessing student achievement, and quality control. Thus, at the outset it is critical to underline the fact that questioning some of the assumptions in the Feet of the Master Myth does not imply a disregard of the importance of faculty.

The myth, however, involves a series of assumptions that add up to the proposition that a really effective education takes place only or primarily in residence on campus, in direct contact with the professor or teacher in traditional classes, laboratories, seminars, and clinical and practical programs carried out under professorial supervision and guidance. Training, even learning, may take place in other settings off campus or on campus and on a part-time basis, but without residence experience on campus and in day-time courses taught by regular faculty, one's education is incomplete. Only if one has the enriching experience of residency and learning at the feet of the master is one worthy of a regular degree. In some instances, this has been carried to the point of insisting, in the case of transfer students, that resident work at the particular institution must include at least the final year or some other terminal time regardless of where one has transferred from or how much work was accomplished on campus there.

The myth can manifest itself in any one or all of four related forms and may be operative at different organizational levels. The policy involved may be explicit, as it usually is in the case of larger operational units, or implicit, the latter most frequently at departmental or individual professorial levels. The four forms might be described as the "who," "how," "where," and "when" forms. The "who" is the collegium of master-teacher-professors (or their designees, who may be teaching fellows, part-time faculty members, or junior instructors) who develop and authenticate the programs and courses. It is they who transmit knowledge, create new knowledge through research, and frequently provide both the substance and the inspiration essential for student achievement. The "how" is through traditional instructional forms, augmented in some cases by new techniques and technologies. The "where" is clearly the campus and the ambience it provides. The "when" is the time—preferably full time—for at least the major portion of the work at undergraduate levels to be accomplished as soon after graduation from high school as possible and with as much continuity to graduation from college or through the next degree as possible.

Any or all of these forms may result in institution-wide policies and practices or, if a number of colleges within a university are involved, in policies and practices of particular colleges that may be implicitly assumed and even applied without being formally stated or adopted. Finally, they may characterize attitudes and actions of particular faculty members in their expectations of their colleagues and students.

That there are real advantages for a good many younger students in being an integral part of the college community, in being involved in direct interaction with regular full-time faculty (when they are available), in being in residence on campus, in committing themselves full-time, and in maintaining the continuity of educational development at least through undergraduate education would be hard to deny. Alexander Astin (1986) points out that there is considerable evidence that "the quality of undergraduate experience, the amount of talent development. that occurs, is enhanced by living on campus" (p. 22). There always will be an important place for the traditional residence college. To insist, however, that all or any of the above are essential to becoming a "truly educated" person would seem not only to be arbitrary but to bar what is in fact the majority of students in postsecondary education today from becoming "truly educated." It thus is basically an elitist and restrictive conception of higher education, with limited relevance for today or for the next century, particularly if the objective is to make quality higher education opportunity available to as wide a range of citizens as possible.

And yet both the argument for and the preference for traditional residential higher education, not only within the academic community but for many people within the larger community, remain strong. In its recommendation to students, the NIE study group urges them "to try to attend college full-time for at least part of your student career even if you are currently

employed full-time and/or have full-time family responsibilities. . . . We believe that the experience of being a full-time
student entails greater gains than costs" (Study Group on the
Conditions of Excellence in American Higher Education, 1984,
p. 78). It would appear that, according to the study group, the
ideal situation is to live in the dormitory, where "effective learning communities" can be established (p. 33). Such communities are particularly important in larger institutions. Recognizing that a good many students cannot live in dormitories, the
report calls for substitute near-equivalents for such students. "But
for the commuter, adult, and part-time students in our institutions, other approaches—such as weekend college and short-
term but intense periods of residence on campus—are necessary" (p. 34).

Howard Bowen, who served as a member of the study
team, was probably one of the most articulate and persistent
proponents of full-time campus residency. Such residency, he
argues, plays a critically important role in establishing student
values. The physical features of the campus, the extracurricu-
lar activities, the contact with and examples provided by administration and faculty, the involvement with student peer
groups, and the impact of campus traditions not only enrich
but are essential to the collegiate experience. Bowen (1982) summarizes both the concern and the objectives of those committed to the essential value of the campus experience as follows:
"It is a pity that college environments have in recent decades
become less effective in the sense that millions of students, the
part-time commuters, cannot partake of them as fully as full-
time resident students. To carry out its responsibility in the formation of values, one of the key tasks before higher education
is to find ways of bringing more students to the campus as full-
time residents or, where this is not possible, of finding substitutes for full-time campus residence. . . . The ideal to be sought
is to bring to large numbers of people the ambience of the
residential campus or the best possible substitutes" (p. 139).

While this ideal of the ivy-covered campus where one sits
at the feet of the master may be unrealistic and actually inhibit
effective planning to deal with the realities of current student

demography or changing societal conditions, it clearly has a great deal of nostalgic appeal. It tends to justify the status quo or what is presumed to be the status quo. In this it is reflected in various types of resistance to academic change ranging from modification in teaching methods to appropriate utilization of technologies and acceptance of nontraditional and experiential types of learning as evidence of achievement of educational competence. Some years back, when language laboratories were first introduced, the language departments at an institution that I was involved with insisted that a language laboratory was essential to effective modern language instruction and that the department had to have one. Once language laboratories were acquired, however, instead of revising their courses to take maximum advantage of their relevance to instruction, the faculty kept the courses exactly the same except for assigning students additional drill time in the laboratories.

This attitude has been reflected more recently in what is still a reluctance on the part of some faculty to utilize telecommunications and even computers as integral to instruction. It was reflected (as noted earlier) in the needs assessment surveys in the Oklahoma project Module II, on program development, in which there was (in 1985–86) remarkable agreement among employers, library patrons, community leaders, and even the educational leaders involved in the leadership development module (Module I) that the traditional classroom setting is the preferred method of instruction for both credit and noncredit work, not just for "traditional" college students but for students of any age and background. Among even the educational leaders, independent study was considered only acceptable and off-campus study utilizing prepackaged materials and media was at best only reluctantly acceptable, as were computer-tutorial programs. This attitude is changing in Oklahoma and elsewhere, but it reflects a basic conservatism and continuing faith in the Feet of the Master Myth.

Closely related has been the reluctance of many, particularly mainline colleges and universities, to accept credit for experiential learning even when carefully validated. This is reflected in the action of some states and accrediting bodies to restrict the amount of credit toward academic degrees not only from experiential learning but from off-campus programs in general. Much of the concern about experiential learning in particular has, as Zelda Gamson (1988) has pointed out, come from the faculty itself: "If education could take place anywhere, as proponents of experiential learning claimed, what was the role of faculty? Experiential education shifted the attention from the teacher to the student. Such a shift required faculty to stop telling students what they wanted them to learn and begin helping students discover what they needed to know in order to understand the realities they experience directly" (p. 9).

The central role of the faculty in developing the content of higher education programs, in utilizing the various technologies in teaching and facilitating learning, and in developing academic policy is not in question. There may well be a question, however, about whether various faculties effectively use the resources available to them in achieving educational objectives relevant to the range of students of all ages involved in various levels of higher education today. There may also be serious questions about whether distinctions in types of instruction and among faculty members teaching what are presumed to be resident students on campus, in contrast to those teaching part-time students, older students, or off-campus students, are not both invidious and counterproductive. We should be talking about one faculty with various functions and not regular faculty and faculty for older, part-time, and continuing education students.

What may much more seriously be questioned is whether, with all due respect to Howard Bowen and the National Institute for Education study group, residence on the traditional campus for a great many institutions is or should be the desideratum as to whether effective education takes place. It may well be that we have outgrown the traditional campus concept with its feet-of-the-master assumptions. If anything is clear (as we stressed in Chapter Two), it is that traditional residential college students are in the minority of those involved in college education. The older concept of the self-contained campus may need to be replaced by what Lynton and Elman and Boyer have called the extended campus. Thus, even in relation to undergraduate education, Boyer (1987) suggests that "The trend is clear. In just a generation, assumptions about time and location of learning that historically have guided undergraduate education have been turned on end. Undergraduate education is beginning to break loose from traditional classroom encounters and even from the notion that all learning must be completed under the formal guidance of a teacher. The nation's colleges are discovering that the campus is as much a state of mind as a place. It exists, or at least *can* exist, wherever the student happens to be" (p. 232).

If what we are concerned with is what the student knows and can do, with attained skills, experiences, and competencies, then the fact of their attainment is far more important than the place or even the method of their attainment. The extended campus does become the community of learners and teachers wherever they may be and whatever the effective mode of communication may be. The distinction between on-campus and off-campus learning, given appropriate recognition and organization of the extended campus, becomes arbitrary. As Lynton and Elman (1987) point out, "the combination of computerization and telecommunications quite literally eliminates the physical boundaries of the university and enables it in principle to expand many of its functions to any desired location" (p. 129) and to do so in such a way that communication and direction remain with a central faculty—or even with a variety of faculties at separate cooperating institutions across the country.

The most striking example of such technology usage is provided by the National Technological University (NTU), which provides advanced engineering education through satellite delivery to many workplaces around the country. It offers its own master's degrees in various types of engineering but has no campus—only an office in Fort Collins, Colorado. While it is an independent accredited institution, it literally is a consortium of some twenty-two prestigious participating universities. Faculty from these institutions serve as instructors in the courses. Twelve participating companies and the U.S. Department of Defense contributed to the establishment of the university (Eurich, 1985, p. 86). Participants must be sponsored by their employers, who must also provide an on-site classroom. In its first year (1985–86) alone, NTU delivered more than three hundred courses and four thousand units of credit (Hirsch, 1987, p. 26).

While still in its developmental stages, the W. K. Kellogg Foundation–sponsored Intermountain Community Learning and Information Services (ICLIS) program provides higher education services and programs for people in more isolated areas of Colorado, Montana, Utah, and Wyoming. As noted earlier, the program involves Colorado State University, Montana State University, Utah State University, and the University of Wyoming, working cooperatively with libraries in the states in question. Quite literally, the campuses of the universities involved potentially extend not only to their individual states as a whole but, through the interlocking network, to the entire intermountain region.

Through its telecommunications network (Module V), the Oklahoma State Regents for Higher Education in cooperation with the Oklahoma Television Authority, the Oklahoma State University Television Service, and the University of Oklahoma Health Services Center have developed a telecommunications network that includes all of the higher education institutions in the state, many of the public libraries, military-base education operations, and various educational guidance centers. Through the network, the various campuses of the system have been augmented for coordinated educational service to all parts of the state. Where one campus ends and another begins thus becomes a matter of function and not of physical limitation.

One particularly striking example of providing higher education opportunity, including degree work that goes considerably beyond the individual professor and the traditional campus, has been the development in Oklahoma of a special program of individualized instruction for the physically handicapped wherever they may be. Through adaptation of the Navy Program for Afloat College Education used on ships at sea, Bruce Wilburn of the Middlesex Research Center, Inc., in Arlington, Virginia, working with the University of Oklahoma, is developing self-contained television-videotape-computer units with "extended" programs in various courses and subjects for the handicapped. Through the computer component particularly, continuing contact with the university and faculty is maintained for correction of assignments and guidance. Within the very near future, full degree programs are expected to be available. In its parent form with the navy under the direction of Defense Activity for Non-Traditional Education Support (DANTES), it has already made it possible for service members at sea to continue their education without interruption. The present program is appropriately called the Naval Electronics Campus System (Defense Activity for Non-Traditional Education Support, 1988). Although more restricted in scope and not geared to credits or degrees at this time, the Personal Adult Learning Lab developed at the University of Georgia Center for Continuing Education with the help of a W. K. Kellogg Foundation grant involves much of the same approach to self-education through computer and videotape instruction.

All of these examples illustrate the growth of the extended campus, the transcendence of the traditional classroom, and the recognition that the teaching roles of faculties have been and will be changing from primarily providing information through lectures to serving as catalysts to learning, whether that learning occurs in traditional classrooms or at remote locations via educational technology or by some other means. While these illustrations involve technologies, it should be pointed out that the recognition of the fact that the primary educational functions of higher education institutions extend far beyond the traditional classroom with students sitting at the feet of the master, while reinforced by technology, is more fundamentally related to the necessity of providing relevant higher education to a far wider clientele than traditional college students. Perhaps the central challenge to the higher education community for the nineties and the next century will be to adapt higher education to the wider community of clients that it must serve if the United States is in fact to remain an educationally competitive nation.

Within the system of higher education, there clearly is a place for traditional institutions — both colleges and universities — but there is a wider function than these encompass that must be not only planned for but implemented. This wider function is evolving today, but the evolution may need acceleration. From this standpoint, we might paraphrase Lynton and Elman (1987, p. 4) by suggesting that what is called for is something different from the old perception of a system of higher education consisting of relatively self-contained isolated campuses populated by research scholars engaged in knowledge for its own sake and young students pursuing undergraduate studies on a full-time basis. Even at present, this is less and less the case, and the assumption that it is or should be the paradigm for higher education as a whole is the kind of myth that constitutes a serious barrier to meeting higher education's real objectives today — let alone in the future.

Summary

A series of key factors have emerged that are important to the kind of curricular development desirable for the future. Such curricular development requires both the appropriate perspectives, value awareness and social commitment, and the specialized and professional accomplishment that is essential to effective operation of individuals in an increasingly complex and internationally competitive world. Among the key factors are the following, some first suggested by recent reports calling for higher education reform and some with much deeper roots.

1. What constitutes liberal education cannot be defined in terms of a specific set of courses or curriculum in the narrow sense but rather involves a series of skills, attitudes, achievements, experiences, and competencies that may be developed in a variety of different ways.
2. The old division between liberal and professional education is an anachronism. Professional education can and frequently does have liberal outcomes, and arts and sciences education can lead to highly restrictive types of overspecialization. Whitehead's (1932) statement that the antithesis between technical and liberal education is fallacious is even more relevant today than it was in 1932. Some grasp of the perspectives of professional fields may be as important

to the liberal education of arts and sciences students as general cultural perspectives are to students in professional fields.

3. The concept of career, rather than being the antithesis of liberal education, may well constitute the appropriate paradigm for integrating liberal and general education and specialized or professional education into effective life-span learning for each individual, adapted to his or her interests, needs, and objectives.

4. As valuable as campus residence may be for some students, the mark of an educated person, if we are serious about skills, competencies, types of experiences, and achievements, is not the where or even the how of instruction but whether a student has the appropriate skills, competencies, types of experiences, and achievements regardless of how these are attained or continue to develop.

5. The concept of the campus as the single place where higher learning occurs is thus as anachronistic for many people and purposes as the division between liberal and technical or professional education. We should welcome and utilize the extended campus, including the technologies that enhance its range and effectiveness, as the real campus of the future.

5

The Quality Quagmire

The key education issue of the present era, if one is to be guided by the various reports, studies, and polls of the last few years, is quality. The current wave of concern with quality at the national level began with elementary-secondary education and was spurred on by the publication in 1983 of the report of the National Commission on Excellence in Education (1983), *A Nation at Risk,* with its warning against "a rising tide of mediocrity" in education that "threatens our very future as a Nation and a people" (p. 5). Although aimed at the public schools, it had advice for the collegiate community as well, calling on colleges and universities to "adopt more rigorous and measurable standards . . . higher expectations for academic performance. . . . and . . . raise requirements for admission" (p. 27). It called for a focus on "excellence" and quality improvement. One direct result of *A Nation at Risk* was the appointment by the National Institute for Education of the Study Group on the Conditions of Excellence in American Higher Education (1984), whose report, *Involvement in Learning,* called for the improvement of the quality of American undergraduate education in particular.

Involvement in Learning was followed by a series of reports dealing with various aspects of the quality issue and in most cases calling for educational reform. These included the National

Endowment for the Humanities report *To Reclaim a Legacy* (Bennett, 1984); the Association of American Colleges (1985) report *Integrity in the College Curriculum;* a report from the Southern Regional Education Board *Access to Quality Undergraduate Education* (Commission on Educational Quality, 1986); the Education Commission of the States (1986) report *Transforming the State Role in Undergraduate Education;* the National Governors' Association Task Force on College Quality (1986) report *Time for Results: The Governors' 1991 Report on Education;* a report of the Council on Postsecondary Accreditation (1986), *Educational Quality and Accreditation;* and a report from the Carnegie Foundation for the Advancement of Teaching by Ernest Boyer (1987), *College: The Undergraduate Experience in America.* The concerns about quality expressed in these reports were reinforced by two books that reached considerably beyond the academic community and were high on the best-seller lists in 1987, Allen Bloom's (1987) *Closing of the American Mind* and E. D. Hirsch, Jr.'s (1987) *Cultural Literacy.* This partial list does not include reports in special areas such as teacher education and mathematics and sciences.

The issue of quality obviously is not something new in higher education. It is as old as higher education itself. However, there appear to have been periods, particularly in the history of the United States, when concern with quality, however defined at the time, has tended to predominate and periods when other issues, such as equity, have been primary matters of attention. In Chapter Two, we dealt with some of the shifts in the nineteenth and twentieth centuries in concerns about quality and access. The Yale faculty in 1828, for example, was undoubtedly convinced that it was acting in defense of preserving quality, whereas the Congress in passing the Land-Grant Act of 1862 was clearly extending access as well as changing the conception of quality.

In an analysis based primarily on forms of federal and state support, W. Lee Hansen and Jacob O. Stampen (1987) maintain that there have been three major periods since World War II when the predominant interest has shifted from concern with quality to concern with access and equity and then back to quality. From World War II until 1967–68, partly as a response to *Sputnik* but carrying over into the period of higher education expansion, the emphasis tended to be on quality. From 1967–68 to 1980–81, the primary focus was on access, spurred on in part at least by the civil rights movement and student unrest. Since 1980–81, the pendulum has swung back to quality, beginning, not coincidentally, with the Reagan election of 1980 and the national shift to a more conservative political stance.

Our concern at this point is not primarily with the relationship between quality and equity (we will return to that issue in Chapter Six). Rather, we are concerned with the issues raised in the academic community generally related to what quality is, how to preserve or strengthen it, and how to increase it. Even within this framework, our concern is primarily with some of the assumptions involved that may be counterproductive to encouraging the kind of further higher education evolution or development that is commensurate with dealing effectively with the changing demographic and economic conditions.

The issue of quality became a central issue, at least rhetorically, during the eighties, and it probably will remain a central issue for some time to come. Thus, in *The Memorandum to the 41st President of the United States,* the Commission on National Challenges in Higher Education (1988) states: "We realize that the vitality of the United States is, in crucial ways, directly dependent on the quality of our institutions and their graduates. To insure that quality is our obligation; we pledge to you our determination to maintain it" (p. 11). That quality is a continuing major concern in higher education today is clear. However, *what* is meant by *quality* as the term is used, for example, by the Commission on National Challenges in Higher Education (1988), the various reports, and the members of the academic communities generally is far from clear. In some cases, the concepts of quality involved seem to be in conflict with each other. In other cases, there is a great deal of talk about quality without any specification of what is meant. In still other cases, even if *quality* is defined, how one attains it is far from clear.

In connection with a major study of perceptions of and experience with campus planning, Frank Schmidtlein (1988) of the National Center for Postsecondary Governance and Finance at the University of Maryland and members of his staff conducted extensive interviews on 16 campuses involving more than 248 people (13 to 19 per campus). The 16 campuses were chosen from a pool of 256 polled in an earlier survey. While not intended to be a statistically representative sample, the 16 included 4 research universities, 4 independent colleges, 4 state universities, and 4 community colleges. Among these were public and private, historically black, religious, and geographically distributed institutions. A central question asked in the interviews was "How does your campus define quality?" There was very little overlap in the answers; in fact, there was very little in the way of definitions. Representatives from 3 institutions suggested that quality is difficult, if not impossible, to define or that it cannot be defined in any one way. Instead of defining quality, most of the respondents offered some factor or factors that might in their views characterize quality, such as economic resources (funding level, facilities and equipment, fund raising, and so on) or even political resources.

What is fascinating is that most of the answers assumed implicit definitions of quality that would support the characteristics specified rather than explicitly providing the definition and then specifying conditions that would indicate its presence. This does not mean that among these answers, as in other current discussions, certain patterns or families of answers about the nature and characteristics of educational quality are not present. What it does seem to suggest is that, in spite of all the discussion about quality and concern with its attainment, there is surprisingly little explicit agreement on what it is or how you know when you have it. At the same time, there are certain kinds of assumptions that persist through much of the current quality discussion and activities that need to be made explicit and to be examined more carefully. In some cases, these assumptions have been around a long time quite independently of current commissions and reports. In others, the assumptions appear to be at least in part report-induced. In a few instances, the term *quality* itself seems to have become a code word for actions and attitudes that have little to do with quality itself.

The Reputational Input Myth

We have something of a love affair if not a fetish with rankings in this country. Alexander Astin (1985) has described the situation as follows: "We Americans seem preoccupied with being the best, whether in sports, automobile manufacture, military weaponry, television shows, or morality. And in higher education, as in society as a whole, the competition frequently focuses on the acquisition of material resources and the enhancement of image or reputation" (pp. 13–14). Both in the public mind and in the academic community, there tends to be a status hierarchy of academic institutions based on reputation that remains amazingly constant over the years. Quality tends to be defined as or identified with position in this hierarchy. Astin suggests that the hierarchy exists as part of our folklore and belief system and includes "a few well known elite institutions, a large sort of bourgeois with modest reputations, and a very large number of institutions that are virtually unknown outside their geographic regions" (p. 15). At the bottom, Astin suggests, are commuting institutions, community colleges, and some state colleges.

In *The Academic Revolution*, Jencks and Riesman (1968) celebrated the triumph of the hierarchy as embodying and demonstrating the meritocratic system. At the top are elite universities and university colleges. Jencks and Riesman noted as one impact of the hierarchy the tendency toward duplication and homogenization on the part of institutions trying to rise in the hierarchy. Much more recently, Frank Newman (1987) has described the hierarchy in terms of a single pyramid of prestige (p. 45) and noted its negative impact on those not at the top. As a counteractant — in fact, as a necessity if the full potential of the higher education institutions in this country is to be realized — he suggests the necessity of creating multiple pyramids of prestige based on differentiation of missions.

As Astin points out, the rankings of graduate institutions particularly have remained remarkably constant over the years. Of the top twenty institutions as reported by R. M. Hughes in 1925, sixteen were also among the top thirty in the 1982 National Academy of Science ratings (Astin, 1985, p. 31). As a result of what Astin calls the halo effect, the general rating of an institution tends in turn to influence the rating of specific departments within the school in comparison with other schools. This halo effect also has an impact on ratings of undergraduate schools. The seven top institutions in the 1980 comprehensive undergraduate rating carried out by Astin and Solomon (1981) are seven of the eight top institutions in the National Academy of Sciences (1983) composite ratings for graduate programs. Yet some of these are among the institutions that in other contexts have been criticized for large classes and for relegating undergraduate courses to teaching assistants.

That the seven institutions at the top of the graduate and undergraduate lists have worldwide reputations as high-quality institutions is clearly the case. That they and the most selective undergraduate institutions may in fact be the best of their types may also be the case. That their quality is either defined by or a function of their reputations or that reputation is or should be the prime indicator of quality is highly questionable. Further, to assume that high quality or excellence is epitomized by such institutions and thus that the characteristics of these institutions should be used as a basis for determining quality in all other institutions would, as Frank Newman (1987), among others, suggests, seems to undermine the very diversity and genius of American higher education itself.

Reputation as the basis for quality judgment is not the only means of determining or defining quality that needs to be questioned. Astin identified five of what he calls traditional approaches to measuring quality in an article in *Educational Record* (Astin, 1982), to which he added a sixth in *Achieving Educational Excellence* (Astin, 1985). These he identifies as the nihilistic view, reputational measures, resources measures, outcome measures, value-added measures, and academic content. In contrast to these, in *Achieving Academic Excellence* and in his address to the leadership development seminars in Oklahoma in 1986, he proposed his own view, which he describes as the talent-development view. The first three—the nihilistic, the reputational, and the resources views—are particularly relevant to this discussion. The academic content view, which ascribes quality to the liberal arts and engineering subjects in contrast to business and teacher education, was dealt with in substance in the previous chapter. We will come back to outcomes in connection with the issues involved in assessment. The concept of value added we will consider as a special issue in Chapter Six. Astin's talent-development approach, however, is relevant to placing reputation and resources in perspective.

The nihilistic view is essentially the position that quality cannot be defined or measured. It may rest, as Astin (1982, p. 10) suggests, on an argument that higher education institutions are far too complex and varied to be summed up in a quality judgment or on the philosophical position that quality is an ineffable characteristic of something—in this case, higher education—that is recognized intuitively. Something either has it or does not. As suggested by one former college president, quality is like pornography—I may not be able to define it, but I know it when I see it (Enarson, 1983, p. 7). The currency of the nihilistic position is reflected in some of the answers in the Schmidtlein (1988) interviews. The major difficulty with the nihilistic view is that it does not get us very far and hardly constitutes an acceptable answer to questions of accountability, wherever they may come from. If quality is whatever you perceive it to be, then when serious people disagree on quality judgments, there is no means of resolution—*de gustibus non disputandum est* (there is no accounting for taste). In practice, those who hold to the nihilistic or intuitive view rather easily shift to the reputational view for reasons not too difficult to see.

Reputation, particularly when it is accepted not just as an indication but as in some sense a definition of quality, tends to be a communal generalization of the intuitive or nihilistic view. As Astin (1985, p. 25) points out, "quality, in this view, is whatever people think it is." The people in this case may be the public in general, the academic community, or specialized communities, such as college presidents, academic vice-presidents and deans, or faculty in particular fields. We have already indicated some of the difficulties in using reputation either as a definition or as sole or primary indicator of quality. It not only helps to account for but reinforces what Astin (1985, p. 93) calls the higher education folklore of the institutional hierarchy. Reputation, ranking, and the hierarchy are inevitably bound up together.

Reputation at best involves a time lag. Actual performance tends to change more rapidly than reputation. The stability of the hierarchy indicates that even time provides no assurance that change in quality will always be generally recognized. Far too frequently, reputation is related to one aspect of a program — faculty research and publications or selectivity of the student body — but has very little to do with the effectiveness of the institution or program in enabling students to reach their educational objectives (Millard, 1983, pp. 24–25). National reputation is related to general visibility and is unattainable for quality programs in institutions that are geographically limited or isolated. Perhaps most serious is the lack of adaptability of reputation even as a quality indicator to widely divergent types of institutions with differing missions that may be providing superior education in the light of those missions.

Reputation and resources in many respects go hand in hand. Reputation makes it easier to obtain resources, and resource augmentation tends to reinforce reputation (Astin, 1986, p. 16). In fact, as Astin points out, reputation and resources far too frequently become ends in themselves rather than means to obtain educational objectives (pp. 24–25). Three obvious kinds of resources or inputs tend to be considered crucial as quality indicators: faculty and staff, funds and facilities, and students. According to Astin, the students may be "seen as resources either in terms of bodies that bring money or high quality bodies that reflect well on our institutions" (p. 16).

Resources are clearly relevant to quality and have been taken as proxies for quality for a long time. Accrediting bodies are sometimes criticized (not necessarily accurately) for confusing the proxies with quality. And yet it is fairly evident that resources alone are no assurance of quality. Faculty members with highly impressive résumés who are unable to work effectively together and are only peripherally interested in students do not ensure a high-quality educational institution. A highly selective student body may be able to fend for itself in spite of what sometimes is close to institutional indifference to their concerns. This may speak well for the students, but it is clearly not an indication of institutional quality, regardless of reputation.

An institution can be well endowed and have large and dependable sources of income and yet be far from realizing its educational potential. A large but underutilized library may be a reputational asset but can hardly be considered a guarantee of quality education. The critical question is not the presence of resources but how effectively they are utilized to achieve appropriate educational objectives. An institution with limited resources and clear objectives that uses the resources effectively to achieve the objectives is far more likely to provide quality education than some of its more affluent counterparts. Without adequate resources to achieve its objectives, an institution cannot achieve quality, but the presence of these resources alone is no guarantee that quality education is taking place.

The major problem with the reputational and resource approaches to quality determination, according to Astin (1986), is that they do not tell us much of anything about "the quality of education that we offer. . . . We do not know from an institution's reputation or resources how effectively that institution educates its students or develops the talent of its students" (p. 17). Such talent development, Astin believes, is the primary reason for being of higher education institutions themselves. Thus he suggests that quality and true excellence lie "in the institution's ability to have a favorable impact, to enhance the intellectual and scholarly development of the student, to make a positive difference in the students' life" (p. 17).

That talent development is one of the major aims of higher education would be hard to deny. If it is, then to the extent that an institution is effective in such talent development, the institution, regardless of its reputation or the size of its resources is, according to Astin, a quality institution. By underlining the relevance of quality to objectives and their accomplishment, Astin is clearly pointing toward a definition of quality that is based not on how institutions are thought of but on what they do; not on what they have but how they use what they have to achieve their educational objectives.

The problem with Astin's definition may be that it is too restrictive in one sense and too broad in another. While talent development may be the central function of most institutions, the definition of quality must be broad enough to encompass all of the institution's activities, including, for example, research and community service, to the extent that these are part of its mission. At the same time, various institutions are concerned with talent development as related to different objectives, in some cases even different talents. Talent development occurs not in the abstract but in the concrete context of individual and social career objectives. It is this fact that to a large extent does or should provide the rationale, even the necessity, for the diversity of types of higher education institutions and programs with their various and unique missions. If we incorporate but move beyond Astin's definition, quality can be viewed as a function of—in fact, defined as—the extent to which an institution or program effectively utilizes its resources to achieve its appropriate educational objectives. Quality thus is a matter of educational achievement in kind.

"An institution's or program's norm is implicit within it, and its quality is determined by how well its various components cohere in achieving its educational objective or objectives. Students, faculty, resources, location or locations, and results are integral to the quality of the operation, and the key to interpretation of all these elements in quality is mission or objective and its educational appropriateness" (Millard, 1983, p. 21). What this suggests is that one can equally expect or demand quality from a variety of institutions with different missions—from research universities, complex regional universities, community colleges, selective liberal arts colleges, open-admission institutions, professional schools, special-purpose institutions, occupational and technical institutes, and adult and continuing education centers. The definition applies equally to programs as to institutions, whether the programs are on- or off-campus, remedial or doctoral research, preparation for particular occupations and professions, or personal enrichment in career development in the broad sense.

This does not, as is sometimes argued, reduce quality and standards to relativism and subjectivity. Quality is contextual, but it is an objective characteristic of the relationships among processes, objectives, and results. Standards are not quantitative prescriptions applicable to all cases irrespective of objectives but rather are generalizable conditions of accomplishment of objectives. To utilize the characteristics of one type of institution to assess the quality of another type of institution may be to compare apples and oranges and is fair to neither institution. However, institutions of different types may legitimately be compared qualitatively in the light of how effectively each accomplishes its appropriate educational objectives.

If we are correct, what all of this means is not that reputation and resources are not important. They clearly are. While resources in particular do not define or serve as a clear indication of quality, they are, up to a reasonable level, a necessary condition of quality. It does mean, however, that Astin's traditional reputational hierarchy and Frank Newman's single pyramid of prestige, as they suggest, need to be challenged not as partial indicators of the presence of quality in certain types of institutions but as definitions or even indicators of quality in higher education in general. Here Frank Newman's call for developing multiple pyramids of prestige related to diverse higher educational missions may be very much to the point.

It seems clear that unless we are able to get beyond the Reputational Input Myth and as academic and political communities to seriously consider quality in terms of achievement of appropriate educational objectives through effective utilization of resources — human and material — our ability as a higher education community and as a nation to meet changing internal and external conditions now and in the twenty-first century will be very much curtailed. We can and should demand excellence in all of higher education, but this clearly is not possible if quality is to be defined or determined in terms of the traditional reputational hierarchy.

Some of the most exciting developments in higher education today are taking place not at the institutions at the top of the reputational and traditional hierarchy but at community colleges such as Dade County and Maricopa, at places such as

Alverno and Northeast Missouri, through outreach programs such as the Intermountain Community Learning and Information Services Project, the Program Development Experiments of the Oklahoma Network of Continuing Higher Education, the New York Regents External Degree program, Thomas A. Edison College, the New Rochelle program for inner-city New York—the list could be expanded almost indefinitely. If quality is or involves effective utilization of resources to achieve appropriate educational objectives, the quality of some of these institutions may well exceed that of a number of institutions high in the reputational hierarchy.

The Research-Publication Myth

One of the results of overreliance within the academic community itself on the Reputational Input Myth, reinforced by the Centrality of the University Myth, is the tendency to hold up practices and policies that may be partially relevant and even normative for primarily research universities as equally relevant for other types of higher education institutions. This is perhaps nowhere more clearly illustrated than in the extension of the research-publication criteria for faculty employment, reward, and recognition—and thus for assessment of faculty quality—to something approximating the academic community at large. Granted that there are exceptions to this extension, perhaps the most obvious being among the community colleges, few of the exceptions are among the more prestigious institutions in the academic hierarchy or among those aspiring to higher places within it.

The issue of research versus teaching and whether they are compatible or conflicting is the subject of a long-standing debate that has been highlighted and even exacerbated by the more recent reform reports. Both *To Reclaim a Legacy* (Bennett, 1984, pp. 18–19) and *Humanities in America* (Cheney, 1988), for example, call for greater emphasis on effective teaching. *Humanities in America,* however, points out that "it is much easier to judge whether a faculty member has written a sufficient number of articles than whether he or she reveals to students by

example and through questioning how and why it is that learning matters to life" (Cheney, 1988, p. 11). The Association of
American Colleges (1985) report *Integrity in the College Curriculum* places the major responsibility for what it takes to be the
sad state of the current curriculum on faculty abdications of
teaching responsibilities (pp. 35–36), and its follow-up report,
A New Vitality in General Education (Association of American Colleges, 1988), calls for a major reorienting of teaching itself (pp.
26–33). Most recently, the "roundtable" of the Higher Education Research Program at the University of Pennsylvania, in
a report entitled "The Business of the Business" (Higher Education Research Program, 1989a, p. 1), has called for higher
education institutions to "face squarely the conflict between their
commitment to teaching and their dominant emphasis on research" and to recognize that teaching and learning are "the business of the business." In *Profscam: Professors and the Demise of Higher
Education,* Charles Sykes (1988) places the major responsibility
for that "demise" on what he calls "the flight from teaching"
(p. 33).

In *Achieving Educational Excellence,* Astin (1985) points out
that, while typical job descriptions for new faculty, even at research universities, stress teaching, research, and service to the
university and the wider community, faculty review and promotion committees in fact "frequently use only a simple yard-
stick: The candidate's scholarly record. Not only does this nar-
rowing of focus simplify the decision process, it also focuses on
the one aspect of the candidate's performance that is directly
related to enhancing the institution's resources and reputation.
In short, the typical faculty job description is a fantasy and
smokescreen. While officially rewarding a diverse set of faculty
accomplishments, the institution is, in reality, rewarding only
scholarly activity" (pp. 186–187).

Teaching and research, however, are an area in which
it is much too easy to arrive at answers through oversimplification. It is undoubtedly true that, contrary to the rhetoric in a
good many institutions, the primary criterion for promotion and
other rewards, including salary, is the "scholarly record," which
usually means publication. Where this is the case, a number of

results are likely to occur. Harley Sachs (1988) suggests that "the consequent pressure on scholars to publish has resulted in mountains of articles of dubious scholarship and countless slipshod presentations at academic conventions" (p. B2). In part to counteract the flow of marginal articles, some institutions insist that only articles published in refereed journals be counted. One accrediting body reinforces this by requiring that for graduate programs in its field "a reasonable cross section of the faculty should be regularly engaged in research and publication that is subject to peer review" (American Association of Collegiate Registrars and Admissions Officers, 1988, p. 25). For many institutions, this seems to imply that the primary "business of the business" is not teaching and learning but publication, even though, according to one observer, in most institutions considerably fewer than half the faculty ever published anything (Edgerton, 1985, p. 7). Thus, the teaching and learning essential on the undergraduate level to an institution's existence as a higher education institution may be largely relegated to lesser members of the faculty, those not on tenure tracks, teaching fellows, and part-time faculty. This seems to be a distortion, to confuse a research institute with a higher education institution, and in fact to be out of touch with the current realities and expectations of higher education in this country.

Yet the opposite assumption—that the sole business of the business is teaching and learning—is equally an oversimplification. Research and scholarship are relevant not only to the broader mission of higher education but specifically to teaching and learning as part of that mission. If scholarship is defined not solely in terms of publication but as involvement in the expansion and interpretation of knowledge in a field, then such scholarship is essential to effective teaching and learning. The report of the American Council of Learned Societies (1989), "Speaking for the Humanities," states the matter as follows: "The two activities of teaching and scholarship are properly a continuum, and one that engages the student in the pursuit as well as in the profession of knowledge, in the desire for learning as well as the facts and theories such learning has produced" (p. A20). The same report quotes Timothy Healy, past president of Georgetown University, as saying that "It is not true that . . . teaching bears no relation to research and scholarship. As a matter of fact . . . these two great works stand as cause and effect" (A20). While this may also be an oversimplification unless one distinguishes between proximate and ultimate cause, what Healy is driving at is clearly pertinent. Thus, even primarily teaching institutions—for example, community colleges and vocational schools—while not necessarily engaged directly in research, are dependent on advances in knowledge for their continued vitality.

However, granted the connection, even the continuum, of research or scholarship and teaching-learning, it does not follow that good researchers or even good scholars are necessarily good teachers or that research per se is the best preparation for effective college teaching. There are examples of people who are both brilliant teachers and first-rate scholars, where the two functions mutually reinforce each other, but there are also examples of first-rate researchers who are less than adequate as teachers and of good teachers who will never be great scholars. One thing that seems clear is that getting people to engage in more research is not the answer to improved teaching. In an interview with Russell Edgerton, Patricia Cross points out that "to suggest to the public that our response to their request for better student learning is more faculty research raises serious questions about our ability to manage education in the public interest" (Edgerton, 1985, p. 7).

Improvement in college teaching is a central issue in most of the recent reports calling for higher education reform. *Integrity in the College Curriculum* (Association of American Colleges, 1985), for example, points out that "during the long years of work toward the doctoral degree, the candidate is rarely if ever introduced to any of the ingredients that make up the art, the science, and the special responsibilities of teaching" (p. 7), either in general or in relation to the specific discipline. The report goes on to recommend that the "Ph.D. candidate should be introduced in a systematic way to the profession of teaching. The qualifying process should include acquaintance with the literature on human learning and evaluation as well as apprentice teaching, subject to peer observation and the criticism of veteran teachers" (p. 36). While there are exceptions, such preparation does not take place in most graduate schools today. This suggestion should be taken seriously and implemented.

Beyond the preparation of college teachers, as important as that is, is a more fundamental issue in determining faculty qualifications and quality in particular institutions. This is the appropriateness of faculty characteristics, preparation, and activities to the mission and objectives of the institution itself. Not all potential faculty members, no matter how well prepared, are equally appropriate to all institutions, departments, or programs. This is so obvious that it is frequently overlooked in discussions either of faculty or of institutional quality. Clearly, faculty members should be adequately prepared in their subject areas, but even what constitutes adequate preparation may vary by institutional type and mission. When it comes to other characteristics— relative focus on research and teaching, full-time or part-time status, community interest, and practical or work experience, including affective as well as intellectual characteristics—the question of fit with institutional mission as a condition of quality becomes even more important. Thus, in describing faculty essential to the mission of Metropolitan State University in the Twin Cities, Reatha Clark King (1985), its immediate past president, says that "To serve these new students we need faculty not only capable of understanding and advising older students, women, and minorities, but also able to make course subject-matter speak forcefully to the experience of these students. At Metropolitan State University, we meet this need by employing, in addition to full-time resident faculty, a significant number of part-time instructors who are professional practitioners of the subjects they teach" (p. 25).

What this underlines is that the quality of a faculty cannot be specified in the abstract. A quality faculty is not simply a group of people with impressive résumés and publication records or even people who are well known in their particular fields. For external bodies of any sort, whether they be accrediting bodies, state agencies, or professional societies, to prescribe what characteristics the faculty should have for particular institutions or programs without reference to institutional or program objectives and the functions that faculty are expected to carry out in the light of these can be both arbitrary and counterproductive for assessing or enhancing institutional quality.

What constitutes faculty of high quality is not the same thing for a research university, a community college, a school of social work, a medical school, a Bible college, or a proprietary-vocational school. Geographical location (inner-city commuter institutions versus rural selective residential institutions), student clienteles (minorities and older students versus traditional college-age students), and even size (large, complex universities versus small, limited-purpose colleges) all make a difference not only in institutional or program objectives but in what for the institution in question should constitute a high-quality faculty. Every type of institution should be expected to develop the kind of faculty appropriate to its objectives — a faculty of high quality for that particular institution. The implication of this is that if the faculty reward system is to encourage quality, it should be directly related to and developed in the light of institutional and program objectives.

Research, scholarship, and publications will and should play a far more important role in some institutions and programs than in others. In few if any institutions should research and publication be the sole factors determining the quality of the faculty. Research, scholarship, and publications do not lose their importance but fit into a wider perspective of the many functions of higher education. As illustrated in the Leadership Development Program in Oklahoma (see Chapter One), faculty development and faculty quality assessment require a far wider perspective and range of activities than encouragement of research and publication alone. Perhaps the primary objective of the Oklahoma Leadership Development Program was to provide through thirty-three seminars the opportunities for faculty, administrators, and trustees to develop such a wider perspective in relation to both the broader issues facing higher education and the specific concerns in particular fields and professions.

The Undergraduate Focus Myth

The Undergraduate Focus Myth involves the assumption that the major quality issues facing higher education today lie in undergraduate baccalaureate education. On the solution to the problem of undergraduate education, it is claimed, depends the ability of higher education to deal with the complex of changing conditions of the contemporary world. Thus, for example, the Education Commission of the States (1986) task force report *Transforming the State Role in Undergraduate Education* states that "Throughout this report we have assumed that successful economic development, international competition, school reform and teacher preparation all depend upon excellence in undergraduate education. In a very real sense, then, the future of our nation depends on the quality of undergraduate education — not just in the long term but in the years immediately ahead" (p. 34).

The National Governors' Association Task Force on College Quality (1986) calls on "institutions and the faculty who teach in them" with the strong support of "governors, legislatures, and coordinating boards to hold undergraduate education in special trust and give it special attention" (p. 161). Even in the 1989 report of the National Governors' Association (1989) Task Force on International Education chaired by Governor Thomas Kean of New Jersey, the recommendations to higher education for strengthening international education are focused primarily on undergraduate education (p. 9).

Quite obviously, the major concern of both the NIE report *Involvement in Learning* (Study Group on the Conditions of Excellence in American Higher Education, 1984) and the AAC report *Integrity in the College Curriculum* (Association of American Colleges, 1985) is undergraduate baccalaureate education. The AAC report was specifically the product of a Project on Redefining the Meaning and Purpose of Baccalaureate Degrees. Even on the undergraduate level, the focus in both is primarily on baccalaureate education rather than on associate degrees and community college activities, although community colleges are mentioned (without discussion) in three of the recommendations to "External Agencies" in *Involvement in Learning* (pp. 46, 67, 69).

There is, as noted, recognition of the role of graduate schools in preparation of college teachers in *Integrity of the College Curriculum,* including the call for major improvement in such preparation. *Involvement in Learning* recognizes the importance of higher education research and calls for shifting priorities in such research to the question of how to facilitate greater student learning and development. In neither report is there much recognition of the continuity or the differences in functions and objectives of associate, baccalaureate, graduate, professional, and continuing education—thus of what might be described as the continuity of life-span learning.

This focus on undergraduate education as a critical point of emphasis is both legitimate and salutary. That undergraduate education, particularly if one includes associate degree programs as well as baccalaureate programs, is the primary activity and business of most of higher education would be hard to deny. This is where the enrollments are; it is where many of the problems or issues related to quality are and where they need to be faced; it is the precondition of more advanced education, including preparation for and involvement in research; it provides the basis for and, through tuition, much of the substance of funding for most institutions.

However, to recognize the central and crucial importance of undergraduate education, even the fact that many quality issues are particularly related to undergraduate education, is something quite different from assuming that the quality of an institution is to be determined solely or primarily by its undergraduate programs. In some cases where the sole function of the institution is undergraduate education, this might come close to being the case. But such instances may be considerably fewer than is sometimes assumed. In fact, the lack of any other activity, as Healy indirectly suggests, may itself raise questions about the quality of the undergraduate education (American Council of Learned Societies, 1989).

In any complex institution with graduate, postbaccalaureate professional, research, and other activities, institutional quality involves considerably more than undergraduate education alone. Yet the assessment movement in particular, spurred on by the Governors' Task Force report and *Involvement in Learning* (as will by further noted later), has focused primarily if not exclusively on undergraduate education, as has the curricular reform movement in general. For example, in a glossary on assessment prepared by the ECS for governors, legislators, and state higher education bodies, Boyer and Ewell (1988) define assessment as "any process of gathering concrete evidence about the impact and functioning of undergraduate education" (p.13). In spite of the caveats in some of the reports to the contrary, it is far too easy to assume that assessment and quality pertain primarily to undergraduate, particularly baccalaureate education. When one adds to this the predilection of *Involvement in Learning* for campus residency as a major consideration in educational quality (Study Group on the Conditions of Excellence in American Higher Education, 1984, pp. 33–34, 78; see also Astin, 1986, p. 22), it becomes too easy to conclude that higher education quality is primarily a characteristic of traditional undergraduate residential education.

Such a position, even if implicit, seems to be both misleading and, if translated into policy at institutional or state levels, counterproductive to what the ECS, the National Governors' Association, or those involved in the assessment movement hope to achieve. One might in fact turn the proposition around and at least suggest that, as the Governors' Task Force on College Quality recognizes but does not pursue (National Governors' Association, 1986, p. 16), the quality of undergraduate education at any particular institution is a function in part of the quality of the institution as a whole, of its integrity, and of its total mission and objectives and their relevance to undergraduate education. This does not diminish the importance of undergraduate education, nor does it preclude the possibility and even desirability of dealing with the quality of an institution's undergraduate education as a separate issue related to the mission and objectives of the institution as a whole. It does, however, involve recognizing explicitly that the quality of undergraduate education in complex institutions is affected by the quality of the institution's objectives and activities in other applicable areas as well. Depending on the nature of the institution, these may include graduate education, research programs, professional education, community service, educational outreach, relationships with business and industry, and even athletics.

Such a shifting of focus to the quality of an institution as a whole means that the institution's quality is determined by the range of its activities, including undergraduate education, and its effectiveness in utilizing resources to achieve its complex mission and objectives. An institution thus is qualitatively accountable for all its activities, regardless of location and collaborative sponsorship. While the quality of various activities may vary, they almost inevitably reflect on each other. Thus, an institution that does not consider off-campus programs and operations on military installations as an integral part of its mission but offers them primarily for income purposes, using less qualified faculty without adequate supervision, may well find that it has undermined its own market both for students and for support of its home campus. The same can well apply to continuing education on a campus where it is considered an income-generating auxiliary enterprise rather than a central institutional function. What we are suggesting here is that both the nature of an institutional undergraduate program's objectives and the extent to which they are achieved are directly influenced by the objectives of the institution as a whole and the extent to which the various objectives reinforce each other. The quality of the undergraduate program or programs contributes to the quality of the institution as a whole, but the reverse is equally the case.

While the current educational reform movement with its concern for quality began with elementary and secondary education and then spread to undergraduate higher education and teacher education, if the higher education community today is to deal with the maintenance and improvement of quality, it cannot do so seriatim or on a piecemeal basis or by looking at undergraduate education in isolation from the rest of its activities. Rather, what seems to be called for is a much more extended recognition that quality as a characteristic of an institution applies to the institution as a whole with all of its activities, and not only or primarily to its parts separately.

The Nontraditional Education Myth

In the context of quality issues, the Nontraditional Education Myth involves a set of assumptions that should have been laid to rest long ago. The basic assumption is that "nontraditional" higher education is essentially second-rate, of lower quality than traditional residential education. This, in many respects, is the qualitative counterpart of the Traditional College Student Myth, the Older Student Myth, and the Continuing Education Myth discussed in Chapter Two. Frequently, it is unclear what *non-traditional* means. In fact, the meaning tends to shift with the point of view of the observer. To complicate the matter further, nontraditional education and educational innovation are obviously linked. Few people within or outside the academy would admit to being opposed in principle to "innovation," although the "if it ain't broke, don't fix it" attitude is far from uncommon, and most people would probably agree that change simply for the sake of change is not particularly appealing.

One of the striking characteristics of the 1960s and the 1970s in particular was a development of a number of new nontraditional educational programs and institutions. Much of the impetus for innovation and what has come to be called nontraditional education during that period was provided by student unrest and the civil rights movement. Even where the innovations were not direct reactions to the unrest, they were affected by it. Within a relatively short time, a series of nontraditional programs and colleges appeared. Among these were the New York Regents External Degree Program, Evergreen State College, Empire State College, Thomas A. Edison State College, Metropolitan State University in Minnesota, and the University Without Walls. Some of the new ventures, such as the Experimental College at Berkeley, were relatively short-lived, but a number of them are very much alive and healthy today.

At least two major studies during the 1970s were devoted to the place and importance of nontraditional education within the total framework of higher education. The first was carried out by the Commission on Non-Traditional Study, established in 1971, sponsored by the College Entrance Examination Board and the Educational Testing Service, and funded by the Carnegie Corporation. Its final report, *Diversity by Design* (Commission on Non-Traditional Study, 1973), published in 1973, is in many respects as pertinent today as it was then. The commission described nontraditional education as "more an attitude

than a system," which "can never be defined except tangentially."
Samuel Gould, the commission chair, elaborated this statement
as follows: "This attitude puts the student first and the institution second, concentrates more on the former's need than the
latter's convenience, encourages a diversity of individual opportunity rather than uniform prescription, and deemphasizes time,
space, even course requirements in favor of competence and,
where applicable, performance. It has concern for the learner
of any age and circumstance, for the degree aspirant as well
as the person who finds sufficient reward in enriching life through
constant, periodic, or occasional study" (p. xv). The report points
out that approaches that respond to the "desire of individuals . . .
who seek education without being confined within the space,
time, place, course sequence. and credit framework characteristic of most educational institutions" are not new. But it notes
that while it is not a new concept, "even as an old one it has
never been completely accepted; in some institutions it has not
even been tolerated" (p. 9). In too many instances, this still seems
to be the case. The report offered fifty-seven recommendations,
ranging from the very broad to the quite specific. The first and
broadest is directly relevant to this discussion and to the later
discussion of equity: "Full educational opportunity should be
realistically available and feasible for all who may benefit from
it, whatever their condition of life" (p. 7).

The second study, directed by Grover Andrews (1978)
was a Project to Develop Evaluation Criteria and Procedures
for the Accreditation of Non-Traditional Education. It was carried out under the auspices of the Council on Postsecondary
Accreditation with funding from the W. K. Kellogg Foundation
in 1977–78. The final report in many respects built on *Diversity
by Design* but called for caution in relation to substandard or
fraudulent uses or distortions of nontraditional education by less
than scrupulous operators. It placed particular emphasis on the
importance of "educational accomplishment and performance
(outcomes)" (p. 123) in assessing the quality of nontraditional
education and urged the effective integration of the nontraditional movement into the mainstream of conventional institutions and programs (p. 121).

On the surface, it would appear that considerable progress has been made in incorporating nontraditional education into the mainstream, in recognizing that quality is not a function of being traditional or nontraditional but of educational effectiveness, and in diversifying the higher education system to serve students of all ages on and off campus, part-time and full-time, utilizing appropriate means of instructional delivery and of student involvement. The W. K. Kellogg Foundation has been one of the major catalysts in attempting to bring this about. Through its many grants to institutions, to consortia, to state agencies, and to state and national organizations, the foundation has worked diligently to encourage expansion and incorporation of quality nontraditional education — particularly for older students — into the main fabric of higher education. Its recent grant to Michigan State University to help it become a land-grant model of a lifelong university is a case in point. Equally pertinent are its support for what is now the Council for Adult and Experiential Learning, which has developed procedures for assessing experiential learning, and its involvement as a catalyst to provide education for workers through labor-management agreements. Its support of the Oklahoma Network of Continuing Higher Education has emphasized the state role, as did its earlier grant to the Education Commission of the States. The list of grants in support of expanding the scope, relevance, and quality of higher education to meet the needs of today's higher education clients, most of whom are "nontraditional," is both extensive and impressive.

One might have expected reinforcement in overcoming any tensions between "traditional" and "nontraditional" higher education from the current reports and books calling for higher education reforms. One might also have expected a call for providing quality higher education in whatever form is appropriate (reinforced by the new technologies) to those who need and can benefit from it. This would have called for moving beyond the Nontraditional Education Myth. In a few instances, such reinforcement is present. Lynton and Elman's (1987) concept of the "extended university" and recognition that "the nontraditional student is becoming the norm" provide a case in point.

Interestingly enough, so does Ernest Boyer's (1987) recognition that "the nation's colleges are discovering that the campus is as much a state of mind as a place. It exists, or at least can exist, wherever the student happens to be" (p. 232). However, most of the reform reports, if anything, present more of a retreat than a forward movement in affirming nontraditional approaches, particularly to undergraduate education. Given their affinity for the Golden Era Myth, this is not surprising. As noted earlier, *Integrity in the College Curriculum* (Association of American Colleges, 1985), *To Reclaim a Legacy* (Bennett, 1984), the reports of the National Governors' Association (1986, 1988, 1989) and the Education Commission of the States (1986, 1987), and *Involvement in Learning* (Study Group on the Conditions of Excellence in American Higher Education, 1984) all seem to hold as the ideal something approximating the resident four-year undergraduate campus baccalaureate program for eighteen- to twenty-one-year-olds as defining the universe in which "quality" education can take place. They call for more effective assessment of the learning that occurs. They are not opposed to innovation; in fact, they call for it. But they tend to call for innovation within a traditional framework.

As a result in practice, particularly on the undergraduate level, the term *nontraditional,* rather than being identified with educational innovation in general, has tended to become progressively restricted to programs for nonresidential, "nontraditional" students. These include residential outreach programs, programs for part-time and older students, off-campus programs, non-credit programs, long-distance learning programs via educational technologies, experiential learning, and, somewhat ironically, much of what has traditionally been considered extension, adult, and continuing education. This clearly is rather far removed from the concept of "nontraditional" of the Gould and Andrews reports. And to the extent that it involves an implicit quality judgment, it also appears to represent a step backward to a new academic conservatism.

Perhaps the most striking example among the reports is *Involvement in Learning.* The NIE study group argues that residency on campus is not only desirable but a condition of the quality of undergraduate education. Although recognizing that more than half of today's students are commuters and many of them are part-time, the study group argues that "the power of the campus as an environment for fostering student involvement is crucial. . . . If students are reluctant citizens of a campus, the degree and quality of their involvement will suffer" (Study Group on the Conditions of Excellence in American Higher Education, 1984, p. 24). Astin (1986), one of the study group members, goes even further and insists that "a massive body of research has consistently shown that the quality of undergraduate experience, the amount of talent development that occurs, is enhanced by living on campus" (p. 22). As a result, the study group suggests that substitutes for residency for commuters, "such as weekend colleges and short-term but intense periods of residence on campus" (p. 34), are necessary.

All of this clearly has negative implications for off-campus programs, for experiential learning, for programs on military bases, for programs offered through business and industry, for long-distance learning via telecommunications and other new technologies, and for educational outreach in general. The implication is that learning by such modes is qualitatively inferior. What is fascinating, however, is that Astin consistently extends the negative judgment to community colleges as well. Almost all community college students are commuters, and the majority of them are part-time. "Community colleges are places where the involvement of both faculty members and students appears to be minimal" (Astin, 1985, p. 146). Astin discusses "the negative effects of attending a community college" and comments, "In short, attending a community college — though convenient — exacts a heavy toll" (p. 87).

The question at this point is not whether residency is desirable or even whether resident experience for some students at some types of institutions, given both student and institutional objectives, is not an essential characteristic of the quality of education for those students at those institutions. It clearly is. (We explored the "residency" assumption and its limitations in connection with the Feet of the Master Myth.) Rather, the question here is whether residency and traditional college structures are essential conditions of quality higher education. The answer clearly seems to be no. The experience and success of such experimental colleges as Empire State, Minnesota Metropolitan State, and Evergreen with contract learning and the use of faculty mentors and the effectiveness of external degree programs such as the Regents External Degree Program (now Regents College Degree) and the programs at Thomas A. Edison in New Jersey and Charter Oak in Connecticut make clear that nontraditional education as such, whether on or off campus, need not be second-rate or qualitatively inferior. Rather, as is the case with all higher education institutions and programs, quality is a matter not of traditional or nontraditional structures but of results — the extent to which the institutions' and the students' appropriate educational objectives are in fact being achieved. As both the Gould and the Andrews reports point out, "nontraditional" programs have helped reinforce utilization of outcomes or results in the light of objectives as a primary means of quality determination.

The view that community colleges are somehow qualitatively inferior because their students are nonresident commuting students and most of them are part-time overlooks the primary functions of community colleges and their relations to the communities in which they exist. We have already noted the rapid development of community colleges from a handful of institutions and students in the 1950s to the point that they now enroll more than a quarter of all postsecondary education students. To some extent, they constitute the twentieth-century parallel and extension of the land-grant movement of the nineteenth century. They have opened postsecondary educational opportunity to a wide range of students to whom it was not previously available and have done so in a context of responsiveness to community postsecondary education needs. As comprehensive community colleges, they include in their missions far more than just preparation of students for transfer to four-year institutions. It may well be that the transfer programs, particularly for minority students, need to be strengthened in some community colleges. One of the more relevant discussions of the missions of community colleges, their nontraditional functions, their relationships to their communities, and their differences from traditional baccalaureate institutions is still Edmund Glea-zer's *The Community College: Values, Vision & Vitality* (1980). To assess community college quality on the basis of criteria relevant to some four-year institution without reference to the specific mission of the community colleges in question is to fail to recognize the relevance of quality to function or mission and to move back to the Procrustean bed of externally imposed homogenization.

While institutions of various types, traditional or nontraditional, two-year, four-year, graduate, what have you, vary widely in quality, what is particularly crucial at this point if the postsecondary educational needs of the country and its various populations are to be met is the recognition that quality is a function not of a particular classification of institutions or programs but of how well each achieves its appropriate educational objectives — of results — granted the legitimately wide variety of missions and objectives to be achieved by different institutions.

The Noncredit Course Myth

While the nontraditional education that we have been discussing is primarily education for credit aimed toward degrees or their equivalent, there is another large category of courses and programs offered by colleges and universities that fit neither into traditional modes nor into their usual manner of student awards and recognition. These are noncredit courses and programs. They are sometimes referred to as "the basket-weaving" courses on the assumption that if students are not working for credit, they can hardly be considered serious students. They frequently are looked at as part of community service and only indirectly related to the central academic educational responsibility of the institution. Such courses tend to be considered as peripheral and, by some academicians and administrators, as too frequently diverting resources from more important matters. Some 20 percent of the higher educational leaders interviewed in the Oklahoma Network of Continuing Higher Education needs survey "thought that on-campus classroom instruction was inappropriate to non-credit instruction" (Belt and Sackett, 1987, p. 86).

The position that noncredit courses and programs are not a part of the primary function of higher education institutions tends to be reinforced, perhaps unintentionally, by the accrediting community. While the Council on Postsecondary Accreditation and the regional institutional accrediting bodies all have statements on credit-bearing nontraditional education, none of them mentions noncredit programs. Although such noncredit programs fall under the general requirement that an institution is responsible for all its activities, in practice little attention is paid to the noncredit sphere.

The downgrading of noncredit courses and programs, the assumption that they have little to do with the important central missions of higher education, stands as a myth in its own right. On closer inspection, the noncredit system turns out to be a much more important part of higher education activities than frequently is recognized. In numbers alone, according to Howard Sparks (1985), some ten million people a year (as of 1985) register for such courses, and it is estimated that by the year 2000 this number will double (pp. 8–9). If this is the case, considerably more students will be taking noncredit courses than are enrolled in credit courses in all of higher education. And this does not include people in in-service education in business and industry or noncredit courses and programs offered by other noncollegiate groups. Further, the people involved in such courses are usually not primarily those with little collegiate background, but, as indicated in the Oklahoma survey of the needs of library patrons (Oklahoma Network of Continuing Higher Education, 1987a, p. 45), they tend to be the better educated and frequently those with advanced degrees.

Nationally, many if not most of those taking noncredit programs are involved in continuing professional education in such areas as engineering, law, the health and health-related professions, and other career fields (Sparks, 1985, p. 8). Thus, the noncredit system constitutes one of higher education's most direct and continuing bases of contact with and service to members of the professions and in many cases their professional sociecieties. To the extent that this is the case, noncredit programs take on major importance for the future not just for the professions and professionals but for higher education institutions themselves. In many cases, noncredit programs are reinforced by state licensing laws and boards, particularly in professions that require members to produce evidence of continuing education activity to maintain their professional status. It would thus appear peculiarly self-defeating for many complex institutions to consider noncredit programs peripheral.

This is not to suggest that there are not problems in maintaining quality in noncredit programs. Because they do not involve the same kind of end-of-course or program-completion requirements that are usually involved in degree credit courses, it would appear relatively easy to make the content less than substantial and to use as faculty people with qualifications that would not be acceptable for credit programs. There are, however, a number of factors that militate against this. First, many members of the continuing education community, which includes not only colleges and universities but other providers and interested parties, such as professional associations, business and industry, certification groups, and government organizations, have adopted what is called the Continuing Education Unit (CEU) as an indicator for students of the required amount not of credit but of participation in noncredit programs. The CEU is now defined by the Council on the Continuing Education Unit (which changed its name in 1990 to International Association for Continuing Education and Training) as "ten contact hours of participation in an organized continuing education experience under capable sponsorship, capable direction, and qualified instruction" (Council on the Continuing Education Unit, 1987, p. ii). The Council on the Continuing Education Unit was established in 1977 as a result of the work of a task force sponsored primarily by the National University Continuing Education Association and the Educational Testing Service. Under the council's guidance, a Project to Develop Standards and Criteria for Good Practice in Continuing Education, directed by Grover Andrews (who had previously directed the Council on Postsecondary Accreditation project on Assessing Non-Tra-

ditional Education), developed a series of criteria and guidelines to guide institutions and organizations offering noncredit
continuing education programs. The report, *Principles of Good
Practice in Continuing Education* (Council on the Continuing Education Unit, 1984), was published in 1984, and the principles,
with some elaboration, have been incorporated into subsequent
publications by the council. The principles cover administration, program development, and program evaluation. The council is not an accrediting body and does not itself evaluate programs. However, the principles have been widely accepted and
applied voluntarily, and the CEU has come to be generally
recognized as a reliable indicator of the amount of organized
noncredit continuing education study that a person has completed. Thus, through the work of the council, self-monitoring
within a number of fields by providers of noncredit continuing
education instruction has become more widespread. It should
be clearly recognized that the CEU is not credit but an indication of student participatory time, which is not and should not
be directly converted into credit. This does not mean, however,
that the substance of what is learned may not be relevant through
validated experiential learning for credit under some circumstances.

Second, in the area of noncredit continuing professional
education, a considerably wider group than the offering educational institutions is concerned with the content and quality of
education offered. This includes the national professional associations and their accrediting and certification bodies, the
health professions specialty boards, state or regional professional
associations, and state licensing bodies. In a number of such
professional associations, continuing education is a necessary
condition for individuals to retain certification. In more and
more states, licensing boards also require continuing education
as a condition of continued licensure. These groups obviously
are concerned with the integrity and quality of the programs
as essential to public health and welfare and continuing professional competence.

The importance of effective cooperation among institutions, professional associations, state licensing agencies, and the

primary state higher education board or agency in developing adequate quality coordination of professional continuing education programs on the state level was clearly demonstrated in Oklahoma by forty-three position papers from twenty-three fields on continuing professional education needs in the state. These were prepared for the module on program development under the Oklahoma Network of Continuing Higher Education by educators, practitioners, and professional association representatives in fields ranging from accounting to veterinary medicine. Among the many constructive comments and recommendations, perhaps the most frequently heard was the call for continued and strengthened coordination under the leadership of the regents of the efforts of institutions, professional associations, and other state agencies in ensuring quality continuing professional education and developing such coordination in fields where it does not now exist. There were caveats, particularly in accounting and public administration, that such coordination should not lead to or be brought about by more regulation and bureaucratic control but should be developed through incentives to cooperation.

Third, an increasing number of major universities across the country are recognizing their obligations to carry out a leadership role in continuing professional education and interprofessional education and to do so as an integral part of their missions and objectives. Here again, the W. K. Kellogg Foundation has played a major catalytic role in focusing attention on continuing professional education, helping to bring it into the sphere of recognized academic responsibility, and encouraging colleges and universities to recognize this responsibility as part of their overall mission and objectives. This role began with the establishment of the Kellogg continuing education centers in the fifties and sixties. More recently, it has become a major concern of the foundation, which has awarded a series of grants to institutions directed primarily at continuing professional education. These include grants to Ohio State University and Pennsylvania State University, one part of the grant to the University of Georgia, Module VII of the Oklahoma grant, and, most recently, the grant to Michigan State University to enable it to become a land-grant model of a "lifelong" university. This does not mean that all of the programs under these grants or the appropriate parts of such grants involve noncredit courses or programs. Some of them also involve credit. But noncredit programs, seminars, and other activities are major components in all of them.

The focus of the various grants differs. At Ohio State, for example, the primary focus is on the interprofessional aspects of continuing professional education. Module VII of the Oklahoma grant devoted to interprofessional continuing education is carried out under the auspices of the Oklahoma University Health Sciences Center and is focused on health care professionals. The original Pennsylvania State University grant was concerned primarily with collaboration between the university and professional associations in practice-oriented continuing professional education programs. The University of Georgia program, in addition to being concerned with cooperative approaches to continuing professional education, also focuses on improving the competencies of the leaders of continuing professional education in the state. Both the Ohio State and the University of Georgia programs led to the formation of statewide assemblies (Ohio) or councils (Georgia) for involvement of professional organizations in cooperative continuing professional education activities. Both programs have also had national impact, Ohio State through its National Consortium on Interprofessional Education and Practice and Georgia through a National Symposium and National Leadership Institute. Finally, a special Kellogg grant to Pennsylvania State University enables representatives of the various Kellogg projects on continuing professional education, the Intermountain Community Learning and Information Services Project, and the National University Continuing Education Association project on Continuing Higher Education Leadership to meet together to share their common experiences and to carry out National Invitational Conferences on Continuing Professional Education. As the Michigan State project gets under way, it undoubtedly will be represented as well if the interproject cooperation project continues.

What is probably most significant about these various Kellogg projects, including the interproject cooperative group project, is that the universities involved have accepted as integral to their mission and function responsibility not only for involvement in leadership in continuing professional education but for the effectiveness and the quality of the noncredit programs involved as well. What all of this seems to amount to is a growing recognition that noncredit programs, as one important form of nontraditional education, are no longer peripheral or necessarily qualitatively inferior, particularly in the area of professional continuing education. Rather, where appropriate, they need to be recognized as an integral part of college or university missions and objectives. To the extent that this is the case, an institution's integrity and quality are as much involved in such programs as in any other programs it offers.

In summary, the time seems past when questions of traditional or nontraditional, of credit or noncredit as related to programs or students are relevant to the quality of the programs or institutions. If what we are concerned about is what Astin has called talent development or what we have suggested is the somewhat wider conception of educational achievement in kind, then the crucial quality question is a matter of results, not of form. It is in this context that the question of assessment becomes a matter of major importance.

The Assessment Myth

The Assessment Myth has two conflicting, even contradictory forms. Essentially, the first form involves the assumption that most, if not all, of the current quality problems, particularly in undergraduate education, can be solved by effective assessment of student learning. *Effective* in this sense frequently is taken to mean assessment expressed in quantitative terms. The conflicting form involves the assumption that while we have to put up with the rhetoric of assessment for the time being, it is essentially a fad that, given time and shifts in political interests in higher education, will go away. These might be described as the Scylla and Charybdis of assessment.

Extensive analysis of the assessment literature or review of the assessment debate is well beyond the scope of this chapter. Few issues have led to so many meetings and so much commentary in a relatively short period of time as assessment has in the last six years, and the discussion is far from over. Our concern, as with the other myths, is with placing assessment in some kind of perspective so that neither the panacea view of assessment nor the passing fad view inhibits the legitimate and necessary concern with maintaining and improving quality or the importance of results in determining educational quality. Among the factors that we need to remind ourselves of is, first, that no matter how complex and sophisticated what Clifford Adelman (1985, p. 77) calls "the new assessment movement" may be, assessment is not new. As evaluation of student progress, it is about as old as higher education itself and is obviously integral to any form of educational accomplishment. As a means of measuring results as a determinant of educational quality of institutions and programs, it has become a progressively critical factor in both institutional and specialized accreditation at least since the Zook and Haggerty (1936) report to the North Central Association of Colleges and Schools in 1936. In the mid-1970s, Norman Burns (1978), former director of the North Central Association Commission on Institutions of Higher Education, developed an analysis and evaluation of the various types of instruments available at that time for quantitative considerations of outcomes. While the players may be new and the technologies improved, assessment is not.

A second factor to be kept in mind is that, contrary to some current discussion, assessment as such does not change things, nor does it ensure quality. Terry Hartle (1985) may be correct in saying that "what assessment appears to have become in higher education is a catch-all phrase that refers to a wide range of efforts to improve educational quality" (p. 4). If this is the case, it involves a basic confusion between what at best is an evaluation, measuring, or judgmental process in regard to the presence or absence of "quality" and how one uses the results of such assessment. It also tends to lead to the assumption in some quarters that testing equals assessment and thus that testing ensures quality. As Hartle also points out, even as used within the field of psychology, while psychological assessment has focused on individuals, it has involved evaluations using multiple methods, not testing alone. Given the variety of uses even within the higher education community (Hartle identifies six), it becomes particularly important that the means nature of evaluation not be confused with the end of enhancing quality, which requires doing something about the results of the evaluation. This is not to suggest that expectation of evaluation may not be an incentive to quality improvement or a hindrance if the evaluation criteria are too relaxed. It is, however, to recognize that even in such instances, the incentive aspect and the evaluation itself need to be clearly distinguished.

Third, there is a real problem not just in definition but in scope of assessment. At times, assessment seems to be applied almost exclusively to evaluation of individual student learning and educational accomplishment, including attitude changes. As used by businesses and industries and more recently in education, assessment centers focus primarily on individual performance (Hartle, 1985, p. 2; Rossman and El-Khawas, 1987, pp. 16–17). However, as used by various other groups, assessment ranges in scope from individual evaluation to evaluation of systems of higher education. This range is illustrated in the definition of assessment provided in the glossary on assessment developed by Carol Boyer and Peter Ewell for the Education Commission of the States: "Any process of gathering concrete evidence about the impact and functioning of undergraduate education. The term can apply to processes that provide information about individual students, about curricula or programs, about institutions or entire systems of institutions. The term encompasses a range of procedures including testing, survey methods, performance measures or feedback to individual students, resulting in both quantitative and qualitative information" (Education Commission of the States, 1988, p. 13). But even this definition seems overly restrictive, for it limits assessment to "undergraduate education." Yet why assessment is not equally applicable to graduate and postbaccalaureate professional education is not clear.

A number of the reports and commentaries cite accrediting agencies as groups calling for more effective assessment or as among the groups that should do so to a greater extent than they may now be doing. Institutional accrediting bodies are clearly involved in assessment of outcomes, of institutional effectiveness as determinants of institutional quality. Specialized accrediting bodies assess particular undergraduate and graduate professional programs. Thurston E. Manning (1987) points out that "Accrediting associations assess institutions and programs . . . against their stated (and acceptable) purposes. Among those purposes for educational institutions must be goals for the educational achievements of their students. Thus assessing whether an institution or program is achieving its purpose includes whether its students are achieving satisfactory educational goals" (p. 34).

The point of all this is that in dealing with assessment, one needs to be aware that the variance in scope as considered by different scholars, commentators, and groups may change the nature and rules of discussion. Other things being equal, the broader the scope, the more assessment consideration and actions are likely to be directly relevant to institutional quality.

Fourth, one of the factors that is considerably different in the "new assessment movement" is the level of political interest and involvement, at both state and federal levels but particularly the former. From the beginning, the movement has been a political as well as an academic issue. President Reagan came into office in 1981 determined to abolish the new U.S. Department of Education and to reduce federal expenditures for education. In the latter, he was partially successful. In the former, he was not. However, the Reagan administration did manage to have a major impact on the substance of discussions and the shifting of concerns in higher education from access and federal support for the learning society to quality and assessment and from federal responsibility to state and institutional responsibility. Secretary Bell appointed the National Commission on Excellence in Education in 1981 with a mandate to report on the quality of American education in 1983; *A Nation at Risk* was published in 1983. Addressed primarily to elementary and secondary education, it placed primary responsibility for reform and improvement on state and local governments. While it did not use the term *assessment,* it did call for development and use of standardized tests for achievement (p. 28). As a follow-up to *A Nation at Risk* in higher education, the National Institute for Education appointed the Study Group on the Conditions of Excellence in American Higher Education, whose report, *Involvement in Learning,* was published in 1984.

    Involvement in Learning listed "assessment and feedback" as among the three basic conditions for excellence in undergraduate education (p. 2). "We thus believe assessment to be an organic part of learning" (p. 53). Five of the major recommendations are related to assessment, beginning with an admonition to faculty and deans to "design and implement a systematic program to assess the knowledge, capacities, and skills developed in students by academic and curricular programs" (p. 55). The National Institute for Education and the U.S. Department of Education set up a series of conferences across the country on the implementation of the report, in each of which the issue of assessment tended to be dominant. These culminated in a National Conference on Assessment in Higher Education at the University of South Carolina in October 1985. The new secretary Bennett wrote the introduction to the publication growing out of the conference. "Assessment" indeed had become the "hot topic" of the 1980s (Rossman and El-Khawas, 1987, p. 1). Politically, attention had been shifted from primary concern with federal reinforcement of higher education to improve access and achieve equity to self-analysis and assessment carried out by the institutions but in many cases mandated by the states.

    Whereas on the state level, until well into the 1980s, accountability focused on management, finance, and program distribution, assessment has become the new accountability focus, again primarily on the undergraduate level. The National Governors' Association (1986) established a Task Force on College Quality chaired by Governor Ashcroft of Missouri. The task force issued its report in 1986 as part of a series of reports on education. The major thrust of the governors' report was, as might be expected, assessment. The task force enjoined "each college and university" to "implement systematic programs that use multiple measures to assess undergraduate student learning" (p. 161) and suggested that the quality judgments from such assessment "should be made available" to the public. It went on to argue that funding formulas should be adjusted to reward those with positive assessment results and to provide incentives to others for quality improvement (p. 162).

At about the same time, the Education Commission of the States' (1986) "Working Party" chaired by Governor Thomas Kean of New Jersey issued its report, *Transforming the State Role in Undergraduate Education*. The ECS report also considered adequate assessment essential to quality development. Both the NGA report and the ECS report called for multiple means of assessment, warned against confusing testing with assessment, and urged institutions to develop their own assessment process in light of their unique missions and objectives. The ECS report in particular called attention to the fact that assessment is not an end in itself and is not limited to assessment of teaching and learning. "To document performance is not to improve performance. Assessment should not be an end in itself. It should be an integral part of an institution's strategy to improve teaching and learning and of the state's strategy to monitor the effectiveness of its system of higher education" (p. 32).

Regardless of what initially may have led to the "new assessment" movement, it has become a fact of academic and institutional life and one that rather clearly links the academic and political communities. As of 1990, forty states required some form of assessment, either by law or as carried out by the higher education agency (Ewell, Finney, and Lenth, 1990, p. 4). In a few states, such as Florida, Georgia, Tennessee, and New Jersey, this has led to some form of statewide testing, such as the Florida Rising Junior Examination and the Basic Skills Assessment Program in New Jersey, the latter used for entering students to help place them in college courses. However, in most states with assessment requirements, the responsibility for developing appropriate assessment programs lies with the individual institutions (see Paulson, 1990 for individual state profiles).

Campus Trends, 1988 (El-Khawas, 1988) indicates that half of the institutions, public and private, have some form of assessment activity under way. Discussions about assessment are taking place in three-fourths of them, and three-fourths of campus administrators expect to introduce some form of assessment on their campuses in the near future (p. 8). While there is considerable concern among administrators about the possible misuse of assessment or effectiveness reviews by external agencies (72 percent of them express such concern), and more than half (55 percent) have reservations about state requirements to show evidence of institutional effectiveness, most college administrators (95 percent) "support assessment that is clearly tied to efforts to improve education" (El-Khawas, 1987, p. 2). There thus seems to be rather strong support of assessment within the academic community if it is kept within reasonable bounds.

This does not mean that everyone within the academic community is happy with assessment. Different types of institutions have different attitudes toward it. The strongest support tends to come from the community colleges and their faculties (75 percent) and the least support from doctoral and research universities (34 percent) (p. 28). In addition to the concerns about misuse of results and the degree of state involvement, at least one in three administrators believes that, to date, assessment has done little except add to institutional reporting requirements to the state (p. 10). One-third of the administrators believe that what should be assessed is unclear, and a third also believe that there are no good assessment instruments. Three-fifths of the administrators have serious misgivings about using standardized tests in the process (p. 10).

Additional concerns about assessment pertain to costs, faculty and student time involvement, and, in more extreme cases, the rationale or basis of assessment itself. Thus, for example, Jon Westling (1988), executive vice-president of Boston University, asserts not only that most of the people who would impose assessment on the academic community are "incapable of recognizing education" but that "assessment is based on a fundamental misdiagnosis of the malaise of American higher education. Does anyone really believe that the failure of colleges and universities to produce adequately educated young people is the consequence of our failure to develop precise instruments to measure what we are doing? Or that true education requires elaborate technical criteria to evaluate its effectiveness?" (p. B1). Ernest Benjamin (1990), the general secretary of the American Association of University Professors, fears that assessment will "institutionalize mediocrity." He argues that "the fact that many faculty members find mandated assessment offensive affects the quality of teaching and learning. Those faculty members who participate in innovative assessment programs may find the process stimulating, but those who inherit or must conform to another test, text, and curricula will not. Ultimately, assessment requires conformity in curricula and instruction to achieve comparability" (p. B2). In spite of objections such as those of Westling, who seems in his own way to have confused the means of determining whether something has taken place with the results, and Benjamin and others who feel that assessment has only added paperwork and costs and would like to see it go away, it seems that general support within the academic community and the continuing concern about educational results or effectiveness on the part of the political community — the current form of accountability — make it highly improbable that assessment is a fad and will go away. Thus, the belief that it will is one side of the Assessment Myth.

At the same time, it is conceivable that if the focus of assessment remains primarily on undergraduate education, if the tendency grows to rely on or push quantitative results obtained primarily through national tests, or if the process of assessment gets further confused with achieving or maintaining quality rather than indicating its presence, it may well diminish in importance. While evaluation or assessment of educational effectiveness of institutions, programs, and even courses is critical to continued quality improvement, and assessment of student learning is integral to such evaluation, assessment as such does not create or ensure quality. The assumption that it does, that assessment is a panacea to overcome whatever ills may beset higher education, is equally fallacious and the other side of the Assessment Myth.

The renewed emphasis on assessment has indeed made some major contributions to the current higher education scene. Among these contributions are the following:

1. It has refocused attention on the critical importance of clarity in developing and formulating missions, goals, and objectives as the basis for any relevant evaluation of educational outcomes or effectiveness. While some educational results may be accidental, identification of them as educational outcomes involves at least an implicit conception of educational objectives.

2. It has reinforced the recognition that educational quality is a function of effective use of resources to achieve appropriate educational objectives and that this applies to students, programs, institutions, and systems.

3. It has refocused concern with educational accountability, both within the academy and on state and national levels, on the substance of educational accomplishment rather than primarily on fiscal and management practices.

4. In an interesting way, on the state as well as the institutional level, the assessment movement has called attention not only to outcomes or results but to the essential role of resources in achieving educational objectives.

5. Although not necessarily part of the intent of some of its proponents, the assessment movement has helped and will continue to help to weaken or at least to temper reputational and resource conceptions of quality. The emphasis in assessment lies not on reputation but on student and program achievement — on results and on the use of resources, not simply on their presence. Thus, assessment and quality judgment are as relevant to remedial or development programs as to doctoral and research programs, but the conditions of quality achievement are defined in terms of the objectives of each — not in terms of invidious external comparisons or of reputational ratings.

There is evidence that the "new assessment movement" is expanding in scope and, while not abandoning concern with student learning and undergraduate education, at least as it is used on the state level and by accrediting bodies, is focused more on total institutional effectiveness than was originally the case. To the extent that this is so, as James Mingle (1989, p. 14) suggests, assessment will continue to be vital to quality determination at program, institutional, accrediting body, and state levels for the foreseeable future.

Summary

Spurred on by various reports, the issue of quality would seem to have become again a major focus of discussion and concern of the higher education community during the 1980s and an issue in which the political community has taken a progressively active role as well. Even if the focus on quality is to some extent a reaction to what was considered to be overemphasis on access in the previous decade, it seems clear that on the quality of higher education depend not only the future of higher education in our society but very possibly the future of our society itself. And yet quality is an issue about which confusion tends to abound. What it is, what it pertains to, how one recognizes it, and what one does with the results of quality assessment are frequently far from clear. From our review of some of the assumptions about quality, however, some essential themes emerge.

First, contrary to some public and academic perceptions, it seems that educational quality cannot be identified with reputation, resources, or selectivity. While resources are relevant to quality, the critical question is what one does with them, not simply their presence or amount. Quality is a matter of achievement of appropriate educational objectives and in fact appears to be a function of effective use of resources to achieve such appropriate educational objectives. To the extent that this is the case, one can expect quality equally from various types of programs, institutions, and even systems, but the conditions would vary with the legitimate educational objectives of each. Quality thus involves achievement in kind. Legitimate comparative judgments involve not external quantitative formula but relative effectiveness in achieving objectives. What this underlines is the critical, even essential importance of clear and careful formulation of missions and objectives, as well as the legitimacy of a wide variety of missions and objectives corresponding to the diversity of society's postsecondary educational needs.

Second, while research and publication are relevant to faculty evaluation in some types of institutions and programs, they seem to be inadequate as sole criteria even in research universities. The critical quality question concerning faculty members is their qualifications and appropriateness in relation to academic program or institutional objectives. Thus, faculty should be appropriate to the program or institution, mission, and objectives, not vice versa, and the appointment, promotion, and reward system should reflect this.

Third, while the focus of most of the "reform" reports and of parts of the political community on improving undergraduate education is both timely and welcome, there is a real danger of losing sight of the fact that quality (or the lack of it) is a characteristic of an institution as a whole given its role and objectives and not just of undergraduate education, as central as that may be. The quality of undergraduate education will clearly be affected by and must be seen in the context of the other activities of the institution, even if it is primarily an undergraduate institution. In complex institutions, the issue of quality applies to all aspects of the institution's operations, instructional and otherwise. These operations mutually affect each other and the quality of the institution as a whole.

Fourth, the quality of an educational institution or of programs is not determined by whether the institution or the programs are traditional or nontraditional, on or off campus, or carried out with the aid of educational technologies either at a distance or on campus or whether the students are "traditional" or not. Quality rather is a matter of results — the extent to which the institutions' and the students' appropriate educational objectives are achieved. Further, the development of nontraditional forms of education has helped reinforce this recognition, one that is critically important given today's changing student clientele and society's emerging postsecondary education expectations for the future.

Fifth, since noncredit courses and programs are an essential part of much of life-span learning and particularly of continuing professional education, colleges and universities involved in such activities have a clear responsibility to ensure that such programs are recognized as an integral part of their missions and that effectiveness in achieving the objectives of such courses and programs is as relevant to institutional quality as are any other educational activities in which the institution is involved.

Finally, assessment is neither a panacea nor a fad. While neither the process nor the results of assessment create quality, assessment is essential both to the recognition of quality and to providing the kind of information in the light of which quality improvement can occur. However, to be of maximum value, such assessment should include qualitative as well as quantitative information, should be applicable not only to undergraduate teaching and learning but to all the programs and operations of the institutions, and should be clearly related to mission and educational objectives. Assessment so conceived is essential to the health, welfare, and continued relevance of higher education for the foreseeable future.

6

The Equity Dilemma

In a special report to the new president of the College Board, Gladys Hardy (1988) pointed out that "Equity and quality are the overarching twin goals of American education" (p. 26). These goals at least theoretically apply to all levels of education. "The first goal," she suggests, "must be how to make larger proportions of the people who are unsuccessful in school, more successful, and, then, how to make levels of learning obtained among all students, of high quality, without changing the effect of the first goal."

These twin goals were recognized as long ago as the eighteenth century by Thomas Jefferson, who proposed universal education in Virginia and argued that it is a duty of government "to provide that every citizen . . . should receive an education proportioned to the conditions and pursuits of his life" (Padover, 1943, p. 1065). In the bill that he drafted for the Virginia legislature, he argued that those people capable of benefiting from it "regardless of wealth, birth or other accidental conditions or circumstances" should receive a "liberal education" to help guard and ensure the "rights and liberties of their fellow citizens" (p. 1048). Although there were limitations on who were "citizens" in Jefferson's day, the concept of universal education at a level appropriate to the individual's ability to benefit from

172

it without regard to "birth, wealth or other accidental conditions" is even more relevant in today's broader, more complex society than it was then.

It should also be noted that the goals of equity and quality were at least implicit in the actions of Congress soon after the United States became a nation. The Northwest Ordinance (1787), in addition to providing public lands to support education in the new territories, also enjoined the states to support forever education for the sake of the happiness of humankind and as essential to good government (Article III).

We have already noted the evolutionary, although sometimes slow, progressive recognition over the last two centuries and particularly the last forty years of the crucial importance of equity and its relevance to quality in higher education. We also noted the tension between the two and the pendulum effect during the last several years in relation to which of the two concepts seemed to be dominant. In this history, with notable exceptions, the academy on the whole has tended to support whatever the status quo happened to be in the name of quality, whereas the major impetus to change and to stressing access and equity has tended to be from outside the academy — from the public, the nation, and the states.

Today, the questions of equity and quality and their mutual attainment in higher education are not simply a liberal fantasy, a reformer's dream, or "it would be nice but . . . " They are related more directly than ever before to the quality of life and the economic welfare and international competitiveness of the nation, now and for the foreseeable future. Considerable progress toward academic equity with quality was made between 1949 and 1980. This resulted from a series of events and factors, including the GI Bill, *Brown* v. *Board of Education,* the civil rights movement, the Higher Education Act of 1965 and its various amendments, particularly the 1972 amendments establishing the range of student aid programs, and what might be considered on the whole the positive commitments to access and quality from the states and from the academic community. We still have not reached President Nixon's stated objective in 1970 that "no qualified student who wants to go to college should be barred by lack of money" or the ancillary goal of increasing substantially the number of qualified students "who want to go to college," but we have been making progress in that direction.

Equity obviously involves considerably more than access to appropriate higher education, as important as that is. It includes not only providing the opportunity but through that opportunity encouraging the development of the potential of individuals for their own career fulfillment and their contribution to the well-being of society. Equity thus applies to all students and potential students of all ages. It becomes particularly a challenge to society and the educational community as it is related to the educationally, culturally, and/or economically disadvantaged. These include people in the inner cities, people who are geographically isolated, people living at or below the poverty level, people regardless of age who have not been sufficiently challenged to develop their human potential for whatever reason — but especially for reasons frequently beyond their control and their immediate understanding.

The issue of equity is particularly acute as it is related to minorities and their participation, sense of belonging, and essential contribution to society's and the nation's welfare and progress in the next century. While we still have a long way to go, progress in providing educational opportunities for minorities has indeed taken place. Between 1968 and 1980, the proportion of minority students in higher education increased from 9.3 percent to 16.1 percent. Among blacks, the increase was from 6.0 percent to 9.4 percent by 1978. Since 1980, however, we have lost ground. The increase has leveled off and, in the case of blacks (State Higher Education Executive Officers, 1987b, p. 14), has actually been reversed. In 1985, of the 75 percent of eighteen- to twenty-two-year-old blacks who finished high school, only 26 percent went on to some form of college participation. Of the 62 percent of Hispanics who finished high school, again only 26 percent continued in postsecondary education (p. 17). In contrast, white rates of high school graduation were 83 percent and of college participation 34 percent. Not only is the participation rate of blacks and Hispanics low compared to that of whites, the college completion rate is equally low. Out of every one hundred white undergraduates, fifty-nine complete college degrees, in contrast to forty-two blacks and thirty-one Hispanics. Thus, as the Education Commission of the States (1986) report on *Transforming the State Role in Undergraduate Education* points out, "college participation and completion rates, especially for minorities, are declining at a time when educational attainment should be rising" (p. 14). There has been some increase in blacks and Hispanic enrollments since 1987, but it has been modest, and it is not clear yet whether it is a new trend or a temporary adjustment (Magner, 1989a, p. A27).

Four factors should make the equity issue a matter of major national concern. First, the proportion of white males in the work force continues to decrease. Eighty-five percent of the twenty-five million people entering the work force in the next decade will be women, minorities, and new immigrants (Holden, 1989a, p. 1133). Second, the changing nature of the economy, with far greater emphasis on information and services than on manufacturing (Sparks, 1985, p. 6), will require increased preparation and more, not less, postsecondary education. Third, unless we are to face the prospect of an increasingly radical social and economic division with a growing "underclass" unable to support either themselves above the poverty level or the growing numbers of senior citizens under Social Security, it is imperative that the level and the quality of education, both in the schools and in the colleges, continue to improve (Hayes-Bautista, 1988, p. 2) and, on the college level, to expand. Fourth, the possibility of continued national vitality in a progressively competitive world depends on an educated work force capable of higher productivity through increased skills and knowledge.

This is not to suggest that the responsibility for meeting all of the educational needs of the country rests with the colleges and other postsecondary educational institutions alone. The issues involve the entire educational system, as well as public awareness and support. It is, however, to recognize the critical role that colleges and universities must play in cooperation with the schools, with business and industry, and with the political community in helping to ensure appropriate equity, including access to higher education for all who can benefit from it. On the realization of this objective in fact may well depend the survival, defense, and maintenance, let alone improvement, of American society in the next century.

Recognizing the importance of equity in education generally and higher education in particular is considerably different from attaining it. One is faced almost immediately with what appears to be a series of dilemmas related again to assumptions that need to be carefully reviewed. For example, on the surface, it would seem that concern with equity and concern with quality are not necessarily compatible. There clearly are some conceptions of quality that are close to being antithetical to the concept of equity, even to the extent that one may have one or the other but not both. Thus, even Hansen and Stampen (1987), basing their analysis on the pendulum swings of national concern with equity and quality on funding patterns, come close to suggesting that increasing emphasis on the one necessarily means decreasing emphasis on the other (pp. 18–19).

At this point, it seems clear that the basic assumption that needs to be reviewed and challenged and that is at the heart of the "equity dilemma" is in fact the view that equity and quality are antithetical concepts—you cannot have both. The possibility of challenging other, related assumptions depends to a large extent on how one deals with the equity-quality interface.

The Equity Versus Quality Myth

In an address to the Washington, D.C., Business Round Table in June 1989, Ernest Boyer (1989) insisted, "Excellence and quality cannot be divided, and as a national strategy, we must focus on the disadvantaged" (p. 6). Boyer's focus in this address was on elementary and secondary education. He was particularly concerned that recognition and implementation of the concept of the indivisibility of excellence and equality should begin in the schools with early education. The principle involved, however, applies, Boyer believes, to all levels of education, from preschool to graduate and continuing education (Boyer, 1987, p. 276). Part of Boyer's point clearly is that unless it begins early, unless disadvantaged people and minorities are not only included in education but included in quality education from the outset, the problems of ensuring both equity and quality become progressively more difficult at more advanced levels.

The need for such early emphasis on quality as a condition of equity not only is illustrated in the general importance of improving basic skills across the board but is particularly relevant to opening up opportunity for minority students, women, and people from economically disadvantaged backgrounds in such fields as the natural sciences, mathematics, and engineering. Increasing opportunity in these areas for minorities and women is both crucial to education and social equity and very much in the national interest. *Science* estimates that at the present rate, unless more women and minorities move into these fields, there will be a shortage in excess of 675,000 scientists and engineers by the year 2006 (Holden, 1989b, p. 1536).

According to the National Governors' Association Task Force on College Quality (1986), there is necessarily a positive relationship in the American scene between equity and quality in higher education: "It is incorrectly assumed that quality and access are competing, antagonistic values in higher education. . . . It is not true that access causes a decline in the quality of higher education. . . . Access without quality is a cruel deception, while quality without access is a betrayal of the American ideal of equal opportunity, and the belief that it is important to educate all children. In the next decade an increasing proportion of the nation's youth of traditional college attendance age categories will have backgrounds that have provided fewer economic and educational advantages. From moral, economic, and national security perspectives the nation simply cannot afford to sacrifice the next generation of emerging Americans in the name of quality enhancement" (p. 162). To the task force statement it should be added that this applies not only and perhaps not even primarily to the nation's youth of traditional college age but to students and potential students of all ages.

Alexander Astin (1985) agrees with the governors and suggests that "there is something inherently contradictory in a higher education system where quality and opportunity are in conflict rather than in harmony" (p. 100). The Southern Regional Education Board, while calling for higher admissions standards for colleges, nevertheless insists that "Opportunity, quality, and diversity are not contradictory goals. Our commitment . . . [is] to insure that educational opportunity becomes synonymous with achievement" (Southern Regional Education Board, 1988, p. 3). In *To Secure the Blessings of Liberty*, the National Commission on the Role and Future of State Colleges and Universities (1986) argues that "Without quality in education, the nation loses its strength. Without equity in education, democracy ceases to function" (p. 9). It would seem that in parts of the academic and political communities, the recognition of an essential linkage between equity and quality as foundational objectives in American higher education is indeed clear.

And yet the concept that equity and quality are complementary, that they mutually reinforce each other, and particularly that they require each other is a uniquely American one and far from universally accepted even in this country. In fact, one must add immediately that whether they are complementary clearly depends on one's conception or definition of quality and one's view of the objectives or aims of higher education. One of the most striking examples of a concept of quality based on a very different conception of the purpose of higher education is to be found in Great Britain. The British system is self-consciously elitist and anti-egalitarian. The contrast between the British view of quality and the American concern with equity became dramatically clear at an Anglo-American seminar on quality sponsored by the Carnegie Foundation for the Advancement of Teaching held at Oxford in the winter of 1986 and a subsequent meeting at Princeton in September of 1987. The difference was sufficiently great that, particularly at the Oxford session, the United States participants and the British participants tended to talk past each other rather than to each other.

"Quality," according to the prestigious British Committee of Vice-Chancellors and Principals, "has no meaning except in relation to purpose or function" (Committee of Vice-Chancellors and Principals of the Universities of the United Kingdom, 1986, p. 3), a statement with which many of us would agree. The purpose of British higher education, however, as

Martin Trow points out, is "education of leadership — chiefly its professional and political leadership." This is a concept of leadership "that has not even included the leaders of business and industry on the whole" (Trow, 1987, p. 25). Along with this conception of education for leadership goes what Graeme Moodie (1986) has described as "the widely held belief that there is only a limited pool of ability in the population and that therefore . . . 'more means worse'" (p. 3). As a result, the criteria of quality utilized by the now defunct University Grants Committee in the early 1980s to apportion cuts in funds by the Thatcher government while preserving or strengthening "quality" were "amount of income a university received from Research Councils . . . and the quality of students on entry as measured by grades obtained in advanced (18 +) Level examinations" (Harris, 1986, p. 3). A further check on quality is the external examination system, which ensures something approximating uniformity of results on graduation across the university system in particular fields. For the British university and polytechnic system, equity and access are in effect irrelevant.

In sharp contrast to the British system, the American system of higher education has progressively evolved in the direction of attempting to provide higher education opportunity to all who can benefit from it. This has not been a straight-line evolution, and elitist pressures continue. These are clearly aided and abetted by the implicit status hierarchy that Astin (1986, p. 15) identifies as part of our belief system, by the single pyramid of prestige that Frank Newman (1987, p. 45) calls attention to, and by the older Jencks and Riesman (1968) concept of the university colleges, each of which we looked at in connection with the Reputational Input Myth. It is reinforced by authors such as Allan Bloom (1987), who is concerned primarily with revitalizing "the kind of young people who populate the twenty or thirty best universities," the young people "who are most likely . . . to have the greatest moral and intellectual effect on the nation" (p. 22). In a statement that some of the British educators would clearly sympathize with, he argues that "It is sometimes said that these advantaged youths have less need of our attention and resources, that they already have enough. But they, above all, most need education, in as much as the greatest talents are most difficult to perfect, and the more complex the nature the more susceptible it is to perversion" (p. 22).

Without going as far as Bloom or the British system, we can say that on the reputational or resource views of quality or excellence, as Astin (1985) points out and as we noted in the previous chapter, there is a clear conflict between quality and equity, a conflict that is very much alive in the United States today. If only a few institutions have the highest reputation, then most students are condemned to attend mediocre or poor institutions. Resources are, after all, finite. When they are in short supply, increasing the number of students means decreasing the support for students individually. Thus, the Association of American Colleges (1985) report states that "the widening of access . . . has contributed to the confusions that have beset the baccalaureate experience" and goes on to comment that while "the tension between democratic values and the effort to maintain standards . . . can be creative, too often numbers and political considerations have prevailed over quality and rationality" (p. 5). According to Astin, Howard Bowen, while worrying "about those ghetto kids, the people in rural backwaters," nevertheless "fear[s] that equity . . . costs so much . . . that for the foreseeable future, equity is unattainable with quality" (Astin, 1985, pp. 5-6). Carrying the matter one step further, John Kelley, the dean of students at Kendall College, argues that "colleges shouldn't waste their resources on students who aren't qualified to be there in the first place" (Kelley, 1989, p. B2).

Kelley's comment may well be right in relation to any particular institution and some particular group of students. However, it is far too easy to assume that a student is not qualified when in fact the potential for achievement is present but needs reinforcement — even remediation — for its realization. As pointed out elsewhere, one cannot deny the importance of resources (as Howard Bowen suggests) for achievement of quality, even though resources are not a sufficient condition of quality. The critical question, however, is their utilization. We may well be at a point at which restriction in resources — including student aid — can undermine both equity and quality. The question then becomes whether as a nation, for the sake of our own future, we can afford not to make available the resources needed to achieve equity and quality.

It becomes far too easy, as the American Association of State Colleges and Universities report points out rather dramatically, to use "excellence" and "quality" as rationalizations, even code words, for denial of access and opportunity for minorities and for the economic and socially disadvantaged (National Commission on the Role and Future of State Colleges and Universities, 1986, p. 3). To do so is not just to turn back the clock but to undermine the basic role of higher education in this country, including its ability to help the country meet the changing conditions of the twenty-first century. Robert Birnbaum (1988) has pointed out that "The genius of American Higher Education is that it attempts, to a degree not found elsewhere in the world, to support both quality and access. And indeed, in our educational system, neither quality nor access can survive alone, it is only in combination that they define our educational system. When the system emphasizes one to the detriment of the other, both are threatened" (p. 452).

It is particularly important, however, to recognize that while access is essential, it is only one part of equity. Access might be described as a necessary but not a sufficient condition for equity. Access alone all too often leads to the revolving door rather than real opportunity. Such a revolving door is economically wasteful, wasteful of human resources, and frequently devastating to the people involved. Thus, in addition to access, equity needs to be reinforced by a number of things. First, equity calls for early identification of student potential in the schools and nurturing and encouraging of its development. It calls for closer collaboration between the schools and the colleges in strengthening programs relevant to college options. For those approaching college age or beyond it, it calls for the kind of supportive and diagnostic testing, counseling, and guidance that will help them match their abilities and interests with the appropriate postsecondary educational programs. The New Jersey Basic Skills Assessment Program required of entering freshmen for diagnostic purposes, counseling, and planning their college courses to fit their interest and abilities is a positive case in point.

Second, equity requires something that might be described as a system of postsecondary education in the sense of an ensured diversity of institutions and programs to meet both student interests and abilities and society's needs. It may or may not be designated or specifically designed as a system, but it should present multiple options and opportunities. Educational homogeneity, whether imposed by examinations, engendered by imitation, or created by design, is an enemy of equity and quality in a pluralistic society. Diversity in this sense must not be confused with types of institutional governance or control. Rather, it refers to the plurality of legitimate postsecondary educational programs and objectives available. Thus, as noted, the W. K. Kellogg Foundation grant to the Oklahoma Board of Regents involving the whole postsecondary educational system in Oklahoma, with all its inherent diversity, is a clear recognition of this principle.

Third, equity involves ready availability of information to students and potential students about programs, institutions, and opportunities relevant to student interests, abilities, and background. Such information needs to be made available through and be reinforced by an effective guidance and counseling system not only for high school students and traditional college-age students but for adults, part-time students, and people interested or involved in continuing education of any age. As already indicated, such older and part-time students constitute a large proportion, even a majority, of the current postsecondary education population. Equity requires not only access but adequate information, career counseling, and guidance for such older students and potential students.

Module IV of the Oklahoma Network of Continuing Higher Education is a striking example of an effective approach to ensuring that this occurs. Under this module, the network identified and brought together the counselors at fifty-two education information centers at public and private colleges and universities, four military bases, and fourteen participating libraries in the state. With the help of the W. K. Kellogg Foundation grant, the network provided each of the information centers with computerized guidance software — either the Educational Testing Service Sigi-plus or the American College Testing Discover for College and Adults. Under the direction of Professor Jim Seals at Oklahoma State University, an assessment of the needs of the guidance and counseling personnel was carried out, and an effective in-service training program was established for the counselors. The in-service program addressed such issues as information on employment trends, adult learning characteristics, computer literacy, and retention of adult students (Oklahoma Network of Continuing Higher Education, 1988, vol. 1, p. 78). The various education information centers were linked together in the computer network, to which twelve public libraries have more recently been added. The computerized guidance system, which helps individuals reach decisions about career and educational goals through consideration of personal interests, aptitudes, experiences, and values, is supplemented by a common data base that matches institutional information about resources available with these goals (p. 79). Through its information centers and library network, the Oklahoma project not only extends access to adult learners across the state but promotes the kind of information and guidance that make more informed educational and career decisions possible. The directors of the centers and their staffs have found the program of such help and value that they have voluntarily organized themselves to seek additional funding beyond that provided by the state and the W. K. Kellogg Foundation and to make sure that the program continues after the Kellogg grant runs out.

The Intermountain Community Learning and Information Services Project in Utah, Colorado, Wyoming, and Montana, which is also funded by the W. K. Kellogg Foundation, provides some of the same services plus limited actual course work to isolated communities and learners in the four-state area. On a much more limited geographical scale at present, the W. K. Kellogg Foundation–supported Personal Adult Learning Lab at the University of Georgia Center for Continuing Education now provides adults similar computerized counseling, guidance, and program planning. Beyond the guidance and program planning, it also directly offers some noncredit independent study courses. While at present it is available only at the University of Georgia Center for Continuing Education, plans exist eventually to provide such centers in other parts of the state.

Fourth, in addition to access, equity also involves providing reasonable assurance to all students, particularly minority students, that the educational learning environment is what might be described in computer terms as "user friendly." This means that there is respect for cultural diversity, that the institution and programs provide what the National Center for Postsecondary Governance and Finance calls a "supportive learning environment" plus "'comfortability' in the social environment" (Education Commission of the States, 1989, p. 4). Among the recommendations of the State Higher Education Executive Officers Task Force on Minority Student Achievement (1987) is that the state agencies "should support institutional programming that meets two equally important ends: to better equip minority students to function well in the institutional environment, and to adapt that environment to better accommodate the needs and interests of minority students" (p. 48). This does not mean either segregated programs or holding to ethnicity blindness as the objective. What it does mean is mutual respect, cooperative learning, and cultural complementation. Equity, in addition to access, entails such respect and mutual help in educational achievement.

Fifth, Astin (1985, p. 82) distinguishes between what he calls equality of access and equality of opportunity. The first involves spaces: Are there sufficient spaces for all those who want postsecondary education? Are they affordable? The second involves not only spaces available but whether "students have equal access to the best opportunity (for them), regardless of race, gender, income, social class or other personal qualities." Clearly, equity involves the latter. The danger here is a not so subtle form of tracking based not on ability or potential but on the negative impact of selectivity. Thus, a disproportionately large number of black students tend to end up in historically black institutions and community colleges; Hispanics have an even higher percentage of students in community colleges. This is not to suggest that community colleges or historically black institutions are inferior. In fact, for a good many students, whether from minorities, affluent neighborhoods, good secondary schools, or economically disadvantaged groups, a community college may be most appropriate for any number of reasons, including career interests. The argument that community colleges are inferior because they generally have lower instructional costs (Astin, 1985, pp. 98–99) is not necessarily correct. Institutional expenditures per student for community colleges need to be compared not with average undergraduate costs but with costs during the first two years at four-year institutions. Faculty functions differ, institutional overhead differs, and it may just be that at least some community colleges use resources more effectively than some other types of institutions to achieve their objectives. What is at issue, however, is not the quality of community colleges or historically black institutions but whether opportunity commensurate with interests and potential (including choice) is also really available for minority and disadvantaged students in more complex and selective institutions.

That institutions are aware of limitations in opportunity, of the plateau or slowdown in enrollments of the two major minority groups in the last few years, and (whatever their motivations) are concerned with doing something about it is underlined in *Campus Trends, 1989* (El-Khawas, 1989). Eight out of ten institutions reported activity to increase minority enrollments. Efforts to improve the campus climate for minorities were reported by 83 percent of administrators. Eight out of ten institutions were attempting to recruit more minority faculty members but finding it more difficult given the currently limited pool (El-Khawas, 1989, pp. 5–6). Significantly, more doctoral institutions than any other group of institutions see this issue of diversity as a major challenge in the next five years. In fact, the number of doctoral institutions that see this as one of three primary issues in the future almost doubled (from 19 percent to 33 percent) between 1988 and 1989 (El-Khawas, 1989, p. 41). While much more needs to be done, at least the recognition that equity involves access not just to particular types of institutions but to the range of types of institutions commensurate with student interest and potential seems to have again become a major higher education concern. This carries with it the further recognition that if such equity is to be achieved for blacks, Hispanics, and Native American, appropriate reinforcement and learning environment are essential at all institutions, particularly at the complex and more selective ones.

Sixth, equity clearly involves providing the amount and kind of financial support that change access from an empty gesture into real opportunity. This means that if equity is to be attained, there is a public obligation to ensure that student aid — federal, state, and institutional — is available and that it is based on and commensurate with need. Major progress was made in this direction in the 1960s and the 1970s. By the end of the 1970s, we had come reasonably close to fulfilling President Nixon's goal that no student should be barred from higher education for economic reasons. However, the situation since 1980 has, if anything, deteriorated. *The Memorandum to the 41st President* (Commission on National Challenges in Higher Education, 1988) points out that "over the last decade . . . we have seen the resurgence of barriers that threatens the progress made in equalizing opportunity. Disagreement about the adequacy of federal support for student assistance is the most obvious difficulty" (p. 3). According to Hauptman and Andersen (1988), "Although funding levels for student aid programs have generally increased as fast as inflation in recent years, the maximum awards in these programs have not kept pace with the rising costs of attendance or the general cost of living" (p. 45).

As grant programs have not kept pace with the need, loan programs, particularly the Stafford Guaranteed Loan Program, have had to be used more and more extensively to meet the needs of those least able to carry large debts and to repay. Default rates have increased dramatically, and the U.S. Department of Education and the Congress have become so concerned with defaults and the possibility of abuse and even fraud that they have tended to forget the basic purpose of student aid and have not taken appropriate steps to increase the balance between grants and loans. Thus, we find ourselves today in a situation that in the fall of 1989 led the House of Representatives to "send a message to colleges and schools that they must curb student loan defaults and cut fraud in other aid program" by voting 345 to 38 to freeze student aid for the following year (DeLoughry, 1989, p. A13). Unfortunately, those most hurt by such freezes will be the neediest students, including minorities. This tends to make the statement in the 1988 Republican platform sound somewhat hollow: "We will keep resources focused on low-income students and address the barriers that discourage minorities students from entering and succeeding in institutions of higher education" (Saunders, 1988, p. A19). It seems obvious that, without the funds to make opportunity real, equity is a chimera.

Finally, to provide real equity, in contrast to access alone, or to make access real opportunity, quality is required. Access to poor or second-rate programs, to programs that do not do what they say they do or are supposed to do, or to shortcuts that compromise the substance of achievement not only is not equity, it is a hoax. *Involvement in Learning* seems to be quite right in insisting that "greater access to education will be meaningless if colleges, community colleges, and universities do not offer high quality programs to their students. True equity requires that *all* Americans have access to *quality* higher education" (Study Group on the Conditions of Excellence in American Higher Education, 1984, p. 3).

By some definitions of or assumptions about quality, one obviously can have educational quality without equity, as illustrated by British higher education and as required by reputational and resource views of quality. The reverse, however, is not the case. One cannot have equity without quality. But quality in this sense again involves effective use of resources to achieve appropriate educational objectives. Equity requires a fit between the interests, abilities, and career potential of students and the purposes or objectives of appropriate educational programs and institutions. Neither equity nor quality requires that all institutions be alike or that all students or potential students be eligible to attend any particular institution or even any particular type of institution. Rather, they require the opportunity for students to find postsecondary programs and institutions commensurate with their abilities, interests, and needs and institutions with programs capable of guiding them to achievement of their educational goals in the context of the educational needs of society. Since the possibility of a program or institution achieving its appropriate educational objectives depends on identifying students with the potential for the achievement of those educational objectives, quality in this sense does require equity as much as equity requires quality.

The Higher Admissions Standards Myth

To the extent that equity and quality do require each other in the American higher education system, it appears to some that the best way for institutions to ensure that the students they accept can benefit from the type and level of educational programs they offer is through admissions standards and prerequisite requirements. This is not to suggest that admissions requirements should be uniform; even the most zealous proponents of higher admissions standards recognize the need for differences related to diversity of institutional and program functions and objectives. However, for many it does mean that, given that diversity, admissions criteria should be developed in relation to the specific educational objectives of the program or institution and should be sufficiently high to give assurance that accepted students have the ability to benefit from the program and a reasonable chance of succeeding. This is undoubtedly what John Kelley (1989) had in mind when he insisted that colleges should not waste their resources on students not qualified to be there in the first place.

Even the Congress and the U.S. Department of Education have become involved in the issue of ability of students to benefit as it is related to establishing eligibility for student aid. Admittedly, the involvement is at a basic level and applies primarily to students admitted who do not have high school diplomas. Because such students usually are needy and require student aid, the fear is that less than scrupulous institutions will enroll such students to collect student aid whether or not the students can benefit from the program offered. Thus, by federal regulation (Higher Education Act of 1965 as amended, 484 (D)), the department requires that institutions present concrete evidence, by testing or other means, that students without high school diplomas do in fact have potential ability to benefit. To back this up, under the 1988 Department of Education criteria for recognition of accrediting bodies for the purpose of helping to establish institutional eligibility for federal funds (Secretary's Recognition Criteria of Accrediting Agencies, 602–13K), accrediting agencies are expected to provide assurance that institutions they accredit will act responsibly in admitting such students.

While the federal concern about ability to benefit seems to be limited in practice primarily to proprietary institutions and to apply only to students without high school diplomas, it can be argued that the principle of accepting only students with ability to benefit is relevant for all levels and types of institutions and programs. Institutions, regardless of level, that accept students who are clearly unqualified, who cannot benefit from the program, or who have little or no chance of completing it are indeed perpetrating a fraud and simply making the revolving door revolve more rapidly. Neither equity nor quality is served in such circumstances. One of the functions, perhaps the primary function, of admissions standards is to ensure that admitted students do indeed have the ability to benefit from the program.

It is possible, however, to carry the concept of equity as involving primarily ability to benefit, comparability of students, and assurance of success in program completion to a point where it becomes a reaffirmation of elitism. This is illustrated in an interesting way in the British system, where the "more is worse" formula does at least ensure comparability and ability to benefit to those accepted but leaves access and diversity far behind. The closest parallel in the American scene is among some of the most selective institutions. However, these constitute a small proportion of American institutions, and even among such institutions, admissions policies tend to be modified to ensure diversity of students and public responsibility for extending educational opportunity.

One may hold to a view of the importance of admissions standards and of their relevance to equity and quality without accepting an elitist extreme. Such a view involves expecting each institution to develop its own admissions standards in the light of its objectives and mission and to make the standards sufficiently specific so that students know what they are getting into and have a reasonable chance of success after admission. A part of this may well involve recognition of the need for some common or comparable standards related to basic skills and to what is deemed to be adequate preparation for college-level work.

This view of multiple standards related to institutional objectives but with something approximating a common core at the initial undergraduate admittance level tends to be predominant today. The responsibility for setting such standards rests with the institutions in the private sector and with either the institutions, the system, or the state in the public sector. This multiple-standards position has the advantage of recognizing the legitimate diversity of standards to fit the diversity of institutions and students. It can accommodate open admissions institutions so long as there is in such institutions some way of distinguishing diagnostically between those students who are better prepared and those who are not and provision of appropriate remedial work for the latter. In fact, it does not restrict any institution from accepting students with weak or inadequate backgrounds but with potential to benefit if appropriate counseling and remediation are provided. Most of the discussion about raising admissions requirements to improve quality and ensure equity is geared to this multiple-standards position and focuses particularly on the common and basic skill aspects. Within this perspective, there are major pressures and legitimate concerns about raising standards — or at least raising the floor for standards for institutions and for state systems. College faculty who have always had a less than sanguine view of preparation of students by the schools seem even more concerned today. In a Carnegie Foundation for the Advancement of Teaching study of faculty, Ernest Boyer reports that "nearly three-fourths of faculty members think undergraduates at their institutions are seriously underprepared in terms of basic skills," and two-thirds of the faculty believe that institutions "are spending too much time and money teaching students what they should have learned before entering college" (Mooney, 1989b, p. A13).

To remedy the situation, many members of the academic and political communities believe that the standards for admission to college-level work must be raised and appropriate pressures brought on the schools to ensure that adequate preparation takes place there. In the interim, remedial work both in the schools and in college will be necessary. The Southern Regional Education Board (SREB), for example, insists that "Standards are needed that address basic academic skills, such as reading and writing. These skill standards should go beyond course requirements for the high school diploma to insure that students can benefit from an upgraded college curriculum, and that faculty are not presented with an impossible range of learning abilities" (Southern Regional Education Board, 1988, p. 8). The SREB argues that the situation is sufficiently critical that the states as well as the institutions have a responsibility to ensure that standards are raised.

Raising or for the first time imposing admissions standards at public institutions is exactly what has been happening in a good many states. In 1986, the Education Commission of the States (1986) reported that "States are raising requirements for admission to college or imposing requirements for the first time. Nearly half the states currently set minimum admissions standards. As of 1984–85, sixteen states had either recently enacted or were considering more stringent standards. In every case, the policies imposed a strengthened or prescribed pattern of high school coursework" (p. 13).

In 1988, the National Governors' Association (1988, p. 40) reported that this movement was continuing. In a number of states that have not raised requirements for admission to public institutions, individual public institutions and particularly the flagship institutions have. While in many cases, as the ECS reports, this has involved increasing required high school work, in others the change has involved requiring higher grade point averages and improved scores on standardized tests. In a number of states, this has involved a departure from a tradition in which the major state universities have taken any state residents with high school diplomas.

Informing students of what will be expected of them, of the backgrounds or prerequisites appropriate to or even necessary for achieving their academic goals, obviously is crucial to equity and quality. To the extent that raising admissions standards serves such an informational function, the results may well be salutary — provided that students with deficiencies but potential for success are given adequate guidance and remedial help to reach a satisfactory level of college performance. Also to the extent that raising standards encourages more adequate preparation, particularly in the basic skills, on the elementary and secondary school levels, it may be a step in the right direction when accompanied by greater school-college exchange of information and cooperation. To assume, however, that raising admissions standards by itself will advance either quality or equity may be seriously misguided. In the first place, without adequate early identification of student potential, without diagnosis of deficiencies and strengths at the college admittance level, and without provision for remedial work to overcome academic deficiencies, the access part of equity is sharply curtailed and, with it, equity itself. (We shall return to this shortly.)

Second, to rely on admissions standards to define either quality or equity is to return to or to perpetuate a reliance on the resources views of quality, on inputs rather than results. It is to fail to recognize that an institution's or program's quality is a function of results, or how well it uses its resources to achieve those results, and not of uniformity of inputs. The NIE study group, while encouraging more study in basic academic disciplines for college preparation on the secondary level, considers "imposing higher admissions *standards* in . . . cutoff scores on standardized tests and grade point averages . . . an inappropriate response" to attain "more rigor in subject matter preparation" (Study Group on the Conditions of Excellence in American Higher Education, 1984, p. 13). It expresses its concern about "the tendency of colleges to control 'inputs,' such as the characteristics of the students they *admit,* while paying insufficient attention to their '*outputs*' — in particular, the learning of the students that *graduate*" (p. 14).

Third, even if admissions requirements are focused on years of study in basic academic disciplines, this becomes discriminatory for students from small secondary schools, particularly rural ones, that are unable because of limited income or size to offer the range and level of programs called for (Humphries, 1987, p. 19). At least one of the functions of the Intermountain Community Learning and Information Service program is to help remedy such deficiencies. It should be noted, however, that inability to offer the appropriate background courses is not limited to rural schools. It may apply to any school system with inadequate financial support, including particularly some inner-city schools.

Fourth, while basic skills are critical not only to all post-secondary programs but to the world of work (Carnevale, Gainer, and Meltzer, n.d., pp. 1–7), the kind of preparation desirable for various types of postsecondary and higher education programs does vary, and any single set of content prerequisites is likely to exclude students who have not received appropriate advice early enough, students who change their intention at a late date, and particularly older and part-time students whose patterns of education and experience frequently do not fit into traditional modes. High or arbitrary admissions requirements can all too easily restrict access for such people, who might be capable not only of benefiting from the program but of excelling in it.

Finally, what is critical both to equity and to quality is not admissions standards, as valuable as they may be in some cases as guidelines for preparation for college, but results or outcomes at graduation and beyond. It is thus exit or graduation requirements and expectations that count, that determine the context for quality and are crucial for equity. One can expect all students completing a program to reach certain levels of accomplishment. It would be inequitable to expect lower levels of accomplishment for one group — whether minorities, women, the economically disadvantaged, or older or part-time students — than from others. To do so is to perpetuate inequities. If we are correct, the quality of a program or institution is directly related to the level of exit expectations and the program's or institution's ability to enable students to achieve these results.

Thus, in a basic sense, admissions requirements alone are irrelevant to institutional quality. Admissions requirements that restrict access of people with the potential for the academic achievement called for in the program are inequitable and need to be reexamined, modified, or done away with.

While admissions requirements are not in themselves indices of quality and if rigidly applied may be restrictive of access and equity, when carefully formulated, they can serve as indices of minimum levels of preparation appropriate to a particular course of study and thus have implications for equity. But to the extent that they do, if equity is in fact to be served, it is vital to provide effective means for people who have the potential to benefit from the program to attain the necessary level of preparation even if this has not been supplied by the secondary schools. Far more important, however, than admissions requirements in ensuring quality and equity are standards of accomplishment of educational objectives at the point of completion or exit from the course, program, or institution.

The Remedial Work Myth

There are relatively few areas in which there is as much uneasiness, inconsistency in attitudes and actions, and ambivalence in the academic community, the political community, and even the general community as in remedial or developmental education. And yet there are also probably few areas more crucial to providing real educational opportunity, equity, and achievement of national educational goals. The uneasiness, the concern, a feeling for the scope of the problem, and, to a certain extent, the inconsistency are reflected in current faculty attitudes. While three-fourths of faculty consider today's undergraduates seriously underprepared in basic skills, two-thirds of them believe that colleges and universities are spending too much time and money teaching students what they should have learned before entering college (Mooney, 1989b, p. A13).

The scope of the problem is clear. According to the Education Commission of the States (1986, p. 13), by 1983–84, 94 percent of all public colleges and universities offered some remedial courses in basic skill areas. A Southern Regional Education Board (1988) study shows that in its fifteen member states, "in almost thirty percent of the institutions, at least half of the first-time freshmen were in need of remedial education" (p. 1). Among the 404 reporting institutions, 35.7 percent of all entering freshmen need additional support in reading, writing, or mathematics. The percentage varies by state and by type of institution, but even for research universities, with the lowest overall figures, 22.3 percent, or more than one in five freshmen, require remedial work (p. 3). This phenomenon is not unique to the South. A 1983 report released by the Institutional Resource Center at the City University of New York indicated that 30 percent of all first-time college students in the nation were academically deficient (Southern Regional Education Board, 1988, p. 1). From these figures alone, it seems obvious that the problem is almost universal, that almost all higher education institutions are involved, and that the number of students is considerable — about one-third of entering freshmen.

There are at least two other important pieces of information to note from the SREB and New York studies that tend to be contrary to what some people seem to expect. The first of these, as noted by the Education Commission of the States (1986, p. 13), is that remediation is not just a minority issue: "Although minorities may be overrepresented among freshmen with serious deficiencies in preparation, the problem of poor preparation cuts across all types of institutions and all student groups. There has been a tendency to explain away the remediation issue as a 'minorities issue,' but that clearly is not the case." Recognition of this should help to overcome what Gladys Hardy (1988) calls "negative sensitivity to 'remedial programs' which appeared to stigmatize minorities students" (p. 38). As a result of such "negative sensitivity," Hardy points out, a number of colleges eliminated or reduced remedial programs in the early 1980s. The fact that the need for remediation applies to students of all groups, including older students, makes it a universal problem and should obviate any tendency to treat remedial or developmental education as somehow a form of racial segregation, tracking, or bias. While there is certainly a need for positive environmental support and reinforcement for some minority students, such programs should not be confused with programs to overcome academic deficiencies. Both are necessary conditions of equity.

The second piece of information from the SREB study that is surprising to many people is that the proportion of first-time freshmen needing remedial work at community colleges (33.7 percent) and of those at liberal arts or comprehensive colleges in the South is essentially the same. Even granted differences in objectives — for example, the generally higher interest in vocational programs in community colleges — this seems to indicate that students coming to community colleges are not noticeably inferior in preparation to those in other types of institutions. If, as has been proposed in some states, community colleges were to be given the primary responsibility for remedial education, this might require a considerable shift in student attendance patterns at both community colleges and other institutions.

The faculty belief that too much time and money are spent by colleges and universities "teaching students what they should have learned before entering college" raises a number of issues. If three-quarters of the faculty believe that entering students are unprepared, then it would seem that faculty and colleges generally should be concerned with providing opportunities to make up the deficiencies while working with the schools to strengthen their preparatory work. Yet some faculty members and even legislators seem to be saying that colleges should get out of remedial work and leave it to the schools. As the ECS points out, there is real concern among many state officials that the states "increasingly 'pay twice' for education, once when students are in the public schools and again when they enroll in remedial programs in college" (Education Commission of the States, 1986, p. 13), and it is at least valid to ask "why should they?" Why not hold the schools responsible and let it go at that? While the flagship institutions have the lowest percentage (22 percent) of unprepared students, according to the SREB report, this still amounts to one in five. Nevertheless, it is particularly in these institutions that "some go so far as to suggest that they should not admit any student who is not ready for college work" (Southern Regional Education Board, 1988, p. 3). Even Ernest Boyer (1987), while recognizing that the need for remedial programs is a fact of life, argues that "it is unacceptable to ask colleges to continue to play endless academic catch up" (pp. 77–78).

It undoubtedly is the case, as Paul E. Barton of the Educational Testing Service Policy Information Center insists, that "the reform efforts of the 1980s are resulting in more high school graduates who are better prepared in academics" (Leatherman, 1989, p. A2). It may also be the case, as Boyer (1987) suggests, that "the long term answer is better precollege education" (p. 78). Few people (except at tax-paying time) would deny that the schools should be strengthened monetarily and educationally to enable them to better prepare students for college work in general and in mathematics and the sciences in particular. It undoubtedly is the case, as the American Association of State Colleges and Universities' national commission argues, that "more school/college cooperative programs should be developed that not only stimulate the talented, but also guide, enrich and raise the performance level of underperforming students" (National Commission on the Role and Future of State Colleges and Universities, 1986, p. 18). All of these and other suggestions, as important and valid as they may be, miss the point if they are used, not necessarily by their authors but by others, as arguments that colleges should get out of the remedial education business.

To propose such a withdrawal is, we would suggest, to propose educational, financial, and social disaster. If, for example, the 75 percent of faculty who believe that today's undergraduates are seriously underprepared are even remotely correct, and if the SREB's estimate that 36 percent of entering freshmen need remedial work to do college level work is correct, then to cut out remedial work on the college level would have a number of startling results. If the unprepared students were not admitted, as some propose, the impact on enrollments would be financially catastrophic. Institutions even partially dependent on tuition would find themselves in a real new depression, as would public institutions where state funding is related to full-time-equivalent enrollment. Institutions would find themselves with excess faculty, excess space, and excess services. Even research universities would be affected, although not as severely as four-year colleges and community colleges. Only the most selective and expensive private institutions would probably be relatively unaffected.

If the unprepared students were admitted but without provision for remediation, one of two results and perhaps both are likely. The first is that the revolving door would swing remarkably fast, with all the discontent, unhappiness, and resentment that that would cause. The second is a real lowering of achievement expectations and a movement not unlike what has been called "social promotion" on the elementary and secondary school level. According to the American College Testing Program (1989), even with some 94 percent of institutions providing some remedial work, in institutions with liberal or open admissions (those that accept students with average SAT scores of 800 or below and ACT scores of 17.9 or below), some 42 percent of the students drop out between the freshman and sophomore years. Even in relatively selective institutions (those with average SAT scores of between 950 and 1100 and ACT scores of between 21.9 and 26), the dropout rate is close to 20 percent, or one in five. Admittedly, other reasons than academic deficiency may be involved in dropping out; however, the correlation between low entry scores and dropout rates is such as to suggest that, in some cases, other reasons may be rationalizations for discouragement resulting from academic deficiencies. Even with such dropout rates, concern about grade inflation is real and is one of the factors leading to the various reports. Thus, for example, the American Association of State Colleges and Universities report insists that "college grades have gone up and up, even as Scholastic Aptitude Tests and the American College Testing scores have gone down and the pressure on teachers to ease their students' paths to graduate schools have increased" (National Commission on the Role and Future of State Colleges and Universities, 1986, p. 1).

The most serious impact from taking colleges out of the remedial education business, however, would be the impact on society. Improvement in secondary school preparation of potential college students is not something that takes place overnight or in all high schools. To insist that college-age and older students return to high school for remediation is not realistic, either psychologically or financially, for the schools or for the students. The alternative of accepting unprepared students and inflating grades would undermine the benefits of higher education to both students and society. The alternative of not admitting students who need remediation would educationally disenfranchise approximately one-third of entering college students. At the very time when the need for more and more adequate education as a condition not just of social equity but of national productivity and competitiveness (Carnevale, Gainer, and Meltzer, n.d.) is particularly acute, when as a result of demographic changes the structure of the work force for the twenty-first century will be considerably different from that of today, when the need to increase minority participation in all levels of society is essential to social welfare, to propose either seriously curtailing or cutting out remedial or developmental work in colleges is a recipe for social and economic disaster.

From the standpoint of equity, the first part of the admonition of the National Commission on the Role and Future of State Colleges and Universities (1986) is very much to the point: "In a society in which knowledge is a source of wealth, deprivation of access to higher education is a form of bondage" (p. 14). From an economic, social, and political standpoint, the second part of the quotation is equally relevant: "The social, economic, political, and cultural complexity of contemporary America requires a much higher level of education for everyone than was before envisioned." Looked at in this context, remedial or developmental education is neither a luxury nor a condescension but a necessity for higher education in the present and for some time to come. It should not be considered as an addendum assigned to adjunct, part-time, or less qualified faculty. One can expect and should in fact demand quality as much in remedial or developmental programs as in any other programs, for it is in such programs that achieving the educational objectives is in many ways a precondition of quality throughout the institution and system. But this means recognizing and developing the continuity between developmental programs and subsequent programs. It means, as the National Institute for Education study group points out, that "remedial courses should be accompanied by a variety of means (including support groups and greater use of peer tutors) to enhance students' self-esteem, academic identity, and sense of direction in life" (Study Group on the Conditions of Excellence in American Higher Education, 1984, p. 48).

It also means a need for effective use of technologies in helping students and counselors to identify deficiencies and strengths and to build appropriate programs. This again is one of the exciting aspects of the Adult Guidance and Counseling System utilizing education information centers (Module IV) and even the advisory potential in the library network system (Module VI) in Oklahoma. Through providing not only advice but video courses, the Intermountain Community Learning and Information Services Project extends help to people in isolated rural communities in Utah, Colorado, Wyoming, and Montana. The Personal Adult Learning Services Lab at the University of Georgia provides such help to adults seeking new educational opportunities. All four of these projects illustrate the importance of developmental education for students of all ages. Effective use of technology in support of remediation should also be as important for entering freshmen on campus as for older and part-time students.

To be effective, remedial programs must be adequately funded. The tendency in some states not to fund remedial programs or not to count students in remedial programs as part of the full-time-equivalent funding formula (where such formulas persist) means either that the programs are not offered or that the other regular programs suffer as funds are diverted into remedial programs and/or that the courses are taught by the least experienced, least prepared members of the faculty. Under such circumstances, it is not surprising that the programs are resented, are less than successful, and carry with them the stigma that Gladys Hardy (1988) refers to not only for minorities but for other students as well. The SREB report on remedial education states that the faculty involved should be specifically trained and qualified in remedial and developmental techniques and "should be recognized fully by the department and institution" (Southern Regional Education Board, 1988, p. 7). As to funding, the report insists that "Funding for remedial/developmental programs should reflect the fact that it can require comparatively greater efforts and costs to develop instruction and programs for teaching students who are academically deficient. Funding should at least be at a level commensurate with lower-division non-remedial courses and students" (p. 6). Both the Southern Regional Education Board (1988, p. 10) and the ECS insist that it is a state responsibility at public institutions to provide explicit and adequate funding for the purpose. The ECS report adds that "These programs are necessary regardless of institutional mission or selectivity; a student in a major research university may be strong in mathematics but need remedial work in writing, for example" (Education Commission of the States, 1988, p. 25). Finally, effective remediation requires diagnostic testing, counseling, and placement, all of which cost money. Perhaps the critical question is not whether the states, the institutions, and the public can afford remedial and developmental programs but whether they can afford not to have them.

One further remedial and developmental education issue is whether such courses or programs should give college credit. It seems clear that credit for such courses should not be accepted as a substitute for other degree requirements and expectations. That they are part of the requirements for obtaining a degree for those people who need them or must take them is indeed the case. There may be some reinforcement advantages in specifying credit for such courses or programs; specifying them as noncredit courses may indicate to students taking them that they are only marking time and may confuse such courses with the highly important legitimate areas of noncredit courses we discussed earlier, including those in continuing professional education. If, however, as we suggested in discussing the High Admissions Standards Myth, what is critical is the exit requirements — what one is supposed to have accomplished — rather than the admissions requirements, then unless one holds to a rigid credit-hour- or time-based degree structure, whether remedial and developmental education is counted as credit toward a degree is somewhat irrelevant. It is not just how far a person has come but the skills and knowledge actually attained that should constitute the conditions or requirements for graduation.

It seems apparent that without remedial and developmental programs, access and equity are severely limited, far beyond what we can afford in the twenty-first century, and quality becomes a progressively elitist attainment. To the contrary, we would strongly argue that high quality should be as characteristic of remedial programs as of doctoral programs and for most institutions must be an essential part of total institutional quality.

The Value-Added Myth

The concept of "value added" as a key to higher education quality and accomplishment in assessing students and institutions is particularly attractive to those concerned with equity. It complements the concept involved in remedial or developmental education that even unprepared people with the interest and potential to benefit from postsecondary education should have the opportunity to do so and the requisite help to overcome their deficiencies. What is important is what happens to students, what skills are attained, what knowledge is mastered, what talents have been developed.

At one of the Oklahoma leadership seminars, Alexander Astin characterized the value-added position as follows: "True excellence lies in the institution's ability to have a favorable impact to enhance the intellectual and scholarly development of the student to make a positive difference in a student's life. The most excellent institutions in this view are those that have the greatest impact, or add the greatest value, as economists would say, to the student's knowledge or personal development" (Astin, 1986, p. 17). If one rejects the reputational and resources views of quality on the grounds that they do not yield information about how effective an institution is in educating its students or helping them to realize their potential, then the value-added position is clearly integral to any adequate definition or conception of institutional educational quality. Astin's "talent development" view of educational excellence or quality is a modified form of the value-added position (see Chapter Five). Collegiate interest in value-added approaches has substantially increased, particularly in relation to curricular reviews. *Campus Trends, 1987* (El-Khawas, 1987) reported that although in such curricular reviews prior to 1987, only 9 percent of institutions used "value-added" approaches, in 1987 some 36 percent of institutions undertaking such reviews were considering using them (p. 6).

As Astin notes, effective value-added measurement can be a time-consuming and expensive method of determining quality. It requires initial assessment and testing to determine the base from which the student starts, with follow-up assessment over time to determine the extent of student achievement or accomplishment. At the least, it involves determining how the student's intellectual skills and knowledge have increased; it may also involve assessing changes in interests, aspirations, and personal values and attitudes (Astin, 1982, p. 12). This information about progress needs to be fed back to the student and used in his or her further educational planning and actions. In some of the most often cited cases, such as Alverno and Northeast Missouri, such continuing student awareness of progress becomes a crucial part of the educational process itself (National Governors' Association, 1986, p. 156). Both Alverno and Northeast Missouri involve elaborate and well-developed systems geared to value-added assessment considerations. Without going as far as these institutions, and quite apart from cost, some determination of the extent to which student and institutional educational objectives are being attained — the extent of educational development beyond the point of entry — is essential to institutional and program quality determination.

There are, however, additional characteristics of the value-added approach that directly involve the question of equity in at least two senses. The first and positive factor is that the emphasis is placed on individual advancement and improvement regardless of background, rather than on prior knowledge as such. Value added does not presuppose liberal or open admissions policies but is clearly compatible with them and is attractive to institutions with such policies. The question of value added is in fact relevant to all students but is perhaps particularly critical for underprepared and disadvantaged students.

The second characteristic, however, underlines a real danger in value-added approaches, one that has at least the potential for perpetuating inequality and that reflects the concerns expressed in our discussions of the Remedial Education and Higher Admissions Standards Myths about the difference between admissions and exit requirements. While it may also apply to groups, value added is basically individual, the progress made beyond the starting point by a particular student. The weaker the student's background, the more value will need to be added before he or she reaches a level of achievement commensurate with the skills, competencies, and knowledge required by the program, course, or field in question and thus its educational objectives. The danger lies in assuming that it is the progress the student has made per se rather than the achievement of the objectives that is important in determining educational credentials.

Such a view can too quickly lead to a phenomenon not unlike social promotion on the elementary and secondary levels. Progress should indeed be recognized, but when the progress toward objectives is confused with achievement of the objectives or progress alone is conceived of as the desired primary objective, the end result is likely to be a perpetuation of differences in levels of accomplishment and the inequity with which one started. While there may be few if any institutions that would explicitly acknowledge that they are operating on an assumption of value added in this sense, some institutions do tend to lower expectations or standards for graduation or program completion on the assumption, usually implicit rather than explicit, that the lower standards are all that can be expected given the students' backgrounds. Unfortunately, this has sometimes been explicitly advocated in academic programs for students involved in intercollegiate athletics. To some extent, remedial and developmental programs are designed to help resist such temptations.

There is also the related matter of reasonable public expectations about the competence of college graduates. While

David Webster of the University of Pennsylvania is primarily concerned with institutional rankings, he points out that value-added assessments that show how much student groups have learned over time "ignore the fact that in many cases the most important outcome is the end-point ability of the student we graduate — not how much he or she has learned since some point in time. In selecting a heart surgeon, for example, most people will insist on a fully competent practitioner, not the one who improved most since his or her first day of medical school" (Webster, 1986, p. 41).

To avoid the relativistic side of the value-added position, Astin (1986) includes as one of the critical factors in his talent-development version of the value-added view high institutional and program expectations. Such expectations, he insists, "include graduation requirements, that is the 'what' of learning and standards, a category of expectation that refers to the level of performance, the 'how well' of learning as well." He adds, "student performance clearly rises to these expectations and students respond positively to reasonable challenges. When we expect too little we seldom get disappointed" (p. 20). Northeast Missouri reinforces its value-added program with a comprehensive examination in the major field, required of all seniors. Alverno insists that "learners have a sense of what they are setting out to learn, a statement of explicit standards they must meet, and a way of seeing what they have learned" (Loacker, Cromwell, and O'Brien, 1985, p. 47).

As with assessment in general, there is some danger in relying too heavily on external examinations and quantitative results in determining value added. Among the tests frequently used as measures of the student's abilities on entrance are the SAT and the ACT. At the completion end of the program, the Educational Testing Service's Graduate Record Examination and ACT's College Outcomes Measurement Project Test (COMP) can be used, the latter primarily measuring general education knowledge and skills and sometimes used prior to graduation. In addition, entrance examinations for professional education in special fields, such as the MCAT and the LSAT, may be used. While there is nothing wrong with such tests, they have serious limitations as means of determining "value added" in any particular case. They may be, as Webster (1986) points out, only more or less related to the curriculum and educational objectives of the institution in question (p. 41) and thus may or may not give an accurate picture of what has been learned. There is also the danger of teaching specifically for the tests. Perhaps more seriously, a number of the "values" added and even skills acquired may not be quantitatively determinable by such tests. The results may at least need to be modified by interviews and skill demonstrations.

The most serious problem with value added as a means of reinforcing equity or of determining quality is not that it is wrong but that it is incomplete. To the extent that the primary concern in value-added approaches is to demonstrate and encourage student accomplishment, it is an integral part also of demonstrating institutional effectiveness and can be of major importance in furthering equity by encouraging continuing achievement regardless of adequacy of preparation or of ethnic or economic background. However, to reinforce accomplishment of either of these, value-added approaches must be placed in a context of clearly defined educational objectives or standards relevant to the type and level of preparation involved. This includes achieving the skills and knowledge relevant to the field or the profession concerned. This again reinforces the importance of clearly defined objectives, standards, or levels of accomplishment as exit or completion requirements, in contrast to entrance requirements, as a condition of equity, including providing the reinforcement necessary to their achievement. Placed in such a context of well-defined objectives with emphasis not only on progress toward those objectives but on achievement of them, value added is an integral part of equity and quality.

Summary

The two primary goals of the American higher education system today, with roots going back to the eighteenth century, are quality and equity—this in contrast to most other countries.

While one or the other of these has tended to dominate in particular historical periods (including recent history), the basic question that must be addressed if we are to meet changing demographic, social, economic, and political conditions, including the demand for a more highly educated work force and citizenry, is whether the two are antithetical or compatible — whether, in fact, we can sacrifice either or whether they require each other.

It would appear that some views of quality are in fact antithetical to equity, particularly those based primarily on reputation and resources. In turn, if equity is conceived of solely in terms of access, it may in fact undermine quality. On the other hand, if quality is conceived of in terms of effective use of resources to achieve appropriate educational objectives and equity is recognized as involving considerably more than access, then it becomes clear that equity does in fact require high quality in higher education programs — and, given the variety of higher education objectives related to social needs, fulfillment of these objectives and thus of quality depends on equity.

Access is an essential but not a sufficient condition of equity. Equity in addition involves at least the following:

1. Early identification of student potential and encouragement to actualize that potential.
2. Not just more places but equality of opportunity in the light of ability and interest. Equity is not served by using a revolving door or tracking students of any age into particular institutions and programs without regard to their interests and abilities.
3. A diverse system of postsecondary education capable of meeting multiple educational interests, needs, and opportunities.
4. Adequate information and counseling about the types of higher education opportunities that are available and their relevance to student interests, abilities, and needs.
5. A supportive environment for all students.
6. The kind of financial support that changes access from an empty gesture to real opportunity.

7. Assurance that whatever the program a student enters, from
    developmental to graduate, and regardless of subject area,
    it is a high-quality program.

Further, to the extent that the achievement of a program's or
institution's appropriate educational objectives depends on identifying students' potential for achievement, quality also requires
equity.

The recognition of the reciprocal relationship between
equity and quality has implications in related areas. For one
thing, raising admissions standards alone will not achieve either
quality or equity. Far more important are completion or exit
requirements. To compromise these is to perpetuate inequality. In addition, developmental or remedial education is not a
luxury but a necessity if the basic educational needs of the country for the next decades are to be met. This is a condition not
only of equity but very possibly of national survival. But to be
effective, remedial or developmental education needs to reinforce student self-esteem; to be staffed by qualified, expert faculty; to provide adequate diagnosis and counseling; and to be
adequately funded. We cannot afford anything less. Thus, to
fulfill its function, to reinforce equity, remedial or developmental
education must be high-quality education.

All of these factors point to the critical importance of a
value-added approach to student encouragement and accomplishment, even to the relevance of value added to an adequate
conception of educational quality. But they also point to the fact
that value added is not a sufficient condition of educational quality, student accomplishment, or equity. To confuse progress
toward accomplishment of educational objectives with achievement of those objectives can itself perpetuate inequality. Placed
within a context of clearly defined educational objectives and
with emphasis not only on progress toward but on achieving
those objectives, value added can be an integral part of equity
and quality; in fact, it comes close then to defining quality itself.

7

The Technology Threat

It is almost a cliché at this point to suggest that one of the most remarkable occurrences of the last half of the twentieth century has been the information revolution and the development of the technology that not only has made this revolution possible but is an integral part of it. Some of the technologies — television and the earlier forms of computers — have been around for some time, but their rapid development, their increasing complexity yet simplification and extension of use, and their progressive adaption in wider ranges of industrial, business, individual, and social functions in the last fifteen or twenty years is unprecedented. This information-technology revolution is to the last half of the twentieth century and the twenty-first century what the Industrial Revolution was to the nineteenth century and the first half of the twentieth century.

This technological development obviously has had considerable impact on some aspects of higher education, and its potential for further impact is almost unlimited. To date, that impact has perhaps been most direct and pervasive in higher education administration and management and in research. The development has, however, also given rise to new academic fields, such as computer science, and has had some impact, experimentally at least, on teaching and learning. Computer lit-

209

eracy is on the way to becoming one of the basic skills expected of most college graduates. Whether, however, the technology has brought about major or extended changes in higher education instruction for most students and professors is another matter.

It is clear that technological developments have the potential for revolutionizing teaching and learning. A number of higher education institutions and even systems have made considerable progress in this direction. For example, the use of computers in instruction as well as research at places such as Carnegie-Mellon, MIT, and Brown seems at this point to be considerably beyond the experimental stage (Turner, 1989, p. A9). The potential not just of computers but of the whole range of applicable technologies to further higher education learning objectives is well stated by Donald R. McNeil (1988) who has long been a pioneer and leader in attempting to integrate technology with teaching and learning: "For education, technology can improve access, raise quality, update the knowledge pool, and facilitate research. It can help individualize instruction, offer educational opportunity at the time and place convenient to the learner, provide rapid feedback, furnish access to remote databases, and enhance counseling and evaluation. Telecourses, video conferencing, the video disc, the electronic blackboard, computer networking and conference telephone hookups, and voice-data transmission can be used separately or together to modify the delivery system" (p. 2). Yet, given the advanced state of the technologies, the many experiments, and even the few relatively well-established programs using the various technologies separately or in combination, there remains for major sections of higher education a real gap between the potential uses of technology and their actualization.

McNeil (1989b) rightly questions why the educational use of integrated technologies remains primarily experimental and restricted to relatively few institutions or even departments within institutions: "Why then is the actual impact on higher education so minimal? Why do so few of the 12.5 million students and 400,000 faculty members in American colleges and universities actually use the technologies available to them?"

(p. A44). To try to get at answers to the question, to identify some of the obstacles to more effective use of technologies, and to suggest ways of overcoming them, McNeil, under the egis of the Academy for Educational Development, called together a group of twenty-eight leaders in the uses of technology in higher education for a conference called the Technology Round Table in December of 1988 (McNeil, 1990). Prior to the conference, Raymond Lewis and Milan Wall (1988) developed an analysis of a series of primary obstacles to "appropriate and effective institutional uses of information technologies" (p. 2). They identified three general types of obstacles related to on-campus and off-campus learning: technical obstacles — those related to the adequacy or inadequacy of the technology itself, structural obstacles — obstacles related to the policies and procedures of colleges, universities, and states; and attitudinal obstacles on the part of faculty, students, and administrators concerned with higher education and its functioning. In the course of the analysis and the round-table discussion, it became obvious that the three types of obstacles are intimately connected, overlapping, and to some extent causally related to each other. The attitudinal obstacles specifically tend to inhibit use of technologies that would enhance higher education effectiveness.

Technical obstacles can be overcome. In fact, considerable progress in reducing some of the technical obstacles has taken place in the past few years (McNeil, 1988, pp. 4–5). McNeil points out that, while problems still remain, computers on the whole have become considerably more user friendly even since 1985. While standardization of hardware and software among computer companies is highly unlikely, computers are being made more compatible with each other, partly as a result of user demand. Earlier complaints about the inadequacy and low quality of software are being alleviated as more good software continues to come into the market.

Access has been considerably increased through the formation of telecommunications consortia, the development and experience of state telecommunications networks, and the creation of regional networks such as the Intermountain Community Learning and Information Services Program. Statewide telecommunications systems have existed for some time in such states as Indiana, Kentucky, Alaska, Wisconsin, Oklahoma, and Kansas. In Oklahoma, the further development of the statewide telecommunications network is in many respects the key to integrating the various modules of the Oklahoma Network for Continuing Higher Education. Access through consortia and networks has been progressively facilitated by such technical improvements as the continuing development of multichannel cable systems, further evolution of direct broadcast satellite facilities, increased use of fiber optics, growth in networking among computers, and further expansion of microwave instruction television fixed services (ITFS) systems, such as the Oklahoma talk-back television system (McNeil, 1988, p. 5).

The technical obstacles reflect the state of the art; ironically, the rapidity of changes in technology constitutes one of the obstacles. No sooner is a system or new technology installed than it may be out of date and its installation a costly mistake (Lewis and Wall, 1988, pp. 4–5). However, the very dynamics of the field provide reasonable expectations that technical obstacles can be progressively overcome. The structural obstacles are related to policies and procedures or the lack of them in colleges and universities and, in some cases, states. Structural obstacles include such matters as traditional budgeting procedures, lack of incentives, lack of adequate training, poor support services, and lack of access or disproportionate access in particular academic fields or programs. Bureaucratic conditions may reflect as well as cause attitudinal obstacles. Overcoming structural obstacles may well depend on changing administration as well as faculty attitudinal obstacles.

Lewis and Wall (1988) describe some illustrative concerns that become attitudinal obstacles: "Apprehension about change, fear of technically complex devices, concerns about job security, resistance to being in the learning mode, worry that students are too uncomfortable with new devices, skepticism about claims made in the name of technology, and previous negative experiences are among the many attitudes that slow the pace of technological advancement in academia" (p. 8). These attitudes, induced in part at least by technical and structural obstacles, are related to and justified by certain assumptions held by some faculty and shared by some students and administrators. These assumptions constitute beliefs that have some basis in fact and underline certain cautions. But taken as matters of fact, these assumptions become myths that in some cases inhibit the very realization of the goals and objectives of those who hold them.

The Sanctity of the Classroom Myth

The Sanctity of the Classroom Myth has both its more naive and its more sophisticated aspects. That the classroom is the unique domain of the professor, which others do not enter without an invitation or expressed permission, has been a long-standing custom and academic prerogative in most collegiate institutions. This concept applies not just to the physical place of the class but to the autonomy of the instructor in developing and presenting the subject matter, both content and instructional mode. Even when a common syllabus is used in multiple sessions of the same course but taught by different instructors, how the individual instructor develops the material in the syllabus is usually considered the prerogative of that instructor.

Obviously, there are exceptions. In the case of multiple sections, comparability may be encouraged by a common syllabus and staff conferences and in some cases by common examinations. Instructors in individual courses may seek advice and help from those with more experience, including asking them to sit in and critique their teaching approaches as well as content development. Institutions may provide professional development activities to increase teaching effectiveness, including videotaping of classroom performance for later critiquing by the instructor and his or her peers. An effective teaching assistant program may well include class visitations and review and suggestions by senior faculty. The current emphasis on assessment places a premium on outcomes or results and thus on evidence of classroom effectiveness. Yet these seeming exceptions tend in most cases to be voluntary, to be designed to strengthen the teaching effectiveness of the instructor, and to reinforce the instructor's classroom authority and control. Anything that seems to threaten the authority of the instructor, it can be argued, undermines his or her role and teaching effectiveness and student respect for the professional expertise and authority within the academic field.

While this tendency might seem to reflect an overconcern with turf and resistance to pedagogical change, it is also clearly related to at least two concepts fundamental to collegiate instructional and research integrity: academic freedom and the authority derived from knowledge or expertise in a field. The second in many respects is what higher education is all about; the first is a condition of its attainment. The argument can be made that when the new technologies, as valuable as they may be for administrative and even research purposes, are introduced into the classroom, they can and perhaps inevitably do change the nature of the classroom in such a way as to undermine the authority of the instructor and to limit the instructor's freedom to develop the course as he or she sees fit. It should be recognized that some faculty are predisposed against further use of technologies on the basis of disappointment engendered by past claims for technology that have not materialized, their own negative experiences with some forms of technology, limitations on the availability and quality of software, and what frequently has been limited access to the technologies by students and even the instructors themselves.

Far more serious, however, than such predispositions are aspects of these technologies that appear to some people, whether correctly or not, to diminish the instructor's central role and authority in the instructional process. First and most serious of these is the perception that the faculty member no longer is primarily responsible for developing or delivering his or her own material but must work in collaboration with technicians and instructional designers regardless of what technologies are involved. David Grossman (1987) points out that "Faculty who embark upon course development for technological delivery are often in for a rude awakening. They find that they are submerged in the course developmental process, taking a back seat to production and technical personnel. Faculty are relegated to the role of content consultant while the media course takes on a life of its own" (p. 9). Further, as Lewis and Wall (1988) point out, it seems to many that such technology "removes from faculty members their control of their intellectual property as their course is transferred to video or some other technology" (p. 9).

Second, with the new technologies, not just course development but instructional effectiveness depends not only and in some cases not even primarily on the instructor but on support personnel and services and on the equipment itself. A breakdown in the delivery system ends or delays instruction and is not under the control of the instructor in the classroom. Further, effective use, particularly of computer systems, depends on training and technical assistance for faculty and students alike. If such training is not provided or is inadequate, the technology may block rather than assist instruction.

Third, rather than freeing faculty time for research, course content development, and other activities, use of technologies actually increases an instructor's time commitment — sometimes to the detriment of content development itself. Time is essential to becoming proficient in the use of the technology, and considerably more time is continually required for planning, production, and follow-up than in the traditional classroom. "Most faculty members report that use of technologies generally takes more of their time than teaching by conventional methods. This is particularly true for instructors who develop their own software or programming materials. Faculty members who are developing software almost universally report that they are devoting substantial blocks of time for which they receive no additional compensation" (Lewis and Wall, 1988, p. 18).

Fourth, even with the additional faculty time commitment rquired, the end result of using the new technologies is very likely to be that the instructor, rather than "professing," becomes a facilitator, that the class dynamics are changed. The instructor becomes one resource among many, and his or her function becomes guiding students to the appropriate resources provided by and through the technologies. Interestingly enough, the instructor's relationship to students in the learning process is likely to be heightened and the communication more direct and two-way—even one on one—than in the traditional lecture class-room. This is particularly the case with computer conferencing and teleconferencing, although it is obviously much less so with prepackaged telecourses. The distinction between the physically present and the remote student is diminished or even disappears. But this clearly requires a rather radical change from the older conception of the classroom as inviolate and the lecture as the primary vehicle of instruction.

In addition to these more obvious inhibiting factors, there are a series of more subtle aspects of the new technologies that seem to present a danger of limiting the manner, scope, presentation, and even range of subject matter of instruction. According to Lynton and Elman (1987), one of these that is particularly applicable to computers is the tendency "to place a premium on simplicity, on direct causal relationships, on unambiguous, yes or no situations, on hard facts and figures" (p. 129). Even Derek Bok, former president of Harvard University, questions the ability of computers to "contribute much to the learning of open-ended subjects like moral philosophy, religion, historical interpretation, literary criticism, or social theory—fields of knowledge that can not be reduced to formal rules and procedures" (cited in Lynton and Elman, 1987, pp. 129–130). Lynton and Elman suggest that one of the major advantages of the new technology, its tremendous capacity for information retrieval, may constitute an additional limitation, for it "places a premium on the accumulation rather than the selection of information, on data rather than on the interpretation and synthesis" (p. 130).

In relation to prepackaged courses, whether television courses or computer-assisted courses, David Grossman, who directs the University of Minnesota Independent Study Program, warns particularly against the dangers of using such packages for introductory courses. To do so, he believes, tends to lead to the "trivialization of instruction" (Grossman, 1987, pp. 5–6) by removing the live instructor and replacing the kind of instruction that is the "creative dynamic process which has an impact on the life of the mind" with standardized machine presentations and further reducing faculty instructional involvement. He also suggests that as such courses are used more widely, there is a real danger of homogenization and loss of timeliness of instruction.

All of these constitute important cautions. There is little question that failure to take some of these cautions into account in the past has been one of the factors that have inhibited greater realization of the educational potential of the technologies themselves. Concern about the sanctity of the classroom is real. The concern for academic freedom and autonomy and the empowering function of knowledge and skills, on which the concept of the sanctity of the classroom in its best form rests, is fundamental to higher education itself. What seems to be amiss is that, carried to extremes, these concerns seem themselves to involve questionable assumptions and confusions.

One of these assumptions, sometimes implicit and at other times explicit, is the view that the classroom must be a single physical place, preferably on campus, with an instructor lecturing to students, and that this is somehow the ideal learning situation. This is at least implicit in the concern that the faculty member is no longer primarily or solely responsible for what takes place and becomes a facilitator rather than a "professor." Somewhat ironically, in the needs assessment survey of academic leaders carried out in 1986–87 in connection with Module II, on program development, of the Oklahoma Project, the traditional classroom setting was overwhelmingly preferred by the "academic leaders" for both credit and noncredit course work. Even independent study, while acceptable, was not preferred, and televised instruction and computer-assisted instruction were at best viewed as "reluctantly acceptable" (Oklahoma Network of Continuing Higher Education, 1987a, vol. 1, p. 41). These reactions come in spite of the fact that, quite apart from current technologies, there have long been alternative teaching and learning approaches that do not involve the traditional classroom or lecture. Tutorial and independent study and even correspondence study are cases in point.

What the new technologies are capable of doing is literally indefinitely extending the "classroom" as the place of learning and in the process actually increasing the interaction between student and faculty. In connection with computer conferencing,

for example, McNeil (1989c) points out that "the most powerful argument for computer conferencing rests . . . on its ability
to empower the professor and students to interact with each other
rapidly and extemporaneously, to gather around the electronic
table those people who wish to participate and . . . communi-
cate with anyone else in the group — each doing so at his or her
convenience" (p. 18). The various aspects of telecommunications and computers particularly have opened new horizons in
teaching and, as Lynton and Elman (1987) point out, brought
about "renewed attention to the process of learning and teaching" (p. 122) itself.

Quite obviously, the technologies include far more than
computers and computer conferencing. Two-way video, talk-
back television, and satellite conferencing all provide both for
extending the classroom and for enhancing or enriching the
learning experience through visual and audio interchange. The
professor, even if only as a facilitator, is able not only to shape
the content of the course or program and provide the relevant
information but also to make available a far wider range of
resources to reinforce and add to the substance and the excite-
ment of the subject than has ever before been the case. This,
however, suggests another confusion among the concerns. The
various technologies are different, and both their potentials and
their limitations differ. It is far too easy to assume that a critique of one type of technology somehow applies to all technologies. A recognition of the limitations of packaged telecourses
has little relevance for interactive videodiscs. Recognizing what
appears to be the tendencies of certain types of computer-assisted
instruction to rely more heavily on simplified and quantitative
information may have little relevance for computer conferencing, Derek Bok to the contrary not withstanding. What is important is to recognize both the potential and the limitations
of the various technologies and at the same time see how they
can reinforce each other.

All of this points to a fundamental issue that is relevant
to the real "sanctity" of the classroom, now viewed not in terms
of fear of external interference but in terms of the integrity of
the teaching-learning process. This is the question of whether

in some sense the academic content is manipulated to demonstrate the technology or whether the technology is used to supplement and enrich instruction and its academic content. In the past, the technology has far too frequently come first, has even been implemented without faculty involvement or academic content development until after the fact. The result might be described as technology in search of content and use. Such cart-before-the-horse situations have at least contributed to the feeling that technologies invade rather than support the classroom and that they weaken its integrity.

In the early 1970s, the State University of Nebraska (SUN) project came close to illustrating the perils of developing a technology-based program without including the faculty in the development of its academic content in the planning and early development stages. Inspired by the announcement that the British were inaugurating an open university, D. B. Varner, then president of the University of Nebraska, undertook in 1971 the development of a similar program in the Middle West using the Nebraska educational television network. The appropriate mechanisms were put into place; the nominal support of the presidents of the Big Eight Athletic Conference was obtained; the U.S. Office of Education and subsequently the newly formed National Institute for Education provided financial support; and SUN became the University of Mid-America. Although teams of specialists, professors, producers, and instructional designers were enlisted, the faculty at the University of Nebraska was virtually ignored, with the result that SUN did not have the support and involvement of the academic community itself. As a result, by 1974 it had to be restructured (McNeil and Wall, 1983, pp. 49–50).

The crucial issue seems to be ensuring that the decision to use technology and the selection of the appropriate type of technology are based on the educational objectives and the problem or problems to be solved. The participants in the Round Table on Technology and Higher Education agreed "that technology, if used properly and appropriately, could enhance the quality of instruction either on campus or off campus . . . [T]echnology should not be a solution going in search of a problem,

but . . . identification of the problem should come first with identification of appropriate technologies to use to solve the problem coming next" (McNeil, 1990, p. 4). The technologies should
be used to supplement and enrich education and the learning
process in the light of the academic educational objectives. This
is what the NIE study group was driving at in its insistence that
"administrators and faculty must plan more carefully for the introduction and application of learning technologies so as to enhance the quality of undergraduate learning, and to foster interaction between students and faculty and among students" (Study
Group on the Conditions of Excellence in American Higher Education, 1984, p. 29).

McNeil (1985) thus summarizes the situation: "For educators to use technology effectively, they must relate each specific
technology or combination of technologies to what they hope to
accomplish. Their objectives must come first" (p. 8). To the extent
that this is the case, then, rather than undermining or destroying
the "sanctity of the classroom," the new technologies reinforce and
extend it. But in this case, "sanctity" is conceived of not in terms of
classroom isolation but in terms of the integrity of the learning
process itself. Through effective use of the appropriate technologies, the integrity of the learning process can be extended to the
wider community, to the five-sixths of the current students who
are not full-time resident eighteen- to twenty-one-year-olds, to the
various groups for whom postsecondary education is more crucial
than ever before. At the same time, technologies can enhance
the content of traditional classes. It thus makes the extended
university or college of Lynton and Elman (1987) a practical reality: "It is very evident that the combination of computerization
and telecommunications quite literally eliminates the physical
boundaries of the university and enables it in principle to extend many of its functions to any desired location while at the
same time maintaining electronically, considerable contact and
communication with on-campus faculty" (p. 129).

The Threatened Faculty Myth

The close relationship between the Threatened Faculty
Myth and the Sanctity of the Classroom Myth is fairly obvious.

The faculty is likely to feel threatened whenever the instructional process and what is perceived as the integrity of the learning process are threatened. Thus, it seems to follow that if the various technologies are used to enhance or strengthen teaching and learning, are chosen and developed in the light of sound educational objectives, and are used to supplement rather than replace the function of the instructor, then the feeling of being threatened would diminish or disappear. To some extent and for some faculty, this may well be the case. For some, however, the feeling of threat is unfortunately not so easily dissipated. The threat for some faculty members seems to lie in the technologies themselves, in a feeling of inadequacy related to the need to master new techniques and approaches, even in concern by some faculty that "they will be embarrassed by a master teacher's input" (McNeil, 1985, p. 13). In a few cases, the threat may involve a fear of change itself. In still other cases, the fear may persist that the technologies will make at least some faculty superfluous and thus threaten employment.

It is a fact that earlier concerns about television courses replacing faculty turned out to be groundless. To the extent that television courses have been included as a regular part of the curriculum, they have in fact supplemented rather than replaced faculty. Faculty have been involved in their production, in academic course guidance, and in assessment of student accomplishment. Television courses available to the wider community for which credit has been granted by particular colleges have reached a broader clientele, many of whom would not have been served otherwise but who are encouraged to continue their education at the institution in question. As for computer conferencing, computer-assisted instruction, or use of computers in general, there is, as McNeil (1989a, p. 8) points out, little or no evidence that these have resulted in the elimination of any faculty position to date. In fact, as noted earlier, the technologies, including development of computer software, place additional demands on faculty time and thus in the short run may call for faculty reinforcement rather than reduction.

If, in spite of expectations to the contrary, the various technologies and their increased sophistication have not endangered faculty positions, and if most of the other fears can be diminished through experience or overcome through faculty development, is the Threatened Faculty Myth something that can be dismissed as likely to disappear? The answer to this question is not quite as obvious as on the surface it might seem. The reason for this is a changing set of circumstances that place the technologies in a somewhat different perspective, which may paradoxically in the short run increase some faculty anxieties but may in the long term alleviate them. These changing circumstances are both political and economic. One of these is the public and political concern with the increasing costs of higher education and a resulting perceived need for cost containment. This has resulted in a growing call for increased higher education productivity to deal not only with cost containment but also with the increasing demand for higher education resulting from changing demographic and social conditions. Technology may well be a key factor in resolving the problems growing out of the circumstances.

Cost containment does carry with it the threat of retrenchment and reduction in force. It also carries with it a concern for increasing faculty productivity. One way to increase such productivity is through broader and more effective utilization of technologies. Thus, for example, *Policy Perspectives,* published by the Higher Education Research Program (1989b) at the University of Pennsylvania, argues that "Increasingly, colleges and universities will turn to technology as well as part-time and adjunct faculty, many of whom will not have been trained as research scholars. Institutions will learn from necessity how to make do with fewer faculty" (p. 6).

While increased productivity through technologies is perhaps more obvious in engineering and the sciences, it is not limited to these. Terry Gildea (1987) of Hewlett-Packard insists that "we need to use the same technologies in teaching humanities" (p. 6).

At first glance, it would appear to some faculty that the technologies would further contribute to institutional ability to reduce faculty without seriously curtailing instruction and services. At the very least, the technologies would decrease the need for faculty expansion. Thus, the uneasiness and feeling of threat in relation to the technologies tends to continue. It may, however, just be the case that, instead of constituting a threat, the technologies provide an opportunity for dealing with the cost-containment issue without faculty curtailment and may thus be part of the answer rather than part of the problem. Admittedly, they may reduce the need for major faculty additions, but with the faculty shortages expected to occur in the late 1990s, such an increase in productivity may be an advantage rather than a peril. In anticipation of the current concern with cost containment, Gildea argued in 1987 that "the solution boils down to getting more output from the same resources; what those of us in industry call productivity improvements. The way to free faculty time for self-improvement is to find ways to teach more per hour. The way to find more money for faculty salaries is to make each faculty member more productive" (p. 6). Gildea also notes that this is not an argument easily sold to faculties.

One needs to add to the picture the fact that, in spite of some aspects of the current political scene, there is a general recognition even within the political community, particularly at the state level, of the need for broader postsecondary educational opportunity, for meeting the needs of older students, and for providing an increasingly educated and adaptable work force. Further, these objectives need to be accomplished without reproducing every program at every institution. They can be obtained through program and faculty sharing via the new technologies while maintaining the unique mission and objectives of the various institutions in the state or system. Given these factors, it would appear that the increased productivity potential provided by the new technologies will reinforce rather than threaten the role, importance, and job security of faculty in the period ahead.

The Collegiate Service Station Myth

The charge that colleges and universities have become supermarkets or service stations offering whatever will sell is not particularly new. From the introduction of the elective system in the late nineteenth century, critics have periodically charged that the curriculum has become a kind of smorgasbord where one picks and chooses courses rather than follows a coherent program. The report of the National Commission on the Role and Future of State Colleges and Universities (1986) rather nicely summarized what it considers to be the thrust of its predecessor reports (those of the National Endowment for the Humanities, the Association of American Colleges, and the National Institute for Education) as follows: "American colleges and universities have become too utilitarian, too vocational in their orientation, too parochial in their outlook, with their curricula incoherent and in a state of disarray. Campuses have become 'supermarkets,' the critics charged, with narrow specialties the order of the day" (p. 28).

Robert Zemsky (1988) of the University of Pennsylvania has phrased the matter somewhat differently: "Institutions of higher education are becoming, and in the case of large research universities, have already become, complex service bureaus" (p. 47). Finally, in discussing commuting students in particular, the Association of American Colleges (1988) suggests in its second report, *A New Vitality in General Education,* that "many commuting students see their institution as a service station, and they may view its efforts to encourage their [broader] development as interference" (p. 45).

While none of the above statements is specifically directed at the impact of technologies, if the service-station perception is present among commuters, it may be further exacerbated for people involved in long-distance learning via technologies. The possibility of picking and choosing among credit courses and programs offered through television, audio, computers, and correspondence by students of whatever age without completing a degree or even developing a coherent sequence of experiences is likely to be increased. When to these multiple choices are added noncredit courses, counseling, and data-base access, the variety of services offered, many of them only indirectly (if at all) related to instruction, is as Zemsky (1988) suggests, considerable.

The technologies will continue to play a major role in increasing access, in extending the classroom, in removing the physical limitations of the traditional campus. But for many people, including some faculty, this has its negative aspects. The importance of the campus appears to be diminished. The series of services offered on and off campus comes close to defining the institution. In some instances—for example, the National Technological University—there may not even be a campus. Under such circumstances, the possibility of developing any feeling of identification with the institution, of being involved in a collegiate experience, is minimal if not missing altogether. Through its very extension, the institution becomes less personal and less important except as a brand name, and one picks the services, not the institutional ambience. All of these factors seem to raise real concerns about institutional integrity and quality control.

A number of comments seem relevant to such concerns. First, it is clear that the technologies make possible and reinforce not only the extended classroom but the "extended university" that Lynton and Elman describe and advocate. They open up access to a far wider range of students of all ages in increasingly remote places. Technologies provide an infrastructure for more effective liaison and cooperation among institutions and between institutions and business and industry, government, the professions, and the public in general than could have been imagined only a few years ago. This calls, however, for clearly developed missions and objectives, for careful selection and development of technologies on the basis of educational and research objectives, and for careful planning. It also strongly suggests the advantages of a cooperative system or of state involvement in the development of telecommunications to take advantage of the unique resources and missions of various institutions in complementation of each other rather than relying on a separate and single institution's operations, no matter how central that institution may be.

Second, the use of technologies does not mean that campuses will disappear or that the traditional campus does not have major advantages for many students. It does mean that these advantages can be reinforced by appropriate on-campus technologies—particularly computers with their various uses. Use of the various technologies opens up possibilities through computer conferencing, two-way audio and video, and talk-back television, for example, of more closely relating the on-campus students with their off-campus counterparts and even of sharing or participating in the same classes (McNeil, 1989c, p. 2) through continuing discussion and mutual involvement. It also helps ensure that off-campus students, courses, and programs are in fact the equivalent of those on campus and that they are considered so by all concerned.

Third, the fact that off-campus students can pick and choose, can take only one course or part of a program or utilize only one service, is not substantially different from the situation on campus, particularly at community colleges and comprehensive colleges and universities. It may well be that such students are getting exactly what they want or need and that this does not require completion of a degree or specific program. However, such selection does not diminish the importance of counseling for off-campus as well as on-campus students. Through the education information centers and libraries in Oklahoma, with their utilization of Sigi-Plus and Discover, and through the Adult Learning Lab at the University of Georgia, such counseling may in fact be more readily available, more complete, and more relevant for adult and off-campus students than what ordinarily is available even for resident students on campus.

Fourth, as discussed in Chapter Four, as valuable as campus residence may be for some students, the mark of an educated person is not the where or the how of instruction but whether that person has the skills, the competencies, the types of experience, and the achievements commensurate with educational accomplishment regardless of how these are attained or continue to develop. We should welcome and utilize the extended campus, including the technologies that enhance its range and effectiveness, as the developing campus of the future.

Fifth, it is clear that in both private and public institutions and systems, the market plays a role in the development of higher education programs and services. Institutional, system, or statewide planning done without regard to the market is apt to be an exercise in futility. In explaining the merits and defects of the American higher education system to British educators, Sheldon Rothblatt (1989) of the University of California, Berkeley, characterized the situation as follows: "To suggest that American institutions have been and remain responsive to market forces does not . . . deny their independence or freedom of action. Rather it means that our universities and colleges are and have been continually engaged in a process of negotiation with their publics, redefining themselves accordingly but manipulating the market wherever possible. Since there are many and varied publics in America, there are many and varied colleges and institutions, either in competition with one another or in search of a special niche in the academic market" (p. 25). It is important for an institution to recognize relevant trends as they relate to the type of institution in question. This is an essential part of strategic planning. Not to do so is, in fact, likely to be self-defeating for planning on an individual institutional basis or an entire system. It is crucial that "market trends" are seen in a context not just of the moment but of the long-term interests, concerns, and needs of the public, including the states and nation, that these interests, concerns, and needs are reflected in institutional and system objectives, and that appropriate technologies are identified and developed to aid institutions and systems in achieving these objectives.

Sixth, there clearly is an important aspect of the service-station concept that is not or should not be considered a myth. This is the recognition that higher education institutions are not ends in themselves but means of serving society, of promoting the education and research essential to national and social as well as individual well-being. From this perspective, institutions are legitimate service stations, and the technologies extend and reinforce their service functions. Service in this sense includes instruction, research, and community reinforcement. The service-station concept runs aground when higher education activities are considered piecemeal and picking and choosing is the only order of the day. One of the advantages of the technologies is the fact that when appropriately used, they tend to reinforce the concept of community and cooperation through the very fact that they transcend older limitations of time and place, involve common data bases, and even involve sharing of unique instructional resources not only within the state but with the nation and the world. Use of the technologies may result in a loss of a sense of unique campus identity for some people, but this may well be compensated for by the potential increase in resources made available to the users.

Finally, as we have stressed so frequently, the question for institutional integrity and quality control is the direct relevance of the program, the service, and the use of the technology to institutional or system educational missions and objectives. Such missions and objectives obviously include specifications of instruction, research, and community service. To the extent that the objectives are coherent and reinforce each other in institutional and system missions and the various technologies are effectively used to achieve these objectives, both integrity and quality are present. To the extent that the technologies somehow become ends in themselves to which content becomes subservient, that externally developed products such as telecourses are not integrated into the total instructional program with faculty approval and guidance, or that parts of the programs or courses operating through technologies involving educational outreach are considered somehow second-class, serious questions about integrity and quality are pertinent. In relation to long-distance learning and faculty involvement in particular, David Grossman (1987) states, "In short, an institution will be high quality to the extent that distance learning programs and technology delivered instruction allow faculty . . . to achieve full realization of their professional responsibilities. To the extent that technology and distance learning compromises the professionalism and subverts the role of faculty, then no standard measure of quality will have any meaning" (p. 12). From this standpoint, how the issues of institutional or system quality and integrity are related to the use of technologies is no different from how they are related to anything else the institution or system does. The institution's integrity is directly involved in how it uses technology and for what purpose or objectives. Quality is a function of how effectively technologies are used as important resources to achieve appropriate educational and research objectives.

Given the range of the technologies, their costs, their interinstitutional implications (including their relevance to institutional cooperation and reinforcement), and their potential for network development, it may well be that the most effective use of them cannot be achieved by any institution in isolation and clearly cannot even be attempted by many smaller or less affluent institutions. If this is the case, then the potential role of the state or of consortia of institutions in making their effective institutional use possible is critical. We have already indicated that a number of states, including Indiana, Kentucky, Alaska, Wisconsin, Kansas, and Oklahoma, have moved in this direction (Cross and McCartan, 1984).

The Oklahoma Telecommunications Network

What can be done with the help of educational technology both to enrich the offerings of individual institutions and to develop a system to meet the higher education interests and needs of the citizens of a state as a whole is strikingly illustrated by the Oklahoma Network of Continuing Higher Education. The telecommunications network (Module V) constitutes the technical backbone of the project. It provides the vehicle for linking together the Education Information Centers of Module IV, on educational guidance and counseling. It is the precondition for the development of the public and academic libraries supporting system of Module VI, on library collaboration. Five of the demonstration projects in Module II, on program development, relate to, expand, and depend on the utilization of the network. It was undoubtedly this potential of the network not only to extend higher education opportunity to as wide a range of Oklahomans as possible but to strengthen the Oklahoma State System of Higher Education through increased opportunities for interinstitutional cooperation and collaboration that led the W. K. Kellogg Foundation, the State of Oklahoma, and the Sarkeys and Noble foundations to support the network project. The telecommunications network provided the basis for achieving the project objectives in a cost-effective manner through extension of access to courses, to counseling, to information, and to continuing education throughout the state.

Even prior to the project, the Oklahoma State System of Higher Education was no stranger to telecommunications and educational technologies. It pioneered in developing a microwave instructional television system. Beginning with state authorization legislation in 1970, and with help from the U.S. Office of Education, the state regents developed the Oklahoma Televised Instruction System, known as "Talkback Television," as an integral part of the state higher education system. It linked public and private colleges, universities, community colleges, and technical institutes. It made possible exchange of educational programs among institutions, thus decreasing course duplication and increasing mutual program enrichment. It also enabled the system's institutions to provide education at remote off-campus locations, to business and industry, the professions, health care services, law enforcement agencies, and state government and correctional institutions ("Telecommunications in Oklahoma—Special Report," 1985, p. 4). Today, this talk-back television system alone involves fifteen transmitting studios at thirteen locations and can be received at more than 120 classrooms at seventy locations around the state.

The telecommunications network, however, involves considerably more than the regents' televised instruction system. It also includes and is linked with the Oklahoma Educational Television Authority (OETA), which became in 1953 the first statewide educational television system provided for by state law. Through four stations plus a series of translator stations, OETA covers the entire state. In 1982, in cooperation with the state's higher education institutions and their faculties, it began offering telecourses that by 1985 were utilized in some twenty institutions around the state and enrolled more than 2,000 students; the number has increased considerably since then.

The third component of the network is the Oklahoma State University Educational Television Services (OSU-ETS). OSU-ETS has specialized in satellite teleconferencing not only in Oklahoma but nationally. It serves as the home of the National University Teleconferencing Network (NUTN), established in 1982, when it linked together sixty-seven major universities and colleges concerned with sharing continuing education programs.

Today it includes more than six hundred colleges and universities around the country involved in a variety of telecommunications activities (Oklahoma Network of Continuing Higher Education, 1988). Thus, through NUTN, the Oklahoma network has a national, even international dimension. Programs developed in Oklahoma can be shared with the rest of the country, and programs from the rest of the country can be rebroadcast by OSU for Oklahoma use. The OSU-ETS has major state-of-the-art production facilities available to state and out-of-state institutions and organizations. The stated purpose of OSU-ETS is "to provide quality broadcast and non-broadcast educational and/or instructional programming to serve the needs and interests" (Oklahoma State University, 1988, p. 3) of OSU, the regents, the communities of the state, and the nation. In addition, through a special W. K. Kellogg Foundation grant, Oklahoma State University has been able to create a field network through the Cooperative Extension Service by providing fifty-eight county extension offices within the state with satellite receiving stations. These also have become part of the overall network.

The fourth partner in the network is the Oklahoma University Health Sciences Center's Department of Media Production and Television Services. Like OSU-ETS, it has a state-of-the-art studio. Its activities are particularly geared to the development and training of health care professionals and making available to such professionals throughout the state the latest in-depth information and instruction in medicine and other health care areas.

The network also has a fifth partner, whose involvement not only has facilitated development of the network to date but has made possible planning and implementation to increase the scope and effectiveness of the system now and in the future considerably beyond that proposed and developed under the W. K. Kellogg grant. This is the Oklahoma Office of State Finance. With the help of this office, the capacity of the system has been and will be considerably increased to enable state agencies as well as the higher education system to utilize the communications network. A six-year plan to further improve the system is under consideration by the state legislature.

The network currently is what might be described as a system of interlocked systems. These involve a fiber-optic system (Oklahoma City, Norman, Stillwater, Tulsa), simplex, duplex, and digital microwave systems, instructional television fixed services, satellite up- and down-links, production facilities, and various telephone connections. The system provides telephone service, computer networking, data exchange, library networking, counseling support, teleconferencing, and vastly increased programming for the expanded video system. The potential of the telecommunications network is almost unlimited.

One major advantage of the Oklahoma telecommunications network is the very fact that it has been put together out of a series of existing yet changing systems, each of which was developed originally to meet specified needs and attain particular objectives, as, for example, is the case with the regent's Talkback Television System. Parts of the network and the network as a whole have been modified as new or additional needs and objectives have emerged. This is not a case of designing a network because it was a good idea and then trying to find a use for it, as has sometimes been the case in other places. Rather, it is a case of developing a coordinated network out of systems designed to meet specific educational needs. Its expanded uses and even in some cases its rough edges reflect this. The appointment of telecommunications coordinators by the presidents of each of the campuses and the development of telecommunications committees at each institution have helped to ensure institutional identification with the network and to keep it relevant to its educational purposes.

An example of such application is the computer network reinforcement of the guidance and counseling activities of the Educational Information Centers (Module IV), including the tie-in of fourteen public libraries in Module VI. Among other things, the network has enabled students at the four interinstitutional higher education centers—Ardmore, McCurtin, Enid, and Tulsa—not only to receive guidance and counseling but to participate through interactive video in programs and courses originating at the cooperating institutions. On the research level, it has enabled faculty at the three research universities—the

University of Oklahoma, Oklahoma State, and Tulsa—to work cooperatively on research projects and to vastly expand their research data bases.

Even more striking is the expansion of the library network at both public and academic libraries. At the public libraries in particular, the guidance functions related to the Educational Information Centers have been reinforced by expanded bibliographical search capabilities. In addition, instead of being hooked into the talk-back television as originally proposed, the libraries received satellite dishes that connect them with a wide range of teleconferencing opportunities. Each of the fourteen libraries has also received telefacsimile machines to facilitate their intercommunication. Through the Tulsa Area Library Cooperative (TALC), the cooperating libraries (some collegiate, some public, some "other") have gained group access to the Online Computer Library Center with its national and international bibliographical data base. The current value as well as the potential of the public library network is well summarized in the report of the Public Library Training Project: "By providing microcomputer and distance telecommunication through satellite dishes, public libraries in Oklahoma can now interface with each other, campus programs, and the individual adult learner. Education for the remainder of this century need no longer be campus bound; it need no longer be directed toward the 18–24 year old college student. Opportunities for educational experiences can now be directed towards the entire adult population . . . education for everyone, everywhere, everyday in Oklahoma" ("The Professional Library Training Project Report and Evaluation," 1988, p. 6). This obviously equally applies to the colleges and college libraries.

Spurred on in part by the success of a common computerized catalogue demonstration project (under Module II) carried out by Northeastern State University in cooperation with Cameron University and Rose State University, a major proposal for a statewide higher educational library network tied in with the public library network has been developed and is under consideration for legislative funding. Among other things, this would involve developing means of linking the nine different

automation systems currently in use in Oklahoma institutions
and ensuring that all Oklahoma higher education institutions
are members of the Online Computer Library Centers through
the regional center, AMIGOS (fifty are now members). Small
libraries with limited budgets would be included through group-
access arrangements.

Instead of constituting a threat to faculty position, an intrusion into the classroom, or a threat to the quality of education offered on or off campus, the Oklahoma telecommunications network has already proved itself to be exactly the opposite.
Rather than undermining the sanctity of the classroom, it has
extended the classroom to the state as a whole, maintaining and
in some cases actually increasing the involvement of and interchange between students and faculty. It has made the academic
resources of the various Oklahoma institutions, including courses
that would otherwise not be available and would be costly to
duplicate, available to the higher education institutions throughout the state and to students of all ages, full- or part-time, on
or off campus, in remote locations, and in business and industrial settings, without losing student and faculty involvement.
Instead of threatening faculty positions, the network has underlined the central and critical role of faculty as crucial to the
reason for being of the telecommunications network itself. In
this respect, instead of weakening quality control, the network
has heightened faculty and institutional awareness of the importance of outcomes or results and reinforced faculty and institutional responsibility for ensuring program effectiveness in
achieving them. Finally, if by being a "service station" one means
extending opportunities for postsecondary education beyond the
bounds of the traditional campus to a much wider range of
citizens who can benefit from it, then the Oklahoma telecommunications network should probably plead guilty. However,
if by "service station" one means an impersonal, piecemeal,
mechanistic substitution of machines for personal contact, interchange, and guidance, one can make a strong case that, to
the contrary, both on and off campus, the telecommunications
network can and does, when effectively utilized, increase not
only the resources available to students but the contact with and
direction of faculty and counseling mentors as well.

Much of the value of the Oklahoma Telecommunications Network lies in the fact that it is a statewide network under the direction of the regents rather than an individual institutional operation. Under the guidance of the regents, it performs in this respect an essential coordinating function. It operationally makes the resources of each institution available to all of the other institutions and the students of the state. It provides a practical means for reducing unnecessary duplication and sharing of faculty, program, and information resources of unique and expensive programs throughout the state. Through the various national data bases, including the Online Computer Library Center, it enlarges exponentially the information and research resources of all Oklahoma institutions, and through the teleconference capabilities of the National University Teleconferencing Network, it links Oklahoma instructionally to the rest of the nation.

Summary

The information revolution and the technology that has made it possible are one of the most striking characteristics of the last half of the twentieth century. The technologies have had major impact on most aspects of our lives, including higher education. In higher education, they seem to have had less impact on instruction than on administration and research, although their potential for changing the character of instruction, for extending the classroom and campus, and for increasing access is almost unlimited. If, however, the potential of the technologies for enriching the teaching-learning experience and even revitalizing the interest in subject matter itself is to be more fully realized, certain conditions seem to be essential:

1. Academic objectives must remain central and not be subordinated to the technologies.
2. The role of the faculty member as key to content development, as authoritative in the subject field in question, and as facilitator must not be sacrificed to technicians and production managers or others concerned primarily with technology operation.

3. Adequate education or training of faculty and students in
    the various types of technologies and their uses, including
    their relevance to particular subjects and modes of learn-
    ing, is essential.
4. Instructors and students need to recognize the potentials
    and limitations of the different technologies and be aware
    of how and to what extent they can and should reinforce
    each other.

To the extent that the technologies are utilized to enhance and
strengthen teaching and learning, are chosen and developed in
the light of sound academic objectives, and are used to supplement rather than replace the function of the instructors, the feeling of threat on the part of some faculty members should be
ameliorated or eliminated.

   With the new technologies, the older campus boundaries
no longer constitute barriers for institutions. The new campus
may be wherever the learner is. Rather than being a disadvan-
tage or a cause for concern about integrity and quality, this constitutes a major positive step in increasing the relevance of higher
education to the current postsecondary educational needs of the
states and the nation. The new technologies make the extended
classroom, even extended colleges and universities, realities, and
with appropriate planning provide an infrastructure for cooperation, coordination, and liaison among institutions for sharing
resources and meeting the educational and research needs of
the broader society.

   The question of institutional integrity and quality in relation to the use of technologies is the same as it is in relation
to anything else that the institution does. Its integrity is as much
involved in how it uses technologies as it is in how it uses any
other resources. Its quality is a function of the extent to which
the technologies as important resources are effectively utilized
to achieve appropriate educational and research objectives.

   The full potential of technologies and of their effective use
to reinforce higher education instruction and research and to
extend higher education opportunity to the wider community
may be beyond the ability of any single institution to achieve.

Costs alone for individual institutions can quickly become prohibitive. This is particularly the case for smaller, less affluent institutions, public or private, but it extends to larger institutions as well. To the extent that this is the case, then the role of the state (or of consortia of institutions) in making possible effective institutional utilization of technologies on a collaborative basis is crucial.

8

The Commercialization Threat

It would not be too far amiss to suggest that most of the myths
we have been considering involve the feeling or, in some cases,
the strong conviction that higher education is in danger of losing its integrity, of abandoning its high purposes, of selling its
mission and high purposes short. In this sense, most of the myths
deal with factors considered to be tainting higher education,
whether from within academe or from the wider community.
Among the forces frequently conceived of as primarily responsible for such tainting is business and industry. Clearly, one of
the growing concerns in some quarters today is that higher education and higher education institutions are losing their unique
functions as discoverers, developers, and transmitters of knowledge by selling themselves and their services for what in effect
is profit. Business and industry are conceived of as the primary
market for such selling, although government (local, state, and
federal) also plays a major role.

The involvement in the marketplace, however, as Clark
Kerr (1988) points out, is almost as old as higher education itself: "The cherished view of some academics that higher education started out on the Acropolis of scholarship and was de-
secrated by descent into the Agora of materialistic pursuits led
by ungodly commercial interests and scheming public officials

and venal academic leaders is just not true for the university systems that have developed at least since 1200 A.D. If anything higher education started in the Agora, the market place, at the bottom of the hill and ascended to the Acropolis on the top of the hill. . . . Mostly it has lived in tension, at one and the same time at the bottom of the hill, at the top of the hill, and on the many paths in between" (p. 4). The fact, however, that the tensions have been around for a long time does not make them any less real, nor does it mean that some of the concerns involved are cautions against real dangers.

What makes the issues particularly critical at this time is the considerably increased recognition on the part of the political, business, and higher education communities of the importance of higher education to economic health and international competitiveness. The role of higher education research in particular in providing the United States a technologically competitive worldwide advantage until relatively recently has been both taken for granted and at the same time clearly realized.

On the state level, the impact of the Massachusetts Institute of Technology (MIT) and Harvard on the Route 128 complex through spinoff companies and thus on the Massachusetts economy in various periods of its development has been the envy of most other states. Other examples, such as the Silicon Valley in California and Research Triangle in North Carolina, have been equally impressive. Yet on the national level, by 1983 the Business–Higher Education Forum's report to the president of the United States pointed out that the U.S. economy was not keeping pace with its own past or with the economies of other industrialized nations and that a number of U.S. industries had lost their competitive advantage. The report strongly urged more effective collaboration among higher education institutions, industry, and the federal government (Business–Higher Education Forum, 1983, pp. 27–28).

Also on the state level, particularly since the recession of 1981, governors and legislators have argued for support of higher education and education-industrial liaison as crucial to state economic health as well as international competitiveness. A number of states, including Ohio, New Jersey, Pennsylvania, Florida, and Texas, have developed highly effective statewide mechanisms to encourage and support university-business liaisons. In fact, as of 1989, twenty-one states had developed competitive or incentive higher education and business-industry programs to encourage economic growth or technology transfer (Berdahl, 1990). According to Philip Abelson (1988), a deputy editor of *Science,* "The nation will encounter rough global industrial competition for the foreseeable future. In this circumstance, it is the states rather than the federal government that have been highly innovative. Today, there are 500 state and local high-tech programs in forty-five states aimed at improving economic competitiveness" (p. 265).

Higher education institutions have not only responded but in many cases taken the initiative in two major areas. One is the area of research, involving the development of university-industry liaisons for support of research, translation of "pure" research into applied research, and application of research in product development, factors that generally fall under the heading of technology transfer. This obviously applies primarily to research universities and tends to be concentrated in a relatively few major higher education institutions. The other is the area of the development of human resources or of partnerships for educating and training the work force, what sometimes is described as development of human capital, either on or off campus or in the marketplace itself.

These liaisons, cooperative arrangements, and partnerships of higher education institutions with business and industry, as important as they may be in reinforcing the economy at various levels, increasing international competitiveness, and providing additional funds for institutions, have raised serious concerns in some quarters of the academic community and beyond. In three areas, these concerns are based on assumptions or beliefs that when carried to extremes tend to become myths. These are the areas of university-industrial research relations; campus-business instructional linkages; and in-service training and education — the corporate classroom — and its relevance to more traditional postsecondary education.

The Business and Industry Interference Myth

Business and industry support for higher education is not new, nor is development of higher education research directly in service to business and industry. If one includes agriculture, such directed research goes back at least to the Hatch Experimentation Act of 1887 and perhaps in principle to the Morrill Land Grant Act of 1862 (Cheit, 1975, p. 42). The role of higher education research in creating new areas of industrial activity and radically changing older ones in such fields as electronics, biomedical and paramedical manufacturing, agriculture, and petroleum products, to mention only a few, is staggering. It has been such research leadership in the physical sciences and engineering in particular that until relatively recently has made possible the economic competitive advantage of the United States in relation to the rest of the world.

The last two decades have seen a major shift from an industrial to an information economy, a rapid increase in the rate of technological change, the internationalization of the economy, and increased international industrial and business competitiveness (Fairweather, 1988, p. 2). At least partially as a result, "the 1980's have evidenced an evolution (perhaps revolution) in the types and extent" of corporate support for and involvement with higher education (p. 2). The interest of universities in both welcoming and seeking such support has been considerably heightened by a 1980 change in the patent law that allows universities to maintain patents and to commercialize patent discoveries developed with federal funds (Fuchsberg, 1989, p. A28).

The result has been a rapid expansion in university-industry liaison activities to facilitate technology transfer. These activities have perhaps most frequently taken the form of licensing agreements with industry providing for an initial fee and royalties if the product sells, with the university retaining the patent. Other forms of cooperative activity include consortia, spinoff companies, and corporate affiliates for technology transfer. Thus, as Fairweather (1988) reports, "between 1982 and

1985, the number of research and development consortia between industry and academic institutions . . . increased five
times" (p. 7). According to Fuchsberg (1989), the level of involvement is accelerating: "Only in the last three years . . . have
more than a few dozen institutions sought to exploit . . . commercialization rights in an aggressive manner. . . . By some ac-
counts between 150 and 200 institutions are now engaged in
some form of technology transfer" (p. A28).

     Although industrial support for research still tends to be
concentrated in a relatively small number of institutions — MIT,
Stanford, the University of California system, and the Wisconsin system accounted for more than half of university-industry
licensing agreements in 1989 (Anderson and Sugarman, 1989,
p. 6) — and the total industrial contributions to university research is now not much more than 6 percent of total university
research funds (the major portion coming from the federal
government), it is nevertheless the fastest-growing source of support for academic research (Fairweather, 1988, p. 7).

     As already noted, a number of states have not only called
for and encouraged university-industry research liaisons but
committed state funds to their support. For example, Abelson
(1988) points out that "in Ohio several programs foster start up
companies. However, the major emphasis is on future-oriented
major industrial-university interactions. At nine Edison Technology Centers, academic researchers work on industrial problems especially relevant to the state. Each center is built around
the problems of a single set of technologies such as advanced
manufacturing, polymer innovation, or welding engineering.
Each center has a number of companies and academic institutions as members. More than 500 companies and every university in the state participate" (p. 265).

     Research universities are concerned not only or perhaps
not even primarily from an income and fiscal point of view but
also from a public-service point of view. At one of the Oklahoma
leadership seminars, Bryce Jordan (1987), the president of Pennsylvania State University, called attention to "the rapidly growing
national consensus that universities — particularly research universities — can and must play a major role in the economic re-

vitalization of the United States and in insuring American competitiveness in the global economy" (p. 11). While reporting that Pennsylvania State ranks toward the top of higher education institutions in the country in industrial-sponsored research, Jordan believes that even more effort is called for. Thus, as a matter of policy, Jordan pledges that at Pennsylvania State University "we will provide assistance to and — where appropriate — work jointly with the private sector in the development and transfer of technology. . . . And we will assist and encourage faculty, staff, and students to engage in entrepreneurial activities which contribute to our activities in support of economic development" (p. 13).

It is not our intention to offer, nor are we capable of offering, either an analysis or a critique of the various forms of university-industrial research liaison and technical transfer activities. It is, however, important to note some of the kinds of concerns that such liaisons give rise to in the academy — concerns that in many cases are legitimate and serve or should serve as important cautions. As early as 1962, Robert Maynard Hutchins sounded the tocsin about what he considered to be both business and governmental motives for interference in research activities of universities and the universities' response: "The universities have demonstrated their willingness to do almost anything for money. Government and business are not wholly disinterested in their approaches to universities; they are not seeking the truth, but are hiring the universities to promote the ends they have in view. If truth serves these ends, it is merely a coincidence" (cited in Fairweather, 1988, p. 2).

Jordan, who is strongly supportive of increased university-industry liaison, nevertheless calls attention to what he considers three of the most important concerns: "These concerns include the potential loss of institutional independence (with a concurrent increase in dependence on corporate support); the possibility that an already pragmatic university could swing too far toward the practical, losing its dedication to values and ideals; and the possibility that teaching will be slighted as the result of more emphasis on research and entrepreneurial activity" (Jordan, 1987, p. 14). Jordan thus raises the issue of institutional autonomy and the danger of becoming overly dependent on corporate support. This undoubtedly is part of what Hutchins was concerned about. We will note a number of facets of a potential negative impact of university-industrial research relations.

James Fairweather (1988) suggests six of what he considers potential "costs" related to conceptions of institutional autonomy and integrity: "academic freedom, focus of research, secrecy, faculty productivity, intellectual property rights, and the split between the haves and the have nots" (p. 60). To these should be added concern about "conflict of interest," a matter very much on the minds of some congressional committees (see Weiss, 1989, p. A56). Another concern is the danger of alliance with certain types of industries whose activities are perceived by some segments of society as being socially harmful or as favoring some social or industrial groups and objectives at the expense of others. Examples include research that is related to arms production and research the results of which support agribusiness at the expense of the small farmer.

Academic freedom is at least theoretically an issue when the selection of research topics is dictated by the sponsor's goals rather than the researchers' interests (Fairweather, 1988, p. 60). On the surface at least, this would not seem to be very different from governmental or even foundation awards for particular research projects designed to achieve particular government or foundation research objectives rather than institutional or researcher objectives. The point at which academic freedom would most clearly seem to become an issue is when, as a result of the liaison and commitment, the investigator cannot choose not to be involved in the research, is not free to follow the project through to his or her own conclusion or results, or is restricted in his or her use of the results in further research.

The question of focus of research reraises the old issue of "pure" or "basic" research versus "applied" research and may be part of the concern about academic freedom. It is a truism that without basic research, there would be no applied research. If university-industrial research liaisons in fact undermined the possibility of the alternative of basic research, both university and industrial involvement would be amazingly shortsighted.

Without going anywhere near this far, however, Fairweather comments that "on the whole, the applied focus of industry-university research liaisons seems incompatible with many academic research goals, especially for basic research that has a long- rather than a short-term focus" (p. 62).

On the positive side are the following: (1) The university-industry research liaisons may themselves provide the funding necessary for basic research. (2) They may and in some cases do (for example, Monsanto–Washington University; see Kenney, 1986, pp. 67–68) specify that certain percentages of the funds involved shall go to basic research. (3) Under any circumstances, "basic" research and "applied" research tend to constitute a continuum rather than disjunctive and opposing types of activity (Lynton and Elman, 1987, p. 152). (4) In a number of fields, such as engineering, most of what might be considered basic research is in fact applied research. (5) It is frequently in the application of research that new areas or issues in basic research open up. Thus John Crecine, the president of Georgia Tech, is reported as arguing that "For a long time people in academe have had a very precious view of the appropriate use of their intellectual powers. . . . There is a belief that says doing things for a client is somehow evil. . . . [A] cross-disciplinary, industrially-sponsored project is an ideal environment for research. Not only does industry provide more resources (big businesses are more likely to support large, expensive projects than are traditional grant agencies such as the National Science Foundation), but a well-chosen project, with a client and a deadline, is more likely to produce scientific breakthrough than any unrestricted grant" (Turner, 1988, p. A3).

More serious than the focus on applied research and more directly related to academic freedom is concern about secrecy. Again, the issue is not new. Some universities have been involved in classified U.S. Department of Defense research since before World War II. However, because scientific progress does depend to a large degree on the free flow of information and publication of results (Fairweather, 1988, p. 62), a good many institutions will not or will only reluctantly accept classified research. In the university-industry context, the relationship of research to the market, the withholding of information of value to competitors, does in some cases lead to restriction on revealing results even to colleagues. Fairweather points out that industrially funded projects in biotechnology particularly are likely to include restrictions on publication, including delays in or even prohibition of open release of research results (p. 62). When the faculty and the university involved also have a stake in income produced, the temptation to withhold results even from academic and research colleagues may be high. Even doctoral candidates and programs may be affected. Again, citing a paper by Maurice Richter, Fairweather suggests that "proprietary rights and secrecy can adversely affect doctoral education by preventing students from using data for dissertations and by imposing delays on submission of dissertations" (p. 66).

Clearly, the borderline between such secrecy and conflict of interest on the part of faculty members and institutions is a thin one indeed. The potential for conflict of interest between academic research goals and proprietary interest, even when the research results in increased industrial competitiveness on various levels, is relatively high *unless* clear policies are carefully developed beforehand and uniformly adhered to. This applies not only to secrecy but to faculty and institutional involvement in, ownership of, and commitment to spinoff companies; to the industries and businesses with which technology transfer is being carried out; and to the time devoted to industrial research as opposed to other research and academic activities. This is not to suggest that either institutions or faculty should not be involved or that they should not be adequately recompensed for such involvement, including receiving income from patents and royalties. It is, however, to recognize again the crucial importance of developing clear policies that relate such activity to the service functions of the university and faculty, not just to income.

Because industrially supported research and university-industry research liaisons tend to be concentrated in a relatively small number of institutions, there is a real concern in some quarters that such university-industry liaisons will primarily help those institutions that already have major research programs and thus further accentuate the difference between the "have" and the "have-not" institutions. From the standpoint of major research capabilities and commitment, this may well be the case. However, it is important to recognize that the number of major research universities or universities in which research is a primary part of their mission is necessarily limited. Industrial support for such universities does help maintain their viability and make them less dependent on the shifts in federal funding (Fairweather, 1988, p. 63). The fact that other universities and colleges are not primarily oriented toward research does not make them second-class or undermine their quality if they are in fact achieving their unique missions. Lynton and Elman (1987) point out that there are aspects of corporate-university cooperation aside from natural sciences research and high technology that most universities can and should become involved in, including the development of human potential or human capital: "But working closely with the corporate sector at the cutting edge of innovation constitutes only a portion of the knowledge needs to which universities should address themselves. There exist substantial opportunities for the entire range of universities to cooperate with industry as well as with government and other external constituencies in ensuring the rapid transfer and absorption of innovation into all segments of the economy" (pp. 21–22).

These concerns are real and should be taken seriously. Any threat to academic freedom is a threat to the integrity of the university itself and should be carefully guarded against. However, the fact that industrially sponsored research is focused on particular, usually applied research objectives does not restrict academic freedom any more than does responding to requests for proposals from the government or meeting the objectives of particular foundations, so long as the university is not restricted from carrying out other types of research projects. As noted, secrecy and conflict of interest can become serious and real problems. Limitations on secrecy and avoidance of conflict of interest do need to be addressed in clear institutional policies and carefully drawn contracts with business and industry. However, as the National Academy of Sciences pointed out in 1983 in relation to government-university partnerships, the most important safeguard of the integrity of the university "is the integrity of the scientists buttressed by codes of ethics and standards of behavior advocated by faculties and institutions" (National Academy of Sciences, 1983, p. 12, cited in Fairweather, 1988, p. 56).

With these cautions in mind, even with the recognition of what J. Scott Chafin (1989) of the University of Houston System describes as the "dangers lurking in the shadows" (p. B6), the advantages of and even the imperative for continued and extended university-industry research liaisons to help meet the changing economic and social conditions now and in the period ahead seem clear. Katherine Ku (1989), president of the Association of University Technology Managers, recognizes the potential economic benefit to universities of university-industry liaison but points out that "the primary purpose of all university technology programs is to promote and encourage the effective transfer of useful research results, for society's use and benefit. Publications of discoveries in scientific journals has not proven to be a practical way of making such discoveries available to society. Companies need incentives to undertake the financial risks of developing and marketing university discoveries. . . . Intellectual property rights provide such incentives" (p. B5). Chafin (1989) adds that "The efforts of institutions of higher education to commercialize their discoveries, inventions, and innovations are not at all inconsistent with higher education's role in society: the discovery and dissemination of knowledge. The commercialization of university-developed ideas through 'technology-transfer,' particularly in a market economy, is a powerful way of giving tangible meaning to that role" (p. B6).

At an Oklahoma leadership seminar, Bryce Jordan (1987) put the issue in the broader perspective of the next decade and the twenty-first century as follows: "There has probably not been a time in the history of our country when the American society needs effective colleges and universities more than now. And colleges and universities face economic imperatives as well. These can be classified under two strategic questions. One question concerns the financial support for higher education, and the other concerns the potential of colleges and universities to aid in American industry's efforts to become more productive and competitive in the new international economy" (p. 2). Looked at in the broader context of the changed and changing economy, of the increased national and international concern with productivity and competitiveness, of the service functions of the universities, and of the need to increase the financial base for university research, university-industry research liaison activities do not constitute an interference in the internal affairs of higher education or a buying out or prostitution of academic integrity. To the contrary, development of such research liaisons and partnerships constitutes a challenge and is an integral part of the obligation of research universities to the broader society and the future economic health of the nation.

The Captive Classroom Myth

While university-industry research liaisons and technology transfer play an extraordinarily important role in the future economic health and industrial competitiveness of the states and the nation, such research liaisons constitute only one aspect of the business–industry–higher education interface. They involve a relatively small number of institutions and a limited though usually prestigious group of major businesses and industries. A far larger area of campus-business linkages involves the educational process itself and the development of courses and programs designed specifically to meet the education and training needs of future and present employers. By far the majority of the more than twelve hundred community colleges in the country are involved in such campus-business linkages (Eurich, 1985, p. 16), but these linkages are by no means confined to community colleges. Four-year institutions, universities, and professional and graduate schools, particularly in engineering and business administration, are also involved. The courses or programs may be offered without credit, for certificate, or for credit toward degrees at the associate, baccalaureate, professional, or graduate level. They tend to be primarily technical, vocational, occupational, or professional in nature.

The programs are specifically developed in cooperation with the businesses or industries involved. The proposal for such programs may come from the institution or from the business or industry and may be encouraged and even funded by state or federal government, as, for example, under the Job Training Partnership Act. The relationship with the business or industry is usually formal, and the programs tend to be developed under contract. The courses or programs may be offered on campus, in house at the business or industry, or at some third place off campus. They may be aided or in some cases wholly delivered via the technologies discussed in the previous chapter. The Oklahoma Talkback Television System, for example, to a large extent began as a means of providing participatory in-plant courses and programs to business and industry in Oklahoma (see Chapter Seven). The National Technological University is perhaps the most striking example of such technology-based in-plant programs on a national scale (see Chapter Four).

It is not particularly surprising that community colleges are the most heavily involved in campus-business instructional linkages. A basic part of the missions of most of them is clearly service to the community, including the business and industrial communities of which they are a part. Many of them have established formal business, industry, and labor councils on their campuses (Day and Rajasekhara, 1988, p. 65). Many of the urban community colleges in particular have multiple business-campus partnerships. Dale Parnell (1988), the president of the American Association of Community and Junior Colleges, comments, "In meeting this growing responsibility to the employer community, college economic development activities have blossomed into a full array of programs and services in job training technology-transfer and industrial restructuring. Over the past few years many community colleges have become established as partners in economic development efforts" (p. 2). Such partnerships result not only in the "business as direct client" position but in "customized job training," described by Hamm and Tolle-Burger (1988) as follows: "Frequently called on-site or in-plant training services, customized job training programs are designed to provide business with precisely the type of training the firm requires; whatever the subject matter, the community college can design or broker a training program to fit the bill. It is provided under contract between business and community colleges to meet a variety of company needs" (p. 19).

As these programs are applied not just to community colleges but to effective instructional linkages of business and higher education institutions in general, Fenwick and others (1986) underline "the need to build a reciprocal relationship with well-defined mutual expectations and realistic goals within the framework of the needs and demands of business and the available resources of the institutions" (p. 10). They go on to point out that in dealing with business and industry, higher education institutions must overcome industrial conceptions of higher education rigidity and, instead, stress their willingness to be flexible and to tailor-make programs to meet industrial human resource needs—"the educational services of the institution [should be] portrayed as flexible and as capable of being customized to meet their specific needs" (pp. 20–21).

Both the American Association of Community and Junior Colleges (AACJC) and the American Council on Education (ACE) strongly encourage such higher education–business linkages. Both provide guides or manuals for establishing them. The ACE guide, by Dorothy Fenwick and others (1986), was first published in 1983 as a directory of such programs; its second edition, published in 1986, includes an extended section on how such programs can and should be developed. While the directory does not pretend to be exhaustive, it lists well over five hundred programs at a variety of types of institutions. In its current form, it is called *Guide to Campus-Business Linkage Programs: Education and Business Prospering Together*. The AACJC guide, published in 1988, is called *Doing Business with Business: A Handbook for College Planning to Serve Commerce and Industry* and is authored by Russell Hamm and Lynn Tolle-Burger (1988). It includes planning for not only business-college linkages but linkages with labor unions as well—an area in which Morris Keaton and the Council for Adult and Experiential Learning (CAEL) are making major contributions. The W. K. Kellogg Foundation has provided funds through both AACJC and CAEL to encourage such developments.

Today's Myths and Tomorrow's Realities

In addition to its handbook, AACJC has published a series of studies of community college involvement with the private sector, beginning with *Putting America Back to Work: The Kellogg Leadership Initiative* (Mahoney, 1984), followed by *In Search of Community College Partnerships* (Day, 1985), and culminating in *Keeping America Working: Profiles in Partnerships* (Day and Rajasekhara, 1988). While the information is not exhaustive, the 1985 report indicated that 78 percent of the community colleges responding (63.2 percent of the universe) offer training at in-plant or business sites. Forty-one percent provide customized training, 28 percent job-specific training, 14 percent generic training, and 9 percent all three types (Day and Rajasekhara, p. 66). The 1988 study revealed that more than two-thirds (69 percent) of the students in such programs were over twenty-two years of age (p. 9), two-thirds (66.9 percent) were part-time students, and two-thirds (66.3 percent) were employed—44.3 percent of them full-time (p. 8).

As important as such educational instructional liaisons with business and industry seem to be in reinforcing the economy, increasing productivity, and ensuring the relevance of higher education to the world of work and the broader society, they do give rise to a number of concerns. This is particularly the case when talk in some academic quarters turns to "customized" or "tailor-made" programs or "contracts" to meet specific business or industry training requirements or moving from "student as client" to "business [as] direct client," as Dale Parnell suggests (1988, p.2). This seems to many to reraise the issue of excessive vocationalism, to suggest that one is engaged in training rather than education, to raise questions about whether one has not transformed the students into economic productivity units, and to question whether credit hours or continuing education units relate to educational programs or to discreet packages of courses for sale, with the bottom line of income primarily in mind.

The fact that the community colleges have been most responsive to the development of corporate-business linkages or partnerships, have responded to federal concerns under the Job Training Partnership Act, and have tailored programs to meet the unique economic needs of particular communities has opened them up to criticisms and even attacks related to the question of whether they are fulfilling their functions. In some cases, questions have even been raised about their legitimacy as higher education institutions. Two recent publications have been particularly critical, both essentially with the same theme: *The Diverted Dream: Community Colleges and the Promise of Educational Opportunity in America, 1900–1985* (Brint and Karabel, 1989), by Steven Brint of Yale and Jerome Karabel of Berkeley, and a report issued by the College Board and the Academy for Educational Development, *Bridges to Opportunity: Are Community Colleges Meeting the Transfer Needs of Minority Students?* (Pincus and Archer, 1989). The gist of both publications seems to be that because of their emphasis on occupational preparation, including and perhaps further inspired by campus-business linkages, community colleges have let their classrooms be captured and have lost their central purpose, which should be to serve as stepping-stones to four-year colleges (Watkins, 1989b, p. A18), keeping central their transfer function (Pincus and Archer, 1989, p. 3). As a result, both publications argue that community colleges with large minority populations tend to block rather than create opportunity for minority students to attain the baccalaureate degree — thus reducing educational and social mobility rather than increasing it. Both cite decreasing percentages of students who transfer as evidence of this failure. While not fully in agreement on the numbers, both report the general number who transfer now at only around 20 percent.

While it may well be the case that a disproportionately large number of minority students go to community colleges, this may in fact be a function of community colleges' accessibility, their relationships to their communities, and a lack of adequate flexibility in recruitment of minorities at other types of higher education institutions. It may indeed also be the case that more minority students should be encouraged to go into transfer programs and that articulation between community colleges and four-year colleges, including the receptivity of four-year colleges to community college transfers, should be improved. But to argue that transfer programs are or should be the primary function of all community colleges is to overlook (1) the differences in missions among community colleges in light of the communities that they serve, (2) the comprehensive nature of community colleges and their obligations to provide programs relevant to the community, including and in many cases highlighting occupational and vocational programs, given the interests of their students, their constituent citizenry, and local businesses and industries, and (3) the fact that for many students, including some minority students, the objective of attending is not obtaining either an associate or a baccalaureate degree but attaining particular skills in preparation for work. From this perspective, it is a bit ironic that the community colleges may be being challenged for doing well exactly what they were designed to do — to offer a comprehensive series of alternatives related to student and community needs. If anybody has failed in providing wider opportunity for minorities, it is not necessarily the community colleges, whose doors are open and which provide guidance in meeting a wide variety of student and community needs, but the wider academic community. In some cases, including California, legislatively approved master plans make inevitable a concentration of minorities in community colleges. To assume that all or most minority students should be in transfer programs any more than nonminority students should be is to disregard student interest as well as broader institutional functions.

Our concern at this point, however, is with what may be a more basic question of whether community colleges and other institutions engaged in campus-business linkages have somehow sold out to the extent that their classrooms have become captive to business and industry training objectives at the expense of educational objectives. Ernest Boyer (1987), while recognizing the relevance of education to the world of work and vice versa, nevertheless argues that "pushing the boundaries of the campus to the work place has risks. The corporation is concerned with productivity and profits. . . . [T]he goal of collegiate education, at its best, is to show how learning can give meaning to skills, place information in larger context, and discover the relationship of knowledge to life's dilemmas. . . . In the end, colleges and corporations should build connections; but they must also protect their independence" (p. 227). Boyer would thus have serious reservations about too much tailoring and contracts so narrow as to preclude perspective in the training process.

In *New Perspectives on the Education of Adults in the United States,* Huey B. Long (1987) the Kellogg Professor of Continuing Higher Education and director of the Oklahoma Research Center for Continuing and Higher Education at the University of Oklahoma (heading up Module III, on professional development, under the W. K. Kellogg grant), warns particularly against the danger of depersonalizing and fragmenting students in the corporate education context, of what he sees as the danger of making business rather than the student the primary client and considering the student only as "human capital." "Individuals in such a context are not really regarded as people normally are, they are transposed into the category of resources. They are resources that are instrumental in the achievement of corporate goals" (p. 60). Long suggests that there are three dangers in too close a link of education with the corporate structure: "First, education may increasingly become justified by the bottom line syndrome. . . . Second, the traditional educational system may be affected negatively through the competitive strategies that blur the distinction between an education that at least pays lip service to the wholeness of the human being and an education designed only to equip the human as worker. Third, education may become more of a means for constraining humanity than liberating it" (pp. 58–59).

The dangers that Boyer and Long point to are real and need to be guarded against. This does not, however, mean that there is not a place, even a responsibility, for higher education institutions to provide technical education through campus-business linkages when this fits into institutional missions and objectives. Such technical education does need to be put into context, and while, within limits, programs can and should be tailored to the interests and requirements of employers, they need to be developed to achieve mutually agreed upon ends. In some cases, the greatest service to the student, the community, and the business partners is specific skill improvement. However, gaining a more adequate understanding of the relevance of the technology and the job to its business or industrial and social impact may be equally important. Just as the question of university-industry research liaisons has to be put into perspective, so does the question of instructional campus-business linkages. A number of factors are relevant.

First, while far more institutions are involved in instructional campus-business linkages than in research liaison relationships, not all institutions are, and whether they should be is clearly related to their institutional educational missions and objectives.

Second, if, as we suggested in Chapter Three, career development in the broad sense is the primary instructional mission of higher education, then specific preparation for work is an integral part of its function and, it might be added, always has been. "Service to the labor market," Clark Kerr (1988) points out, "has been from the start an important part of higher education in most of the world and has continued to be so at nearly all times and all places" (p. 4). No one questions the legitimacy of the collegiate role in professional education. One of the striking developments of the nineteenth century and the first half of the twentieth was the movement and expansion of what were apprentice occupations into colleges and universities as professions (medicine, law, nursing, pharmacy). Clearly, professional and other types of occupational education and training are on a continuum, and higher education's concern with and service to them should be considered equally legitimate. Clark Kerr again points out that one of the major changes in the relationship of the labor market to higher education in the contemporary world is "the extension of the use of higher education from supplying the ancient professions to supplying hundreds, even thousands, of subprofessions and occupations and vocations" (p. 33).

Third, to the extent that preparing students for professions, subprofessions, occupations, and vocations as a part of career development in the broad sense is one essential function of higher education, then the more relevant such preparation is to jobs and the tasks to be done in them, the more effective the education and training are likely to be. In the case of the professions, the role of professionals as well as educators in helping to determine the relevance of the education to entry into professions is clearly recognized. For subprofessions, occupations, and vocations, the views and requirements of employers may be equally relevant. Thus, campus-business linkages may be extraordinarily important in determining educational and training content, not just for initial entry into the industrial enterprise but for updating, retraining, advancement, and occupational or job change.

Fourth, given the present composition of the higher education student population, with its predominance of older, part-time, and nonresident students, it is important that higher education institutions develop the kinds of programs relevant to their needs. For many people, a large part of those educational needs is job-related, and higher education institutions have an obligation in accepting such students to ensure that their course work does in fact prepare them for the world of work. In the light of their missions, community colleges in particular have a direct obligation to accept such students and provide appropriate occupational preparation. Given the projected demographic changes of the next decades, with a decreasing number of younger members of the work force; an increasing number of women, minorities, and immigrants, many from disadvantaged backgrounds; and more older students involved in occupational changes; the need for close college-business cooperation, planning, and reinforcement becomes progressively more essential to business, to the wider community, and to the economy.

Fifth, those courses designed to be offered on location in business and industry through such campus-business linkages not only serve the employees taking the courses in their jobs but may also encourage such students to expand their educational activities at the institutions providing the courses, thus widening horizons for the students and increasing the colleges' opportunities for service.

Sixth, in providing effective education for people in the work force through campus-business likages, higher education will have a progressively important role in supporting economic development, in increasing productivity, and thus in adding to and reinforcing economic competitiveness on the local, state, and national levels.

The major caution in all this is that in such business- and

industry-oriented education and in the linkage programs, the student as student, as "whole person" and not simply as "human capital," should not be lost sight of. In other words, it is important that such programs be put into perspective, that the courses themselves be developed to provide not only skills but some understanding of the relevance and importance of the skills, and that appropriate academic as well as occupational counseling be available to students. Looked at with these factors in mind, such instructional campus-business linkages, far from making the classroom captive to outside nonacademic interests, open up and thus expand the opportunity for higher education institutions to serve more fully not only students but the wider social and economic community in which they exist.

The Noncomparability of In-Service Education Myth

Those who have reservations about instructional campus-business linkages and the courses and programs offered as a result are likely to be even more concerned about any discussion of equivalence of in-service education or training within or by business and industry itself when higher education institutions in the more traditional sense are not involved at all. The critical question is whether such in-service training and education are relevant to postsecondary or higher education and should be considered for credit toward degrees, certificates, or other forms of academic recognition. This is clearly related to the Transfer of Credit Myth considered in Chapter Two; what was said there in regard both to in-service business education and training and to experiential learning is equally relevant here. A few additional comments, however, may be helpful, given the scope of the issue and its relevance for assessing the postsecondary educational activities and resources of the country. Until relatively recently, corporate in-service education has tended to be largely ignored by the higher education community. In *Corporate Classrooms: The Learning Business,* Nell Eurich (1985) reported the results of a study of education and training by business and industry carried out by the Carnegie Foundation for the Advancement of Teaching. In the foreword to that book, Ernest Boyer rightly comments that "Her study shows that corporate learning has become an absolutely essential part of the educational resources of the nation" (p. ix).

The scope of corporate or business and industry in-service education and training almost parallels that of the higher education community itself. On the financial side, Alan Knox (1987, p. 14) reported that the total amount spent for training and development in 1987 exceeded $100 billion. This figure, it should be noted, includes both public and private employers, but it is with the latter that we are primarily concerned here. It should also be noted that total higher education expenditures for 1985–86 were approximately $98 billion (*The Chronicle of Higher Education Almanac,* 1989, p. 22). Further, the number of students or participants, approximately eight million in 1985 (Eurich, 1985, p. 7), matches or exceeds the number of students in all four-year and graduate colleges and universities in the country, which in 1985 equaled 7,715,978 (Center for Education Statistics, 1987, p. 125). The programs offered by business and industry, as Boyer (1985) points out, range from "remedial English to the Ph.D., from short term intensive training to sophisticated high-tech graduate study" (p. x). The specific operations range from those conducted in plant by company trainers through elaborate learning or educational training centers with their own facilities to degree-granting institutions, which in most cases are accredited by recognized accrediting agencies. Eurich (1985) reports that as of 1985, some four hundred companies operated separate buildings or "campuses" labeled as colleges, universities, institutions, or education centers (p. 48). She also describes some eighteen degree-granting operations, or what she calls corporate colleges (pp. 88–95). According to Mary Jo Elenberg (1987, sec. V) of the Oklahoma City chapter of the American Society for Training and Development, another thirteen corporations were planning to open their own "colleges" by 1988.

Finally, while the primary curricular emphasis in most programs is on application rather than theory, and much of the training is job- and even task-specific, there has been a growing tendency to include a broader perspective, particularly at the learning centers and in degree-granting programs. Thus,

Eurich (1985) reports that "The curriculum of corporate class-rooms has broadened remarkably in recent years. Courses of study now seek to educate the whole person and to put the work of industry in a larger social, economic, and political context. Indeed, the corporate curriculum increasingly parallels the work of the nation's colleges and universities, ranging from the teaching of English and computation to post-doctoral study and research" (p. 59).

It would thus seem progressively obvious that corporate education constitutes, in addition to the elementary and secondary schools and the colleges, a third major segment of education in this country. In fact, where one draws the line between "corporate education" and "higher education" becomes more and more arbitrary. The question of the relationship of this third sector to higher education is a complicated one, much too complicated to deal with here. However, in terms of the educational validity of such corporate education and training and its equivalence to college-level work, particularly as evidenced by transferability to and acceptance at collegiate institutions, the picture is mixed.

Most of the "corporate colleges" or degree-granting programs either have or are in the process of obtaining accreditation by their appropriate regional and specialized accrediting bodies. For all intents and purposes, these have joined the collegiate community. When it comes to the far larger range of business and industry programs provided through company learning centers or directly in plant as in-service training programs, the situation is considerably different. In a broad sense, almost all such programs are part of the continuing education of the participants. Much such work does in fact parallel or expand college-level work. This was specifically recognized by the Carnegie Commission on Non-Traditional Study in 1973. Through its Commission on Accreditation of Service Experience, the American Council on Education has been evaluating military training equivalency for credit since 1945. Accordingly, the Commission on Non-Traditional Study recommended that the techniques used by the American Council "should be used in other alternate systems to establish credit and other equivalencies for courses offered by government, industry, and other sponsors" (Commission on Non-Traditional Study, 1973, p. 89).

In 1974, with the help of funding from the Carnegie Corporation and the Fund for the Improvement of Postsecondary Education, the American Council on Education and the New York Board of Regents undertook a joint Program on Noncollegiate Sponsored Instruction with particular emphasis on courses offered by business and industry. A first guide resulting from the pilot study was jointly published that year. After 1976, the American Council and the board of regents went their separate ways, each publishing its own guide. The American Council calls its guide *The National Guide to Educational Credit for Training Programs* (Galloway and Spille, 1989), and the board of regents uses the title *College Credit Recommendations* (University of the State of New York, 1987). While both are technically national in scope, they tend to complement each other, with the regents' guide concentrating on New York and the American Council guide on the rest of the country, although there is some overlap. In each case, the courses are evaluated and credit recommendations are made by experts from the academic community in the areas in question. Between the two of them, more than 6,000 courses at about 400 organizations have been reviewed through their Program on Noncollegiate Sponsored Instruction (PONSI). The American Council on Education (1988) claims that some 1,500 academic institutions have accepted credits under its program, and the regents claim that some 1,300 have accepted their credit recommendations. Usually, institutions that accept the one also accept the other. The evaluations are paid for by the corporations involved, and the costs range from $2,500 to $3,750 plus the cost of a two-day visit by the evaluators.

In addition to and in reinforcement of its PONSI activities, the American Council on Education has developed a national Registry of Credit Recommendations, which establishes a permanent record or transcript for employee-students of more than fifty sponsoring organizations, including courses completed, outcomes, and credit recommendations. These are available to any college to which the student wishes them sent for evaluation.

To date, the registry contains the records of some 30,000 individuals (Spille, 1989, p. 32).

These various developments in recognizing and evaluating corporate instruction for credit and acceptance of those credits by higher education institutions are highly encouraging. There are two factors, however, that put something of a damper on enthusiasm about them and that suggest that the Noncomparability of In-Service Education Myth is still alive in spite of the major progress that has taken place. One is the concern noted by Nell Eurich (1985, pp. 81–82) and discussed in Chapter Two about the difficulties in obtaining cooperation from some institutions in granting credit as recommended by the two programs for noncollegiate-sponsored instruction. This concern, Eurich suggests, tends to be somewhat typical of higher education institutions.

The second and related factor is that while the number of institutions that have accepted such credit recommendations — at least 1,500 — is impressive, the number and kinds of institutions that have not is also impressive. While there are important exceptions, the 1988 list of institutions accepting American Council on Education credit evaluations does not include either the flagship public institutions or the most prominent private institutions in a number of states. Thus, for example, while most of the California State University colleges do accept such credit, among those not included in the list of accepting institutions are eight of the units of the University of California (the important exception being Berkeley) and Stanford University. In Connecticut, Yale, Trinity, and Wesleyan are among the missing; in Massachusetts, Harvard, MIT, Brandeis, and Tufts are not on the list; in Michigan, the University of Michigan, Ann Arbor, is not present. On the other hand, institutions such as Princeton, Cornell, the University of Wisconsin, Johns Hopkins, and the University of Illinois have accepted or do accept such credits. Thus, while it is a mixed picture that reflects a recognition on the part of much of the academic community of the legitimacy of the equivalent learning and accomplishment of students in relevant programs in business and industry to higher education programs and degrees, it is disturbing that so many of the more prominent and prestigious schools seem not to do so.

We have suggested a number of times that our national postsecondary educational objectives include reinforcement of the learning society and life-span learning as critical, first, for the welfare, accomplishments, and careers of the individuals involved and, second, for the welfare and health of society, including economic development, productivity, and competitiveness of states and the nation. If this is so, then we can ill afford not to recognize the importance and legitimacy of the corporate classroom as the third sector of education in general and postsecondary education in particular. This does not mean that distinctions between the corporate educational system and the higher education system do not exist or should be downplayed any more than distinctions among various types of higher education institutions in the light of their missions and functions should be. What does seem to be called for, on both the research liaison level and the instructional campus-business linkage level, is fostering of more effective understanding and cooperation while maintaining the unique contributions and functions of both the collegiate system and the corporate system.

The fundamental challenge is to build the kinds of linkages or systems that ensure the continuity and accumulative impact of continuing educational experiences, whether in the collegiate sector, in the corporate classroom, in experiential learning, or in all three. This involves recognition that the real and fundamental task is to provide the rigor and flexibility that allow each life-span student, regardless of age, of corporate or collegiate affiliation, or or full- or part-time status, to be assessed and encouraged on the basis of what he or she knows and is capable of doing as that is related to appropriate educational objectives, and not on the basis of structural hurdles that have little to do with the learning process.

Summary

The concern that higher education is somehow being tainted by too close a relationship with business and industry is not new. The current recognition of the relevance of higher education to economic development and international competitiveness by business, industry, and government, on the one hand, and by educators in the higher education community, on the other, has tended both to increase the tension between the two and to offer new and wider opportunities for cooperation and for higher education institutions directly to serve their communities and the nation.

University-industrial research liaison activities have become progressively more important. Today it is crucial for research universities to recognize the advantages of and even the imperative for continuing and extending such industry research liaison activities to help meet changing economic and social conditions, to reinforce economic development, to help increase national economic competitiveness, and thus to be responsible citizens in the contemporary world. However, to ensure institutional and researcher integrity, it is extraordinarily important that each university involved in such research and its faculty develop *beforehand* clear policies in regard to conflict of interest, secrecy, ownership and intellectual property rights, time commitments, and the relationship of research to other academic commitments; that alternative research opportunities for faculty members not be closed off by research liaison agreements; and that the critical role of basic research not be lost sight of in concern for applied research.

Campus-business instructional linkages are extraordinarily important in delivering educational and training content, not just for initial entry into the world of work but for updating, retraining, and occupational and job change. To the extent that preparing students for professions, subprofessions, occupations, and vocations as a part of career development in the broad sense is an essential function of higher education, the more relevant such higher education and training is to the tasks to be performed, the more effective the education and training are likely to be. Given the changing college population, the preponderance of older students, and the increasing numbers of minorities in the population and the work force, the need for close college-business cooperation and planning in meeting both the needs of human beings as people and the needs of business and industry for well-trained, educated workers becomes progressively more crucial.

Two major cautions in relation to campus-business instructional linkages are critical. First, any campus-business instructional linkage must be directly related to the institution's mission and objectives as well as to business and industry objectives. Second, in the development of such institutional campus-business linkages, the students must be considered not simply as human capital or as units of productivity but as whole persons. Thus, part of the colleges' function in the linkage is to insist on the importance of perspective.

If our community, state, and national objectives in postsecondary education include reinforcement of the learning society and life-span learning as critical for the careers and accomplishments of individuals in society and for the economic development, productivity, and competitiveness of society itself, then we can ill afford not to recognize the importance of the corporate classroom as a third critical sector of education in this country. This does not mean disregarding the uniqueness of the collegiate sector or the corporate system any more than one disregards the unique missions of individual higher education institutions. What is called for, as in the university-industrial research liaison and college-business instructional linkage, is more effective cooperative understanding and mutual reinforcement in achieving common goals.

9

Honoring Tradition
While Building the Future

Five central themes have emerged out of this review of higher education myths that might be described as basic perspectives for dealing with the realities of the twenty-first century. They do not involve abandoning tradition. This, by the nature of the case, would be neither desirable nor possible. They do involve transcending or reformulating tradition to deal with the new realities. These perspectives are themselves rooted in traditions, some of which are as old as higher education itself and some much more recent but all of them related to quality, equity, and the comprehensive role that higher education can and should play in the contemporary world. They focus on people in society, not on academic or bureaucratic forms or structures as such; on the service of higher education to society, not on institutional aggrandizement; and on the legitimacy, even the necessity of multiple higher education objectives to meet the complex and varied needs of people in the contemporary world. They emphasize what today should be the continuity of postsecondary education in life-span learning for people of all ages, not just the preparation of the young to enter the adult world. Finally, they place particular emphasis on results or accomplishments rather than the specific means of getting there.

The first of these perspectives involves the recognition that career development extending throughout life is the primary instructional objective of education in general and higher education in particular. It should be the key to curricular organization, to counseling, and to assessment of educational effectiveness. Career in this sense includes far more than work, although occupational preparation, reinforcement, and renewal are an important part of it, whether one is a homemaker, an auto mechanic, a physician, or a research scientist. It includes affective as well as cognitive elements and thus life plan, life-style, and life work. It can and should serve as a paradigm for integrating liberal or general and specialized, professional, or occupational education or programs into relevant wholes adapted to the unique interests and needs of particular individuals. For the individual, career provides the sense of direction that makes it possible to compare and choose among competing values and objectives, not only in formal educational activities but in other areas of experience as well.

The second perspective calls for explicit recognition of not only the legitimacy of but the necessity for a real diversity of postsecondary institutions and programs to meet the variety of appropriate career needs of citizens and the research and public-service needs of society. This implies a real diversity in the instructional, research, and community service objectives of different institutions and not simply or primarily different forms of control or ownership of institutions, as is sometimes argued. In relation to instruction, it calls for a diversity of both subject areas and programs related to different educational objectives, as well as recognition of the legitimacy of the diversity of means for attaining these objectives as long as the appropriate objectives are in fact achieved. What is crucial is the development of clear and explicit institutional and program missions and objectives that are relevant to individual and societal needs. The public, through the states particularly, has an overriding interest in ensuring that this is the case. This includes ensuring that the needs are being met not only instructionally but also in research and public service. At least in the public sector, this should be accomplished through cooperative planning, including mission determination, in which the states are involved through their higher education agencies (where these exist). The private sector of higher education should also be encouraged to participate.

The third perspective concerns quality and involves the recognition that educational quality needs to be defined not in terms of reputation or resources but in terms of excellence in kind and thus in terms of effective use of resources to achieve appropriate educational objectives. Such a conception of educational quality means that one can equally expect high quality in all types of institutions and programs. It eliminates invidious comparisons and the mistaking of reputational hierarchies with the real presence of high quality. Quality comparisons should assess how well each institution or program achieves its appropriate mission and objectives and should be phrased in terms of relative mission accomplishment. For institutions, this means that quality is a function not just of instruction, as central and important as that is, but of all their activities as they are related to their missions and objectives. For students and instructional activities, the "bottom line" is educational accomplishment, or the actual achievement of knowledge, skills, and attitudes defined by the educational objectives — and thus positive outcomes. Assessment in the broad sense, while it is not defining of quality, is crucial to its determination.

The fourth perspective concerns equity and calls for the recognition that while access and its extension are essential to equity, equity is considerably more than access alone. It also requires remedial support when necessary, environmental support, information support, financial support, and, most important, program quality. Equity is fundamental to career development and fulfillment in our society today. It is also crucial to dealing with the demographic changes already occurring, to developing an adequately prepared work force for the next century, to increasing productivity and international competitiveness, and to preparing an educated citizenry capable of dealing with the changing conditions.

The fifth perspective calls for recognizing the critical importance of bringing nontraditional students and nontraditional programs into the mainstream of higher education. "Traditional students" are now a decided minority (less than one-sixth) of the college population, and yet many colleges and universities are organized and operate as though the traditional students were the majority and constituted the norm. In far too many places, adult and continuing education is still considered a kind of auxiliary public-service activity, not part of the major business of the campus. There are still faculty members who consider off-campus operation, programs carried out via the new technologies, and experiential learning as not really part of the mainstream or central educational mission of higher educational institutions. For higher education to be relevant to current and future students and the needs of the contemporary world, it is critically important that the distinctions between traditional and nontraditional students and programs and between adult and continuing education and other central institutional activities at the very least be minimized and perhaps even be recognized as anachronistic and done away with. It is essential that institutions reassess the relevance of their educational programs and structures to the range of their actual students.

Our concern, however, is with the need for the higher education community to recognize far more clearly than it has in the past the continuity of higher education and the need for effective planning to ensure that life-span learning becomes the norm rather than the exception. To the extent that this is done, higher education will not be abandoning but will be broadening and transforming its traditional instructional mission to encompass concern not only with preparation of the young for careers but with providing higher education opportunity for career development, enrichment, and change to people at any age and any stage of life. While progress has been made in this direction, this broadened concept of instructional mission needs to become an integral part of the mission of a considerably wider range of higher education institutions than is now the case. Such an emphasis on career development in the broad sense as the primary instructional mission of higher education in no way diminishes the importance of research and close cooperation between the universities and the industrial and business communities in developing its application. It clearly reinforces the legitimacy and importance of instructional campus-business linkages where they are relevant. It thus recognizes the critical importance of higher education to the economic development of the states and the nation. But it places economic concerns within the much broader perspective of developing the comprehensive careers of people in society — in other words, of providing both personal and social balance and enrichment. To the extent that this goal becomes central and is at least partially achieved, the prospects for the twenty-first century and for the key role that higher education will — in fact, must — play in it look bright indeed. We will then be approximating the Oklahoma Network of Continuing Higher Education objective of providing "relevant higher education opportunity to everyone, everywhere, everyday" on a national scale.

The question remains, however, can we afford it? Perhaps a far more relevant question is whether we can afford not to support the further development of the higher education system to overcome the myths, to accomplish the transition, and to provide the range of opportunity called for. Citing figures from the Institute for Adult Learning at Pennsylvania State University, Senator Paul Simon (1988) pointed out in 1988 that the costs of not educating disadvantaged young men and women for careers and jobs alone is over $255 billion a year in productivity, welfare, and expenses related to crime prevention and the criminal justice system (pp. B2, B3). In *The Memorandum to the 41st President of the United States,* the Commission on National Challenges in Higher Education (1988) points out that between now and the year 2000, "a majority of all new jobs will, for the first time in history, call for some form of postsecondary education" (p. 3). The National Commission on the Role and Future of State Colleges and Universities (1986) points out that "Ignorance is costly — it is the passageway to a disastrous fall from which America may never recover" (p. 2). Nell Eurich (1985) points out that "Urging the restoration of America's leadership and competitive position in the world economy sounds hollow if our educational resources are ignored as the underpinning for development and if training needs are unmet. The nation is weakened by any person unable to contribute to its productivity and enrichment in any sense" (p. 140).

On the positive side, Leslie and Brinkman (1988), in *The Economic Value of Higher Education,* provide extensive documentation to reach the following conclusions:

- College does pay off, in most cases, for the individual who invests in higher education. The payoff typically is quite handsome—a good deal more handsome than most observers perceive (p. 8).
- In terms of social rates of return, society receives a positive payoff on its investment in higher education. Again, the return is far more handsome than commonly perceived (p. 9).
- Education is a major contributor to economic growth in the United States (p. 12).

Finally, Clark Kerr (1988) points out that "Higher education, more than ever before, helps to create the wealth that finances it" (p. 35). The answer seems clear: Not only can we afford to support higher education in facilitating its own transition and the social, economic, and political transitions facing us in the twenty-first century; not to do so can only result in national disaster.

We began by noting the remarkable progress that higher education has made in the United States in the last half of the twentieth century. We have analyzed some of the endemic assumptions that need rethinking if that progress is to continue. We end by insisting not only that many of these traditional assumptions can be and are being transcended in a renewed vision of higher educational objectives but that on the continued evolution and support of higher education depend the future of the nation and the quality of life in the twenty-first century.

References

Abbott, F. C. *Governmental Policy and Higher Education.* Ithaca, N.Y.: Cornell University Press, 1958.

Abelson, P. H. "Academic-Industrial Interactions." *Science,* Apr. 15, 1988, *240,* p. 265.

Adelman, C. "To Imagine an Adverb." In C. Adelman (ed.), *Assessment in American Higher Education.* Washington, D.C.: Office of Educational Research and Improvement, U.S. Department of Education, 1985.

American Association of Collegiate Registrars and Admissions Officers. *Transfer Credit Practices of Designated Educational Institutions.* Washington, D.C.: American Association of Collegiate Registrars and Admission Officers, 1988.

American College Testing Program. "National Dropout Rates" and "National Graduation Rates." Compiled by S. C. Cowart. Iowa City: American College Testing Program, 1989.

American Council of Learned Societies. "Speaking for the Humanities." *Chronicle of Higher Education,* Jan. 11, 1989, pp. A11, A12, A14, A16, A17, A20, A22.

American Council on Education. *Academic Institutions That Have Accepted ACE Credit Recommendations.* Washington, D.C.: American Council on Education, 1988.

"America's Best Colleges." *U.S. News and World Report,* Oct. 10, 1988.

Anderson, R. E., and Sugarman, B. *Options for Technology Transfer.* Capital Ideas, vol. 4, nos. 1 and 2. New York: Forum for College Financing, Teachers College, Columbia University, 1989.

Andrews, G. J. *Assessing Non-Traditional Education.* Vol. 1. Washington, D.C.: Council on Postsecondary Education, 1978.

Apps, J. W. "Adult and Continuing Education." In K. Halstead (ed.), *Higher Education Bibliography Yearbook, 1988.* (2nd ed.) Washington, D.C.: Research Associates of Washington, 1988.

Ashby, E. *Technology and the Academics: An Essay on Universities and the Scientific Revolution.* New York: St. Martin's Press, 1966.

Association of American Colleges. *Integrity in the College Curriculum: A Report to the Academic Community.* Washington, D.C.: Association of American Colleges, 1985.

Association of American Colleges, Task Group on General Education. *A New Vitality in General Education.* Washington, D.C.: Association of American Colleges, 1988.

Astin, A. W. "Why Not Try Some New Ways of Measuring Quality?" *Educational Record,* Spring 1982, pp. 10–15.

Astin, A. W. *Achieving Educational Excellence: A Critical Assessment of Priorities and Practices in Higher Education.* San Francisco: Jossey-Bass, 1985.

Astin, A. W. "Achieving Educational Excellence." In Oklahoma Network for Continuing Higher Education, *The Expanding Knowledge Base.* Oklahoma City: Oklahoma State Regents for Higher Education, 1986.

Astin, A. W., and Solomon, L. "Are Reputational Ratings Needed to Measure Quality?" *Change,* Oct. 1981, pp. 14–19.

Astin, A. W., and others. *The American Freshman: National Norms for Fall 1985.* Los Angeles: Higher Education Research Institute, 1985.

Astin, A. W., and others. *The American Freshman: National Norms for Fall 1988.* Los Angeles: Higher Education Research Institute, 1988.

Belt, J., and Sackett, R. *Priorities for Demonstration Projects in Continuing Education in Oklahoma.* Unpublished report, Oklahoma Network of Continuing Higher Education, 1987.

Benjamin, E. "The Movement to Assess Students' Learning Will Institutionalize Mediocrity in Colleges." *Chronicle of Higher Education,* Jul. 5, 1990, pp. B1–B2.

Bennett, W. J. *To Reclaim a Legacy: A Report on the Humanities in Higher Education.* Washington, D.C.: National Endowment for the Humanities, 1984.

Berdahl, R. O. *Statewide Coordination of Higher Education.* Washington, D.C.: American Council of Education, 1971.

Berdahl, R. O. "Statewide Coordination of Higher Education." *Chronicle of Higher Education,* July 5, 1990, pp. B1–B2.

Bickart, T. "Effective Education, Technology, and Teaching." In National University Continuing Education Association, *Challenges for Continuing Higher Education Leadership: Corporate/ Campus Collaboration.* Washington, D.C.: National University Continuing Education Association, 1987.

Birnbaum, R. "Administrative Commitments and Minority Enrollments: College Presidents' Goals for Quality and Access." *Review of Higher Education,* 1988, 2 (4), 435–457.

Blackwell, J. E. "Faculty Issues: The Impact on Minorities." *Review of Higher Education,* 1988, 2 (4), 417–434.

Bloom, A. *The Closing of the American Mind.* New York: Simon & Schuster, 1987.

Blumenstyk, G. "Many States Are Turning to Science Advisers for Expertise in Crisis and Budget Battles." *Chronicle of Higher Education,* Apr. 19, 1989, pp. A21–A22.

Botstein, L. "The Limits of Technology." In National University Continuing Education Association, *Challenges for Continuing Higher Education Leadership: Corporate/Campus Collaboration.* Washington, D.C.: National University Continuing Education Association, 1987.

Bowen, H. R. *The State of the Nation and the Agenda for Higher Education.* San Francisco: Jossey-Bass, 1982.

Boyer, C., and Ewell, P. *Assessment of Undergraduate Education: A Glossary and Selected References.* Denver, Colorado: Education Commission of the States, 1988.

Boyer, E. *The Control of the Campus.* Princeton, N.J.: Carnegie Foundation for the Advancement of Teaching, 1982.

Boyer, E. "Foreword." In N. P. Eurich, *Corporate Classrooms: The Learning Business.* Princeton, N.J.: Carnegie Foundation for the Advancement of Teaching, 1985.

Boyer, E. *College: The Undergraduate Experience in America.* New York: Harper & Row, 1987.

Boyer, E. "School Reform: A National Strategy." Paper presented at the Business Roundtable, Washington, D.C., June 3, 1989.

Bragg, G. L. "Impact of the Technology Renaissance on Oklahoma Higher Education." Address to the Leadership Development Seminar for Presidents and Governing Boards, Oklahoma State University, Mar. 7, 1987.

Breneman, D. *The Coming Enrollment Crisis: What Every Trustee Should Know.* Washington, D.C.: Association of Governing Boards of Universities and Colleges, 1982.

Brint, S., and Karabel, J. *The Diverted Dream: Community Colleges and the Promise of Educational Opportunity in America, 1900–1985.* New York: Oxford University Press, 1989.

Burns, N. (ed.). *Evaluation of Institutions of Postsecondary Education: An Annotated List of Instruments.* Washington, D.C.: Council on Postsecondary Accreditation, 1975.

Burns, N. *Evaluation of Institutions of Postsecondary Education: Assessment in Terms of Outcomes Through Institutional Self-Study.* Washington, D.C.: Council on Postsecondary Accreditation, 1978.

Business–Higher Education Forum. *America's Competitive Challenge: The Need for a National Response.* Washington, D.C.: Business–Higher Education Forum, 1983.

Cabell, H., and Hickerson, J. H. "Instructional Models: Whys and Hows of Prior Learning Assessment." In S. Simosko and Associates, *Assessing Learning: A CAEL Handbook.* Columbia, Md.: Council for Adult and Experiential Learning, 1988.

Callan, P. "Minority Degree Achievement and the State Policy Environment." *Review of Higher Education,* 1988, *2* (4), 335–364.

Carnevale, A. P., Gainer, L. J., and Meltzer, A. S. *Workplace Basics: The Skills Employers Want.* Alexandria, Va.: American Society for Training and Development, n.d.

Carter, L. *Kellogg Interdisciplinary Task Force on Governance (1985–1987): A Summary of the Final Report.* Athens: University of Georgia, 1988.

Center for Education Statistics. *Digest of Education Statistics, 1987.* Washington, D.C.: Office of Educational Research, U.S. Department of Education, 1987.

Chafin, J. S. Letter to the editor. *Chronicle of Higher Education,* May 3, 1989, pp. B5–B6.

Chait, R. "Assessing Assessment's Future." *Centerpiece,* 1989, *4* (1), 3.

Cheit, E. J. *The New Depression in Higher Education*. New York: McGraw-Hill, 1971.

Cheit, E. J. *The Useful Arts and the Liberal Tradition*. New York: McGraw-Hill, 1975.

Cheney, L. V. *Humanities in America*. Washington, D.C.: National Endowment for the Humanities, 1988.

The Chronicle of Higher Education Almanac. (Special supplement edition.) Sept. 6, 1989.

Cohen, A. M. "Degree Achievement by Minorities in Community Colleges." *Review of Higher Education*, 1988, *2* (4), 383–402.

Collison, M. "Neighborhood Campuses and Flexible Class Schedules Lure New York Adults to College of New Rochelle." *Chronicle of Higher Education*. Oct. 18, 1988, pp. A39–A40.

Commission on Educational Quality. *Access to Quality Undergraduate Education*. Atlanta, Ga.: Southern Regional Education Board, 1986.

Commission on National Challenges in Higher Education. *Memorandum to the 41st President of the United States*. Washington, D.C.: American Council on Education, 1988.

Commission on Non-Traditional Study. *Diversity by Design*. San Francisco: Jossey-Bass, 1973.

Committee of Vice-Chancellors and Principals of the Universities of the United Kingdom. *Academic Standards in Universities*. London: Committee of Vice-Chancellors and Principals of the Universities of the United Kingdom, 1986.

Cordes, C. "Colleges Receive About $289-Million in Earmarked Funds." *Chronicle of Higher Education*, Feb. 1, 1989, pp. A1, A20.

Council for the Advancement and Support of Education, National Task Force on Higher Education and the Public Interest. *Special Advisory for College and University Presidents*. Washington, D.C.: Council for the Advancement and Support of Education, 1988.

Council on Postsecondary Accreditation. *Specialized Accreditation and Liberal Learning*. Washington, D.C.: Council on Postsecondary Accreditation, 1985.

Council on Postsecondary Accreditation. *Educational Quality and Accreditation: A Call for Diversity, Continuity and Innovation*. Washington, D.C.: Council on Postsecondary Accreditation, 1986.

Council on Postsecondary Accreditation. *The COPA Handbook.* Washington, D.C.: Council on Postsecondary Accreditation, 1990.

Council on the Continuing Education Unit, Project to Develop Standards and Criteria for Good Practice in Continuing Education. *Principles of Good Practice in Continuing Education.* Washington, D.C.: Council on the Continuing Education Unit, 1984.

Council on the Continuing Education Unit. *The Continuing Education Unit: Criteria and Guidelines.* Washington, D.C.: Council on the Continuing Education Unit, 1987.

Cross, K. P., and Hilton, W. J. *Enhancing the State Role in Lifelong Learning.* Denver, Colo.: Education Commission of the States, 1983.

Cross, K. P., and McCartan, A. *Adult Learning: State Policies and Institutional Practices.* Washington, D.C.: Association for the Study of Higher Education, 1984.

Danachak, M. "Knowledge Maintenance for the Professional." In National University Continuing Education Association, *Challenges for Continuing Higher Education Leadership: Corporate/ Campus Collaboration.* Washington, D.C.: National University Continuing Education Association, 1987.

Day, P., Jr. *In Search of Community College Partnerships.* Washington, D.C.: American Association of Community and Junior Colleges, 1985.

Day, P. R., Jr., and Rajasekhara, K. *Keeping America Working: Profiles in Partnership.* Washington, D.C.: American Association of Community and Junior Colleges, 1988.

Defense Activity for Non-Traditional Education Support (DANTES). "Naval Electronic Campus System (NECS)/Program for Afloat College Education (PACE II) Aboard Norfolk-based Ships." *Educational Technology Report,* Feb. 1988, no. 13.

DeLoughry, T. J. "Study of Transcript Finds Little Structure in the Liberal Arts." *Chronicle of Higher Education,* June 18, 1988, pp. A1, A32.

DeLoughry, T. J. "House Passes Bill to Freeze Student Aid and Increase Financing of other College Programs and NIH." *Chronicle of Higher Education,* Aug. 9, 1989b, pp. A13, A16.

DeLoughry, T. J. "Education Officials Fear Indifference Among Politicians to College Problems." *Chronicle of Higher Education,* Oct. 11, 1989a, pp. A21, A34.

Edgerton, R. "It All Begins in the Classroom: An Interview with K. Patricia Cross." *AAHE Bulletin,* Sept. 1985, pp. 3–7.

Education Commission of the States. *Challenge: Coordination and Governance in the 80's.* Denver, Colo.: Education Commission of the States, 1980.

Education Commission of the States. *Transforming the State Role in Undergraduate Education: Time for a Different View.* Denver, Colo.: Education Commission of the States, 1986.

Education Commission of the States. *Assessment and Outcomes Measurement: A View from the States.* Denver, Colo.: Education Commission of the States, 1987.

Education Commission of the States. "Boggled by 'Outcomes,' 'Indicators,' 'Gate Keeping,' 'Tracking,'? Assessment Glossary Will Help." *State Education Leader,* 1988, *7* (1).

Education Commission of the States. "Removing Race/Ethnicity as a Factor in College Completion." *State Education Leader,* 1989, *7* (4), pp. 1, 3–5.

Elenberg, M. J. "Business Management, Finance & Marketing Position Paper." *Position Papers: Continuing Professional Education Needs.* Oklahoma City: Oklahoma Network of Continuing Higher Education, section V, 1987.

El-Khawas, E. *Campus Trends, 1985.* Washington, D.C.: American Council on Education, 1985.

El-Khawas, E. *Campus Trends, 1987.* Washington, D.C.: American Council on Education, 1987.

El-Khawas, E. *Campus Trends, 1988.* Washington, D.C.: American Council on Education, 1988.

El-Khawas, E. *Campus Trends, 1989.* Washington, D.C.: American Council on Education, 1989.

Elman, S., and Lynton, E. A. "Assessment in Career-Oriented Education." In C. Adelman (ed.), *Assessment in American Higher Education.* Washington, D.C.: Office of Educational Research and Improvement, U.S. Department of Education, 1985.

Enarson, H. L. "Quality–Indefinable but Not Unattainable." *Educational Record,* Winter 1983, pp. 7–9.

Eurich, N. P. *Corporate Classrooms: The Learning Business.* Princeton, N.J.: Carnegie Foundation for the Advancement of Teaching, 1985.

Evangelauf, J. "Education Department Foresees Slight Fluctuations in Number of College Students over Next Decade." *Chronicle of Higher Education,* Nov. 30, 1988, pp. A33–A34.

Evangelauf, J. "For Most, Cost of Going to College Outpaces Inflation Again." *Chronicle of Higher Education,* Aug. 16, 1989a, pp. A1, A26.

Evangelauf, J. "Record College Enrollments Mask Serious Flaws in Student Admissions Systems, Experts Warn." *Chronicle of Higher Education,* Feb. 8, 1989b, A1, pp. A30–A31.

Ewell, P., Finney, J., and Lenth, C. "Filling in the Mosaic." *AAHE Bulletin,* April 1990, pp. 3–5.

Ewell, P. T., and Jones, D. P. "The Costs of Assessment." In C. Adelman (ed.), *Assessment in American Higher Education.* Washington, D.C.: Office of Educational Research and Improvement, U.S. Department of Education, 1985.

Fairweather, J. S. *Entrepreneurship and Higher Education: Lessons for Colleges, Universities, and Industry.* Washington, D.C.: Association for Higher Education, 1988.

Feistritzer, C. E. "Will American Workers Be Ready for the 21st Century?" *Washington Post,* Education in Review, Aug. 7, 1988, pp. 11–13.

Fenwick, D. C., and others. *Guide to Campus-Business Linkage Programs: Education and Business Prospering Together.* (Rev. ed.) New York: Macmillan, 1986.

Finn, C. E., Jr. "Consumers Need a 'No-Frills University' to Turn the Higher Education Marketplace Upside Down." *Chronicle of Higher Education,* Oct. 26, 1988, pp. B1–B2.

Fisher, J. L. "Social Imperatives in Higher Education in the 1990's." Address to the Leadership Development Seminar, Oklahoma Center for Continuing Education. Norman, Apr. 16, 1987.

Folger, J., and McGuinness, A., Jr. *Catalog of Changes, 1984.* Denver, Colo.: Education Commission of the States, 1984.

Frances, C. "Uses and Misuses of Demographic Projections: Lessons for the 1990s." In A. Levine and Associates, *Shaping*

Higher Education's Future: Demographic Realities and Opportunities, 1990–2000. San Francisco: Jossey-Bass, 1989.

Freedman, L. *Quality in Continuing Education: Principles, Practices, and Standards for Colleges and Universities.* San Francisco: Jossey-Bass, 1987.

Fuchsberg, G. "Universities Said to Go Too Fast in Quest of Profit from Research." *Chronicle of Higher Education.* Apr. 12, 1989, pp. A28–A30.

Fulton, O. "Entry Standards." Unpublished paper prepared for the Anglo-American Seminar on Quality in Higher Education, Templeton College, Oxford University, Dec. 1986.

Galloway, S., and Spille, H. A. *The National Guide to Educational Credit for Training Programs.* New York: American Council on Education/Macmillan, 1989.

Gamson, Z. F. "Education and the Real World." Unpublished manuscript for the Council on Adult and Experiential Learning, 1988.

Giamatti, A. B. "American Colleges and Universities Have Failed to Assert Their Ideals and Purposes Persuasively." *Chronicle of Higher Education,* Nov. 9, 1988, p. B1.

Gildea, T. "High Tech Industries: Staying on the Technological Forefront Through Employee Reeducation: Implications for Academia." In National University Continuing Education Association, *Challenges for Continuing Higher Education Leadership: Corporate/Campus Collaboration.* Washington, D.C.: National University Continuing Education Association, 1987.

Gleazer, E. J., Jr. *The Community College: Values, Vision & Vitality.* Washington, D.C.: American Association of Community and Junior Colleges, 1980.

Glenny, L. "Politics and Current Patterns in Coordinating Higher Education." In J. W. Minter (ed.), *Campus and Capitol.* Boulder, Colo.: Western Interstate Commission on Higher Education, 1966.

The Grant Commission. *The Forgotten Half.* Washington, D.C.: William T. Grant Foundation Commission on Work, Family and Citizenship, 1988.

Gray, H. H. *The Liberal Arts Revisited.* Chicago: University of Illinois, 1981.

Gray, W. H. "America's Rural Economy Under Stress: Challenges for Continuing Higher Education." In National University Continuing Education Association, *Challenges for Continuing Higher Education: The Transformation of Rural America.* Washington, D.C.: National University of Continuing Education Association, 1987.

Grossman, D. M. *Hidden Perils: Instructional Media and Higher Education.* Washington, D.C.: National University Continuing Education Association, 1987.

Halstead, K. (ed.) *Higher Education Bibliography Yearbook, 1988.* (2nd ed.) Washington, D.C.: Research Associates of Washington, 1988.

Hamm, R., and Tolle-Burger, L. *Doing Business with Business.* Washington, D.C.: American Association of Community and Junior Colleges, 1988.

Hansen, W. L., and Stampen, J. O. "Balancing Quality and Access in Financing Higher Education." Unpublished paper, University of Wisconsin, Madison, 1987.

Hardy, G. *External Views.* Report to the Board of Trustees and Donald M. Stewart, president of the College Board. New York: College Entrance Examination Board, 1988.

Harris, J. "Assessing Outcomes in Higher Education." In C. Adelman (ed.), *Assessment in American Higher Education.* Washington, D.C.: Office of Educational Research and Information, U.S. Department of Education, 1985.

Harris, M. "Judgements of Quality in Higher Education: The Role of the University Grants Committee." Unpublished paper prepared for the Anglo-American Seminar on Quality in Higher Education, Templeton College, Oxford University, Dec. 1986.

Hartle, T. W. "The Growing Interest in Measuring Educational Achievement of College Students." In C. Adelman (ed.), *Assessment in American Higher Education.* Washington, D.C.: Office of Educational Research and Information, U.S. Department of Education, 1985.

Harvard Committee. *General Education in a Free Society.* Cambridge, Mass.: Harvard University Press, 1945.

Hauptman, A. M., and Andersen, C. J. "Background Paper

on American Higher Education." In Commission on National Challenges in Higher Education, *Memorandum to the 41st President of the United States.* Washington, D.C.: American Council on Education, 1988.

Hayes-Bautista, D. "Shifting Demographics: Implications for the Community and Higher Education." In National University Continuing Education Association, *Challenges for Continuing Higher Education Leadership: Economic Development in a Multicultural Society.* Washington, D.C.: National University Continuing Education Association, 1988.

Hazeltine, B. "The New Liberal Arts." Unpublished paper, Brown University, 1985.

Heller, S. "Universities Grapple with Academic Politics as They Strive to Change Their Curricula." *Chronicle of Higher Education,* Sept. 7, 1988, pp. A12–A13, A16.

Hesburgh, T. M., Miller, P. A., and Wharton, C. R., Jr. *Patterns for Lifelong Learning.* San Francisco: Jossey-Bass, 1973.

Higher Education Research Program. "The Business of the Business." *Policy Perspectives,* May 1989a, pp. 1–7.

Higher Education Research Program. "Double Trouble." *Policy Perspectives,* Sept. 1989b, pp. 1–8.

Hines, E. R. *Higher Education and State Governments.* Washington, D.C.: Association for the Study of Higher Education, 1988.

Hirsch, E. D., Jr. *Cultural Literacy: What Every American Needs to Know.* Boston: Houghton-Mifflin, 1987.

Hobbs, D. S. *Oklahoma Demographics: Myths and Realities.* Oklahoma City: Oklahoma State Regents for Higher Education, 1986.

Hodgkinson, H. L. *Higher Education: Diversity Is Our Name.* Washington, D.C.: National Institute of Independent Colleges and Universities, 1986.

Hofstadter, R. "Report of the Focus Group on Megatrends Affecting Continuing Professional Education." Unpublished report to the planning committee for the Second National Conference on Continuing Professional Education, 1988.

Hofstadter, R., and Hardy, C. D. *Development and Scope of Higher Education in the United States.* New York: Columbia University Press, 1952.

Hofstadter, R., and Smith, W. (eds.). *American Higher Education: A Documentary History.* 2 vols. Chicago: University of Chicago Press, 1961.

Holden, C. "Radical Reform in Science Education." *Science,* Mar. 3, 1989a, p. 1133.

Holden, C. "Wanted: 675,000 Future Specialists and Engineers." *Science,* June 30, 1989b, *244,* pp. 1536–1537.

Horton, P. E. Letter to J. A. Leone, chancellor of the Oklahoma State Regents for Higher Education. July 16, 1986.

Houle, C. O. *Patterns of Learning: New Perspectives on Life-Span Education.* San Francisco: Jossey-Bass, 1984.

Hughes, R. M. *A Study of Graduate Schools in America.* Oxford, Ohio: Miami University Press, 1925.

Humphries, F. S. "The Academic/Rural Split: How it Happened and Why it Should Change." *Challenges for Higher Education Leadership for Continuing Higher Education: Transforming Rural America.* Washington, D.C.: National Continuing Education Association, 1987, pp. 18–22.

Independent Commission on the Future of the State University of New York. *The Challenge and the Choice: The State University of New York.* Albany State University of New York, 1985.

Jaschik, S. "State-College Officials Call Public's Panic Over Fees Needless." *Chronicle of Higher Education,* May 18, 1988, pp. A1, A22–A23.

Jencks, C., and Riesman, D. *The Academic Revolution.* Garden City, N.Y.: Doubleday, 1968.

Johnson, G. W. *Forging New Relationships Between the Academy and the Community.* Washington, D.C.: National University Continuing Education Association, 1985.

Jonsen, R. "Lifelong Learning: State Policies." *School Review,* 1978, *46,* 360–381.

Jordan, B. "From Now to the Year 2000: Some Strategic Questions." Address at Oklahoma State University, Mar. 7, 1987, and Oklahoma Christian College, Apr. 9, 1987.

Keller, G. *Academic Strategy: The Management Revolution in American Higher Education.* Baltimore, Md.: Johns Hopkins University Press, 1983.

Kelley, J. "Colleges Shouldn't Waste Their Resources on Students Who Aren't Qualified to Be There in the First Place." *Chronicle of Higher Education,* May 17, 1989, p. B2.

Kenney, M. *Biotechnology: The University Industrial Complex.* New Haven, Conn.: Yale University Press, 1986.

Kerr, C. *Governance of Higher Education: Six Priority Problems.* New York: MacGraw-Hill, 1973.

Kerr, C. *Higher Education in Service to the Labor Market: Contributions and Distortions.* Philadelphia: Institute for Research in Higher Education, University of Pennsylvania, 1988.

King, R. "The Changing Student: A Resource for Improvement of Educational Services." *Phi Kappa Phi Journal,* Spring 1985, pp. 22–25.

Knowles, M. S., and Associates. *Androgyny in Action: Applying Modern Principles of Adult Learning.* San Francisco: Jossey-Bass, 1984.

Knox, A. B. "Implications of Societal Myths and Realities for Planning Responsive Continuing Education Opportunities in Oklahoma." In Oklahoma Network of Continuing Higher Education, *1986–87 Annual Report.* Vol. 2. Oklahoma City: Oklahoma State Regents for Higher Education, 1987.

Koerner, J. D. "A Note from the Sloan Foundation." *NLA News,* May 1985, p. 1.

Krotseng, M. U. "Profiles of Quality and Intrusion: The Complex Courtship of State Governments and Higher Education." *Review of Higher Education,* Summer 1990, pp. 557–566.

Ku, K. Letter to the editor. *Chronicle of Higher Education,* May 3, 1989, p. B5.

Leatherman, C. "High-School Students Found Taking More Core-Curriculum Courses." *Chronicle of Higher Education,* Aug. 2, 1989, p. A2.

Leslie, L., and Brinkman, R. T. *The Economic Value of Higher Education.* New York: American Council on Education/Macmillan, 1988.

Levine, A., and Associates. *Shaping Higher Education's Future: Demographic Realities and Opportunities, 1990–2000.* San Francisco: Jossey-Bass, 1989.

Lewis, R. J., and Wall, M. *Exploring Obstacles to Uses of Tech-*

nology in Higher Education. Washington, D.C.: Academy for Educational Development, 1988.

Loacker, G., Cromwell, L., and O'Brien, K. "Assessment in Higher Education: To Serve the Learner." In C. Adelman (ed.), *Assessment in American Higher Education.* Washington, D.C.: Office of Educational Research and Improvement, U.S. Department of Education, 1985.

Long, H. B. *New Perspectives on the Education of Adults in the United States.* New York: Nichols, 1987.

Lynton, E. A., and Elman, S. E. *New Priorities for the University: Meeting Society's Needs for Applied Knowledge and Competent Individuals.* San Francisco: Jossey-Bass, 1987.

McGrath, E. J. *Liberal Learning in the Professions.* New York: Bureau of Publications, Teachers College, Columbia University, 1959.

McInnes, W. C. "The Integration of Liberal and Professional Education." *Change,* June 1982, pp. 206–218.

McNeil, D. R. "The Status of Technology Education in the United States." Unpublished paper prepared for the government of the Netherlands and the European Institute of Education and Policy, 1985.

McNeil, D. R. "Status of Technology in Higher Education: A Reassessment." Unpublished paper prepared for the second annual Conference on Interactive Technology and Communications, Augusta, Me., Sept. 30, 1988.

McNeil, D. R. "Computer Conferencing: The Causes for Delay." Unpublished paper, Academy for Educational Development, 1989a.

McNeil, D. R. "Technology Is a Hot Topic but Its Impact on Higher Education Has Been Minimal." *Chronicle of Higher Education,* June 7, 1989b, p. A44.

McNeil, D. R. *Technology Planning for Waldorf College.* Washington, D.C.: Academy for Educational Development, 1989c.

McNeil, D. R. *Wiring the Ivory Tower: A Round Table on Technology in Higher Education.* Washington, D.C.: Academy for Educational Development, 1990.

McNeil, D. R., and Wall, M. N. "The University of Mid-America: A Personal Postscript." *Change,* May–June 1983, pp. 48–52.

Magner, D. K. "8 in 10 Colleges Have Plans to Boost Minority Presence." *Chronicle of Higher Education,* July 26, 1989a, pp. A27, A28.

Magner, D. K. "Major Changes Set in Admissions Test for Medical School." *Chronicle of Higher Education,* Mar. 22, 1989b, pp. A1, A34.

Mahoney, J. P. *Putting America Back to Work: The Kellogg Leadership Initiative.* Washington, D.C.: American Association of Community and Junior Colleges, 1984.

Manning, T. E. "The Why, What and Who of Assessment: The Accrediting Association Perspective." In *Educational Testing Service Invitational Conference Proceedings.* Princeton, N.J.: Educational Testing Service, 1987.

Massey, W. F. *A Paradigm for Research on Higher Education.* Philadelphia: Institute for Research on Higher Education, University of Pennsylvania, 1988.

Mawby, R. G. "Unfinished Business." Address to the National Adult Education Conference at the American Association for Adult and Continuing Education, Milwaukee, Wis., Nov. 7, 1985.

Melendez, S. "Minority Issues: Central Theme of Footnote?" In National University Continuing Education Association, *Challenges for Continuing Higher Education Leadership: Economic Development in a Multicultural Society,* Washington, D.C.: National University Continuing Education Association, 1988.

Millard, R. M. "Insuring the Future of the Liberal Arts." *Educational Record,* 1964, *45,* 371–378.

Millard, R. M. *Vocation: Central Aim of Education.* Iowa City, Iowa: American College Testing Program, 1973.

Millard, R. M. *State Boards of Higher Education.* Washington, D.C.: American Association for Higher Education, 1976.

Millard, R. M. "Accreditation." In J. R. Warren (ed.), *Meeting the New Demands for Standards.* New Directions for Higher Education, no. 43. San Francisco: Jossey-Bass, 1983.

Millard, R. M. "Relevance of Governance Issues to the Tension Between Quality and Equity." Unpublished paper for the Anglo-American Seminar on Quality in Higher Education. Princeton, N.J., Sept. 1987.

Millard, R. M., and Berve, N. "Higher Education." In R. Weber (ed.), *The Book of the States, 1970–71.* Lexington, Ky.: Council of State Governments, 1970.

Millard, R. M., and Berve, N. "Higher Education." In R. Weber (ed.), *The Book of the States, 1972–73.* Lexington, Ky.: Council of State Governments, 1972.

Miller, P. "What Is an American?" In National University Continuing Education Association, *Challenges for Continuing Higher Education Leadership: Economic Development in a Multicultural Society.* Washington, D.C.: National University Continuing Education Association, 1988.

Millett, J. D. *Conflict in Higher Education: State Government Coordination Versus Institutional Independence.* San Francisco: Jossey-Bass, 1984.

Mills, C. "The Sources of Faculty Resistance to Reform." *Chronicle of Higher Education,* Sept. 28, 1988, p. B3.

Mingle, J. "Shouldering the Social Obligation." In National University Continuing Education Association, *Challenges for Continuing Higher Education Leadership: Economic Development in a Multicultural Society.* Washington, D.C.: National University Continuing Education Association, 1988.

Mingle, J. "The Political Meaning of Quality." Paper prepared for the National Advisory Committee Meeting of the National Center for Postsecondary Governance and Finance, Baltimore, Md., Mar. 16–17, 1989.

Mitchell, B. L. "Higher Education Reform and Ad Hoc Committees: A Question of Legitimacy." *Review of Higher Education,* Winter 1987, pp. 117–135.

Moodie, G. C. "Debates About Quality in Higher Education." Unpublished paper for Anglo-American Seminar on Quality in Higher Education, Templeton College, Oxford University, Dec. 1986.

Mooney, C. J. "Court Says University of California Must Show Agricultural Studies Aid Family Farms." *Chronicle of Higher Education,* Nov. 25, 1987, pp. A19, A23.

Mooney, C. J. "Conservative Scholars Call for a Movement to 'Reclaim' the Academy." *Chronicle of Higher Education,* Nov. 23, 1988, pp. A1, A11.

Mooney, C. J. "Studies Find That Prestige Remains a Key Factor in Determining Professors' Career Patterns." *Chronicle of Higher Education,* Feb. 8, 1989a, pp. A11, A13.

Mooney, C. J. "3 in 4 Professors Think Their Undergraduate Students Are Seriously Underprepared." *Chronicle of Higher Education,* Aug. 16, 1989b, p. A13.

Moos, M. *The Post-Land Grant University: The University of Maryland Report.* Adelphi: University of Maryland, 1981.

National Academy of Sciences. *Strengthening the Governmental-University Partnership in Science.* Washington, D.C.: National Academy Press, 1983.

National Center for Postsecondary Governance and Finance. "State Incentives Funding: Leveraging Quality." *Briefings* (newsletter of the Forum for College and University Governance), Spring 1990, pp. 1–6.

National Commission on Excellence in Education. *A Nation at Risk,* Washington, D.C.: U.S. Department of Education, 1983.

National Commission on the Role and Future of State Colleges and Universities. *To Secure the Blessings of Liberty.* Washington, D.C.: American Association of State Colleges and Universities, 1986.

National Education Association. "Higher Education Reform: New Policy Statements Highlight NEA Perspective." *NEA Higher Education Advocate,* Jan. 30, 1987, pp. 1–10.

National Governors' Association, Task Force on College Quality. *Time for Results: The Governors' 1991 Report on Education.* Washington, D.C.: National Governors' Association, 1986.

National Governors' Association. *Results in Education: 1988. The Governor's 1991 Report on Education.* Washington, D.C.: National Governors' Association, 1988.

National Governors' Association. *America in Transition: The International Frontier. Report of the Task Force on International Education.* Washington, D.C.: National Governors' Association, 1989.

Neusner, J. "It is time to stop apologizing for Western Civilization and to start analyzing why it defines World Culture." *Chronicle of Higher Education,* Feb. 10, 1989, p. B1.

New York State Department of Education. *New York State Goals for Adult Learning Services.* Albany, N.Y.: Office of Adult Learning Services, New York State Department of Education, 1981.

Newman, F. "Rising Expectations: Can States Help Renew Quality?" Interview with Governor Thomas H. Kean of New Jersey. *Change,* Nov.–Dec. 1985, pp. 13–17.

Newman, F. *Choosing Quality: Reducing Conflict Between the State and the University.* Denver, Colo.: Education Commission of the States, 1987.

Niebuhr, H., Jr. *Revitalizing American Learning.* Belmont, Calif.: Wadsworth, 1984.

Ohio Board of Regents. *Toward the Year 2000.* 3 vols. Columbus: Ohio Board of Regents, 1988.

Oklahoma Network of Continuing Higher Education. "Telecommunications in Oklahoma Special Report." *Frontiers in Oklahoma Higher Education,* 1985, *1* (4), pp. 1–6, 9.

Oklahoma Network of Continuing Higher Education. *The Expanding Knowledge Base.* Oklahoma City: Oklahoma Network of Continuing Higher Education, 1986.

Oklahoma Network of Continuing Higher Education. *1986–87 Annual Report.* 3 vols. Oklahoma City: Oklahoma State Regents for Higher Education, 1987a.

Oklahoma Network of Continuing Higher Education. *Position Papers: Continuing Professional Education Needs.* Oklahoma City: Oklahoma State Regents for Higher Education, 1987b.

Oklahoma Network of Continuing Higher Education. "Industrial Cooperation in Oklahoma." Unpublished paper in National Advisory Committee agenda for Apr. 16–17, 1987c.

Oklahoma Network of Continuing Higher Education. *1987–88 Annual Report.* 4 vols. Oklahoma City: Oklahoma State Regents for Higher Education, 1988.

Oklahoma State Regents for Higher Education. "Oklahoma Network of Continuing Education." Unpublished project description sent to members of project National Advisory Board, Jul. 23, 1985.

Oklahoma State Regents for Higher Education. "Educational Outreach General Policy." Oklahoma City: Oklahoma State Regents for Higher Education. Adopted Feb. 22, 1988a.

Oklahoma State Regents for Higher Education. *Telecommuni-*

cations in Oklahoma: User's Handbook. Oklahoma City: Oklahoma State Regents for Higher Education, 1988b.

Oklahoma State University. *Telecommunications Policy and Procedures.* Stillwater, Okla.: Oklahoma State University, 1988.

Ottinger, C. A. *Higher Education Today: Facts in Brief.* Washington, D.C.: American Council on Education, 1987.

Padover, S. K. (ed.). *The Complete Jefferson.* New York: Tudor, 1943.

Parnell, D. "Preface." In R. Hamm and L. Tolle-Burger, *Doing Business with Business.* Washington, D.C.: American Association of Community and Junior Colleges, 1988.

Paulson, C. *State Initiatives in Assessment: Tools for Teaching and Learning in the 1990s.* Denver: Education Commission of the States, 1990.

Pincus, F. L., and Archer, E. *Bridges to Opportunity: Are Community Colleges Meeting the Transfer Needs of Minority Students?* New York: Academy for Educational Development and College Entrance Examination Board, 1989.

"The Professional Library Training Project Report and Evaluation." Appendix Q. *Oklahoma Network of Continuing Higher Education Annual Report.* Vol. 2. 1988.

Quehl, G. H. *Higher Education and the Public Interest: A Report to the Campus.* Washington, D.C.: Council for the Advancement and Support of Education, 1988.

Rhodes, F.H.T. "Foreword." In J. S. Stark and M. Lowther, *Strengthening the Ties That Bind: Integrating Undergraduate Liberal Education and Professional Studies.* Ann Arbor: Regents of the University of Michigan, 1988.

Richardson, R. C., Jr., and de los Santos, A. G. "Guest Editors' Introduction: From Access to Achievement: Fulfilling the Promise." *Review of Higher Education,* Summer 1988, pp. 323-328.

Rosencrance, F. *The American College and Its Teachers.* New York: Macmillan, 1962.

Rossman, J. E., and El-Khawas, E. *Thinking About Assessment: Perspectives for Presidents and Chief Administrative Officers.* Washington, D.C.: American Council on Education, 1987.

Rothblatt, S. "Merits and Defects: The American Educational System." *Liberal Education,* Jan.-Feb. 1989, pp. 22-25.

Sachs, H. "The Publication Requirement Should Not Be Based Solely on Refereed Journals." *Chronicle of Higher Education,* Oct. 19, 1988, p. B2.

Sagen, H. B. "The Professions: A Neglected Model for Undergraduate Education." *Liberal Education,* Dec. 1973, *59* (4), pp. 507–519.

Saunders, C. B., Jr. "Bush and Dukakis Evince Little Understanding of the Real Problem of Colleges and Universities." *Chronicle of Higher Education,* Sept. 1, 1988.

Schmidtlein, F. A. "How Do Higher Education Leaders Define Quality? The Planning Process Perspective." Unpublished paper, National Center for Postsecondary Governance and Finance, University of Maryland, 1988.

Schmidtlein, F., and Milton, T. H. "Campus Planning in the United States: Perspectives from a Nation-wide Survey." Unpublished paper, National Center for Postsecondary Governance and Finance, University of Maryland, 1988.

Schorske, C. E. "Secretary Bennett and His Conservative Supporters Are the New Fundamentalists of Western Culture." *Chronicle of Higher Education,* June 1, 1988, pp. B1–B2.

Schulman, C. H. "Report on Integrating Liberal and Professional Education." Arlie House Conference, Dec. 12–14, 1983. Washington, D.C.: Association of American Colleges and Council on Postsecondary Accreditation, 1983. (Unpublished summary of conference.)

Sharp, P. "Leadership Development Program" *Oklahoma Network of Continuing Higher Education. 1986–87 Annual Report.* Vol. 3. 1988, p. 34.

Simon, P. "Secretary Bennett Is Making All Proprietary Schools the Scapegoats for Loan-Collection Problems of a Few." *Chronicle of Higher Education,* May 25, 1988, pp. B2, B3.

Simosko, S., and Associates. *Assessing Learning: A CAEL Handbook for Faculty.* Columbia, Md.: Council for Adult and Experiential Education, 1988.

Simpson, E. G., Jr., McGinty, J. L., and Morrison, J. L. "Environmental Scanning of the Georgia Center for Continuing Education: A Progress Report." *Continuing Higher Education Review,* Autumn 1987, pp. 1–20.

Solomon, L., and Astin, A. W. "Departments Without Distinguished Graduate Programs." *Change,* Sept. 1981, pp. 23–28.

Southern Regional Education Board. *Remedial Education in College: How Widespread Is It?* Atlanta, Ga.: Southern Regional Education Board, 1988.

Sparks, H. *Tradition, Transformation, and Tomorrow: The Emerging Role of Higher Education.* Washington, D.C.: National University Continuing Education Association, 1985.

Spector, M. "Medical School Test Revised." *Washington Post,* Mar. 14, 1989, pp. A1, A11.

Spille, H. A. *Beyond the Rhetoric: Toward a System of Learning and Credentialling for Adults.* Washington, D.C.: American Council on Education, 1989.

Stark, J. S., and Lowther, M. *Designing the Learning Plan: A Review of Research and Theory Related to College Curricula.* Ann Arbor: Regents of the University of Michigan, 1986.

Stark, J. S., and Lowther, M. *Strengthening the Ties That Bind: Integrating Undergraduate Liberal and Professional Studies.* Ann Arbor: Regents of the University of Michigan, 1988.

State Higher Education Executive Officers. "Statement of Policy by the State Higher Education Executive Officers on Program and Institutional Assessment." Unpublished report, State Higher Education Executive Officers, 1987a.

State Higher Education Executive Officers Task Force on Minority Student Achievement. *A Difference of Degrees: State Initiatives to Improve Minority Student Achievement.* Denver, Colo.: State Higher Education Executive Officers, 1987b.

Stewart, D. M. "Overcoming the Barriers to Successful Participating by Minorities." *Review of Higher Education,* Summer 1988, pp. 329–336.

Study Group on the Conditions of Excellence in American Higher Education. *Involvement in Learning: Realizing the Potential of American Higher Education.* Washington, D.C.: National Institute for Education, 1984.

Sykes, C. J. *Profscam: Professors and the Demise of Higher Education.* Washington, D.C.: Regency Gateway, 1988.

"Telecommunications in Oklahoma—Special Report." *Frontiers,* 1985, *1* (4), pp. 1–6, 9.

Thelin, J. R., Casteen, J. T., III and Bailey, J. M. "After the Academic Revolution: A Retrospective Forum." *Review of Higher Education,* Autumn 1988, pp. 1–16.

Thrash, P. "A Report on the Role of Outcomes Evaluation in the Accreditation Process." *North Central Association Quarterly,* Spring 1987, pp. 481–490.

Thrash, P. "Educational 'Outcomes' in the Accrediting Process." *Academe,* July–Aug. 1988, pp. 16–18.

Trow, M. "Academic Standards and Mass Higher Education." *Higher Education Quarterly,* 1987.

Turnbull, W. H. "Are They Learning Anything in College?" *Change,* Nov.–Dec. 1985, pp. 23–26.

Turner, J. A. "Georgia Tech's Outspoken President Tackles Atlanta." *Chronicle of Higher Education,* Aug. 10, 1988, p. A3.

Turner, J. A. "Projects to Measure the Effects of Computers on Campus Make Major Advances, Leave Several Unsolved Problems." *Chronicle of Higher Education,* June 21, 1989, pp. A9, A12.

Tyson, L. D. "Quality and Equality for Our Work Force." In National University Continuing Education Association, *Challenges for Continuing Higher Education Leadership: Economic Development in a Multicultural Society.* Washington, D.C.: National Continuing Education Association, 1988.

U.S. Department of Education. "Part 602 — Secretary's Procedures and Criteria for Recognition of Accrediting Agencies." Title 34 of Federal Regulations. July 1988.

U.S. Department of Education, National Center for Educational Statistics. *Projections of Education Statistics to 1997–98.* Washington, D.C.: U.S. Government Printing Office, 1988.

University of the State of New York. *College Credit Recommendations.* Albany: National Program on Noncollegiate Sponsored Instruction, University of the State of New York, 1987.

Vandament, W. E. "Point of View: Those Who Would Reform Undergraduate Education Must Recognize the Realities of Academic Governance." *Chronicle of Higher Education,* Nov. 30, 1988, p. A52.

Vobejda, B. "The Great Books Debate: Colleges and Universities Ask What Does It Mean to Be an Educated Person?"

Washington Post, Education Review, Aug. 7, 1988, pp. 4, 16–17.

Warner, L. "Economic Imperatives in the 1990's in Oklahoma." Address to Leadership Development Seminar for Faculty, Oklahoma Center for Continuing Education, Norman, Apr. 16, 1987.

Watkins, B. T. "Colleges Urged to Avow That Teaching Is Central to Their Mission and to Steps to Upgrade It." *Chronicle of Higher Education,* Apr. 26, 1989a, pp. A13, A15.

Watkins, B. T. "Community Colleges' 'Legitimacy' Seen Threatened by Vocational Emphasis." *Chronicle of Higher Education,* Sept. 20, 1989b, pp. A1, A18.

Watkins, B. T. "With More Adult Students on Campus, Some Colleges Are Adjusting Their Curricula and Teaching Methods." *Chronicle of Higher Education,* Jan. 18, 1989c, pp. A27, A32.

Weber, A. R. "Point of View: Colleges Must Begin Weighing Public Perceptions, as Well as Economic Reality, When Setting Tuition." *Chronicle of Higher Education,* Oct. 11, 1989, p. A52.

Webster, D. "Ranking Academic Quality." *Change,* Nov.–Dec. 1986, pp. 34–41.

Weiss, T. "Research That the U.S. Is Paying for Should Not Be Tainted by Any Possible Bias." *Chronicle of Higher Education,* Oct. 4, 1989, p. A56.

Western Association of Schools and Colleges, Accrediting Commission for Senior Colleges and Universities. *Handbook of Accreditation.* Seattle, Wash.: Accrediting Commission for Senior Colleges and Universities, Western Association of Schools and Colleges, 1988.

Westling, J. "The Assessment Movement Is Based on a Misdiagnosis of the Malaise Afflicting American Higher Education." *Chronicle of Higher Education,* Oct. 19, 1988, pp. B1–B2.

Wheeler, D. L. "Pressure to Cash in on Research Stirs Conflict-of-Interest Issues." *Chronicle of Higher Education,* Apr. 12, 1989, pp. A29–A30.

White, T. "Executive Director's Report." *1987–1988 Annual Report.* Vol. I. Oklahoma Network of Continuing Higher Education, 1988, pp. 3–21.

Whitehead, A. N. *The Aims of Education*. London: Williams & Norgate, 1932.

Wilson, R. "For Profit Trade Schools Defraud Students and Waste Federal Student Aid Money, Bennett Charges in Scathing Report." *Chronicle of Higher Education,* Feb. 17, 1988, pp. A1, A21.

Witherspoon, J. P. "Telecommunications and Continuing Education in the 90s." Address to Leadership Development Seminar for Educational Outreach, Oklahoma State University, Stillwater, Sept. 25, 1986.

Zemsky, R. *The Way We Are*. Philadelphia: Institute for Research in Higher Education, University of Pennsylvania, 1988.

Zook, G. F., and Haggerty, M. E. *The Evaluation of Higher Education Institutions*. Chicago: University of Chicago Press, 1936.

Index